74-80

# CITIZENS
# WITHOUT WORK

## A STUDY OF
## THE EFFECTS OF UNEMPLOYMENT
## UPON THE
## WORKERS' SOCIAL RELATIONS
## AND PRACTICES

BY

E. WIGHT BAKKE

ARCHON BOOKS
1969

SBN: 208 00810 1
LIBRARY OF CONGRESS CATALOG CARD NUMBER: 70-85913
PRINTED IN THE UNITED STATES OF AMERICA

# FOREWORD

THIS volume and its companion, *The Unemployed Worker,* present the results of a series of studies that have been carried on at the Institute of Human Relations since 1932. These studies have endeavored to carry the analysis of the problem of unemployment beyond the stage reached by the initial study which was begun in 1929 and reported in 1934 in a volume by Clague, Couper, and Bakke entitled *After the Shutdown.* The research was undertaken for the purpose of discovering the readjustment problems faced by unemployed American workers and their families and the resources which they brought with them to this task. No effort has been made to develop a practical program, yet certain principles have emerged which must be taken into account in the development of a plan for the solution of the problem. These studies represent an effort to see the complex ramifications of the problem through the eyes of the worker himself, and to reveal the self-initiated efforts at readjustment which programs must take into account if they are to be effective.

Every problem of human relations is experienced by an individual or a group of individuals in concrete describable situations. Certain aspects of these situations are determined by general social, economic, and political conditions and are related to certain traditions, beliefs, and values which taken together represent a particular culture. These studies reveal clearly that it is impossible to analyze completely the problems of human relations of a group of unemployed workers without at the same time analyzing the economic, social, political, religious, and cultural setting in which these problems occur. Even a preliminary and tentative analysis of the complexities involved requires an extended descriptive account of the factors that are relevant to the central problem. The space devoted to the description of these factors is justified in order that the specific reactions of workers to particular problems may be seen in perspective and interpreted as a part of a total dynamic life situation.

The staff of the Institute of Human Relations is developing a system of psychological and sociological concepts in the hope that data on problems like the ones reported here can assist in evolving a unified social science. From the point of view of that part of the Institute's program the research embodied in these volumes is exploratory in nature. The realistic description and analysis of the worker adjusting his practice and thought to the factors in his own environment have furnished both a factual corrective and a substantial support for certain of these tentative concepts so far developed. Moreover, the studies suggest a promising line of approach to other problems of American society such as labor organization, to which the author of these volumes now proposes to devote his attention.

The Institute in sponsoring such studies of particular problem areas seeks primarily to discover the fundamental principles which define the interaction of individuals and society, and to develop a science of human relations whose findings will be relevant not alone in the particular situation but wherever human beings must adjust themselves to the physical and cultural environment and to each other.

MARK A. MAY

*New Haven,*
  *July 1, 1940.*

# PREFACE

*Citizens Without Work* and a companion volume, *The Un-employed Worker*, represent the author's attempt to continue in the United States an analysis of unemployment and its effects begun in England in 1931 and embodied in *The Unemployed Man.*[1] The first volume of this present series, *The Unemployed Worker*, portrayed the world of labor from which workers came to unemployment, the goals toward which they direct their energies, the barriers which are placed across their path to those goals, and the customary practices they develop in the effort to surmount or circumvent these barriers. The economic adjustments involved when the worker lost his job, such as work seeking, stretching the income, recourse to unemployment compensation and various forms of relief, were then presented as a continuation under most difficult circumstances of the process of adapting these resources and techniques to the problems raised by lack of work.

The reader who is not familiar with this first volume will find its major ideas embodied in Section III of this book, which is in effect a summary of both volumes.

In *Citizens Without Work* we turn our attention to community and family relationships and practices of the unemployed. The adjustments made by unemployed workers and their families in their relations to the neighborhood, to friendship groups, to religious organizations, to politics and pressure groups, and the rearrangement of the structure of family life are here recorded. The data are obtained from the same sources as those used in the first volume:

1. Participation as unemployed men in the life and practices of the unemployed for several periods during the eight-year interval.

1. E. Wight Bakke, *The Unemployed Man.* Nisbet, London, 1933, and Dutton, New York, 1935.

2. Intensive case studies and budget investigations of twenty-five unemployed families between 1932 and 1939.

3. Testing of hypotheses developed from the foregoing sources by reference to interviews with two hundred "married and together" unemployed families appearing in a random sample of two thousand families in New Haven in 1933.

4. Investigation of a 10-per cent sample of unemployed households in New Haven in 1938.

5. Interviews with social workers, ministers, public officials, and employers to check on the alleged facts disclosed in the contacts with the unemployed.

6. Examination of numerous reports and other documentary evidence on the social and economic environment of New Haven workers and on the operation of the various social services for the benefit of the unemployed.[2]

An account of the procedure followed and forms used in connection with these several investigations has been mimeographed and is available to those who may be interested.[3]

From the data accumulated in the course of these investigations, I have tried to present a picture of what was happening in the unemployed families during this period and to give at least tentative answers to questions of real import for public policy. What functions are performed by community institutions and relations in the efforts of the unemployed to meet their problems? What changes are made by the unemployed in such relations? Is unemploy-

2. Of these documents several were of particular value:
*Human Reactions to Relief.* A study of the reactions of New Haven workers to relief policies and practices, undertaken by the Division of Economic and Social Research of the W.P.A. in collaboration with the staff of the Yale Institute of Human Relations.
*A Handbook of Social Statistics of New Haven, Connecticut,* compiled by Thelma Dreis from census material and a sample investigation of 2,000 New Haven families made in 1931 and again in 1933 by the Yale Institute of Human Relations.
Annual and special reports of the several relief agencies in New Haven.
3. Write Institute of Human Relations, Yale University, New Haven, Conn., and enclose 10 c. to cover mailing.

ment a specific cause of or a general irritant toward change? What is the effect of these changes on the goals men seek and the techniques developed for achieving them? Are there observable periods in the changing pattern of the behavior of the unemployed? What is the mutual effect of family organization and practice and of adjustments to unemployment upon each other? What main sources of stability or instability in community institutions, including the family, show up under the strain of unemployment? In view of the answers to such questions, what is a reasonable judgment as to the effect of unemployment and unemployment relief on the self-reliance of workers, and what tests may appropriately be applied to the policy and practice of relief agencies?

These are large questions, and I can make no claim that the materials of this study give final answers to them. Whatever conclusions are made are presented simply as those suggested by close association with the unemployed and their families in one community over a period of eight years and by an analysis of the large body of data we have collected from attempts to observe objectively the realities of their experience.

We have seen a group of workers functioning as members of a community:

Working toward certain goals;

Within a cultural environment;

In the midst of opportunities offered and restrictions imposed by the conditions of life in the community;

With the use of their personal equipment for the task; and by means of certain practices, economic, familial, recreational, religious, and political.

We have tried to portray the adjustments of citizens to unemployment as a rearrangement of that normal structure of their lives and the effects of unemployment as a modification of that structure under the stress and strain of the absence of a job.

In *The Unemployed Worker,* after describing the nature of the worker's world, the goals which he strives to reach, the practices he and his family develop in the attempt, and the resulting realistic meaning which "getting ahead" has for him, we charted the course of his primarily economic adjustments to unemployment. We described his efforts at job hunting, stretching his income, and making use of available social services as a continuation of the same process of adapting means to ends under circumstances in which the basic means, a job and wages, were absent.

In this present volume we consider the unemployed as citizens and as members of families. What resources did they bring with them in the form of neighborhood, clique, recreational, religious, and political practices and relations? Of what use were these in their efforts to overcome the difficulties of unemployment? What in turn was the effect of unemployment on these resources for personal and social security?

Throughout both volumes has appeared an implication that the worker's world is different at many points from that of other economic groups in the community. Section I of this book is concluded with a discussion of the degree to which workers are becoming conscious of this fact and are developing practices and associations which give reality to the process of the formation of a working class.

Section II is concerned with the effects of unemployment on the stability of the family. Several case histories are presented picturing the reality of these effects on individual families. Generalizations are then attempted as to the cycle of readjustment, first in the areas of living on which family relations are built and then in the area of family relations themselves. The section is concluded with a summary of the nature of the challenge which unemployment makes to family stability and the factors which enable the institution to survive though its pattern is changed by the necessary adjustments to the problem of unemployment.

The final section is a summary not only of this book but of the companion volume, *The Unemployed Worker*. The summary focuses the findings of both volumes on two issues: What are the effects of unemployment on the self-reliance of workers and their families? What tests for social services designed to reduce the unemployed worker's difficulties are appropriate in the light of the findings of this study?

E. WIGHT BAKKE

*New Haven,*
*June, 1940.*

# CONTENTS

# CONTENTS OF

# THE UNEMPLOYED WORKER

## A COMPANION VOLUME

# SECTION I

## THE UNEMPLOYED WORKER AND HIS COMMUNITY

# I

## SPARE-TIME RELATIONS AND PRACTICES

THE most obvious damage to customary living wrought by unemployment is centered on the practices and relationships labeled economic. Normally geared to his fellows in the workaday life of the community, the unemployed man fights with sometimes more, sometimes less, success to avoid the loosening of those economic bonds which hold him to the productive ways of men in society.[1] All other ways by which a man becomes less the individual and more the citizen are based in some fashion on his economic activities and relationships, if for no other reason than that the spending of money is involved in all of them. Yet these latter ways cannot be designated as primarily economic. It is with these practices in essentially noneconomic areas of living that this book is concerned. To what degree do neighborhood associations, the relationships with friends, leisure-time activities, the practices of religion and of politics make it possible for the unemployed worker to further his personal ambitions and social security? How far do the associations in these fields counteract the loosening of community bonds by lack of work? Or do they themselves tend to disintegrate under the impact of necessary adjustments to unemployment?

### The Neighborhood.

One might expect that the associations of neighborhood life would offer many opportunities for such "gearing in." Paradoxically enough, however, the keynote of the worker's relations to the neighborhood is isolation rather than

1. The primarily economic adjustments of the unemployed workers and their families have been discussed in a companion volume, *The Unemployed Worker*, Yale University Press, New Haven, Connecticut, 1940.

intimate association. That isolation is penetrated on occasion. A neighbor is greeted on the street, a short conversation is held over the back fence, children play in each other's houses, illness or accident or death may provoke an inquiry or even the offer of help or that all but universal symbol of sympathy, some cooking. But visiting in each other's homes, sharing of meals, and other relationships of a more intimate nature are reserved for friends. They are not in the folkways of the neighborhood.

The normal types of neighborhood association are not the sort which lead one to feel that his neighbors' opinions are an important item in determining the status which one occupies in the community. They are not of that face-to-face sort which would exercise a very strong stimulating or inhibiting force in the determination of attitudes or behavior.

### Why Isolation in the Neighborhood?

Why this degree of isolation? It cannot be that these neighbors lack common interests. They are, in general, of the same economic status. They face the same problems of low income, the control of others over their jobs and their destinies. They require common services from the government and from the political parties. They are very frequently coreligionists. All of them have similar problems of domestic economy and the raising of children. There are numerous interests, therefore, which they have in common. It appears that something more than common interests is necessary as a basis for intimate association.

What are the reasons which these workers gave for their lack of intimacy? Some of them were merely practical reasons. Said an Italian truck driver:

If you keep away from your neighbors, you stay out of trouble. There are so many chances for squabbling that if you have too many acquaintances among your neighbors you may find that life becomes one big squabble.

The wife of an American factory worker put the matter this way:

What do you suppose we talk about when we talk across the fence here? Well, we're gossiping mostly. Now can't you see that it wouldn't be wise for me to know too many people intimately here because they would all of them know so much about me that they might gossip to other people about me?

A munitions worker indicated a very interesting reason:

You hate to fight with your friends, and in a neighborhood of this kind you live so close together that there are all kinds of opportunities for conflict. Well, if you're not too well acquainted it doesn't hurt you so much if you get into a scrap.

The lack of permanence in residence is another factor which discourages intimacy. As one carpenter put it:

You don't plant permanent shrubs, you know, when you're only going to live a few years in a place and when you rent it. And like with shrubs, it's like with friends.

Very few of the people with whom we were associated owned their own homes; it was altogether likely that in a few years they would move on. It just wasn't worth their while to build up intimate friendships for that short while, even if such relations could be established in a short time. In a few cases neighborhood orchestras or card clubs had been formed at one time or another, but with the moving away of a few individuals the groups broke up. After one or two experiences of that kind they apparently didn't think it was worth the trouble to form another. Mobility does not encourage intimacy.

A plumber who had formerly lived in the country indicated that the very presence of a large number of people decreased one's need for intimate associations. He contrasted this situation with that of the country, in which one so infrequently saw other people that it was a welcome event when anyone stopped in "simply because you were lonely for the sight of some strange face. But," he said, "there are so many strange faces around here that you never feel that need at all." He went on:

In a way, you know, picking friends from this gang which is around you is like picking out a necktie. It wouldn't be so bad if there were fewer to choose from, but when there are so many and such a variety, well, you get all mixed up and in the end you may end up by not choosing any at all. It is a strange fact in our city that we live so close together that we don't have any neighbors.

Many of our informants indicated to us that their ideal of intimate friendship was thoroughly colored by the memory of their youthful companionships. They were so tied up with work and with duties at the present time that they knew they wouldn't have time to make friendships of that sort again.

They tell me there was an English poet once who said, "A little knowledge is a dangerous thing," and I want to tell you that it's the same way with friendships. A little intimacy is worse than none.

Throughout the comments on neighborhood relations, it was clear that individuals desired a greater independence from the judgment of their associates than would be possible if associates "lived too close." The desire for independence is apparently greater than the desire for a complete sharing of all one's affairs. It is difficult for an individual to control the degree of intimacy with "the man next door." With one's friends living at some distance this control is easier to exercise. One steam fitter put it this way:

You don't want just anyone judging that you're good or bad or that you are successful or unsuccessful. You only want those that you can be sure of, that you can trust. Moreover, you don't want people knowing too gol-darned much about you, even your friends. An' it's pretty hard to keep them from knowing that much about you if they live so close to you.

In numerous comments of this sort there is clearly indicated an attempt to control the extent and the membership of the society against whose standards one's status is defined. If that society is too large, judgments made by its members get out of hand and one feels less confident that he will be able to achieve a satisfying status.

Part of the isolation may be due to the lack of sociability on the part of individuals; that is, the causal factors may be within the individual rather than in the circumstances in which he lives. But the same isolation was observed among both introvert and extrovert types. In the case of the first, the comment indicative of isolation was likely to be made without criticism and likely to end in "we like it so." With the second, it was likely to take the form of a complaint; but the fact of isolation stands out in both cases.

### Unemployment and Neighborhood Associations.

The effect of unemployment upon this state of affairs is hard to measure. A variety of comments leaves us with no clear judgment as to the actual effect of idleness upon neighborhood associations. Presumably, having more time to spend would facilitate making new acquaintances, and the fact that men are around home more would make them more likely to "run into" neighbors. Apparently, however, this is not happening. If anything, men tend to hold more to themselves in unemployment than otherwise. Apparently unemployment is not one of those crises which break down the normal isolation of the neighborhood relationship.

This fact is significant. Early in our study we were inclined to give a considerable importance to the fact that unemployed people were tending to concentrate in the same neighborhoods and even in the same tenements, and to indicate that this would probably help to build up a culture which was typically that of unemployed people. There is no lack of evidence that intimate association with others who are experimenting with ways to meet the problems of unemployment results in a cross-fertilization of practices which speeds up the process of adjustment. But that association must be more than residence in close proximity. A degree of intimacy usually lacking among "neighbors," and especially absent among newly made neighbors, is still more necessary for the reinforcement of a successful practice through social approval. It seems to us, therefore, that there is not sufficient sharing of intimate problems and ideas and attitudes and reactions among those who have been thrown spacially close together to make a rapid building of a distinctive culture likely. New friends are made slowly. Some of these are sharing the same problems of readjustment. But any mutual influence on practice and ideas is rooted in these selective contacts rather than in the spacial association with a community of unemployed.

The fact that unemployment pushes people into less desirable neighborhoods is probably more important, at least initially, from the point of view of the damage to their status in the eyes of those with whom they normally associated on intimate terms than from the point of view of the formation of new group contacts which influence ideas and conduct. One's neighborhood is one of the symbols of status in the eyes of the worker's customary associates, and it is these customary associates whose opinions he cherishes and whose criticisms he would like to avoid. Consequently, moving into a neighborhood whose occupants are of a lower economic or cultural status is a severe ordeal from this point of view.

### Cliques and Friendships: Their Bases.

Neighborhood associations, therefore, do not appear to be primarily those which set the standards against which an individual measures his own attitudes and conduct. Intimate friends, sometimes grouped into cliques, come much closer to performing this function. Such cliques are not coextensive with club or church or union membership. Each of these may define certain standards consistent with its own function and purpose, but it does not provide a whole gamut of standards against which the individual can measure his own total life activity. Moreover, it should be noticed that very frequently the husband and the wife may belong to different cliques. Indeed, it would seem to us from our observations that the number of cliques to which husbands and wives belong separately is greater than that to which they belong in common. This is perhaps a natural situation when one considers that close associations had been formed before marriage. Wife or husband may not be a congenial accession to the former circle of the other.

When these friendships and cliques are put under stress and strain by the fact of unemployment, it sometimes becomes possible to see more clearly what are the requirements for their successful functioning and survival. We may distinguish several. The first is that participants shall have enough money to provide for the events on which such friendships thrive. More than occasional contact is necessary if cliques are to hold their membership. Secondly, the economic fortunes of those who participate in the clique must not be too diverse. Mutual independence and mutual dependence must be a reality. In the third place, the members of the clique must have social and moral standards sufficiently similar so that the status of any one of them is not too frequently challenged. Individuals do not join or maintain association with cliques in which they are constantly being criticized. The standards of the group against which they measure their own conduct must not be so dissimilar to their own that they are constantly aware of not "fitting in." Fourth, the friendships must be pleasant and refreshing. There is no place for a friendship in which only misery is shared. Apparently an important function of friendship is to provide one with a type of association which causes him either to forget his troubles or at least to view them from a less discouraging point of view. Finally, the clique offers the individual a chance to be admired; it must keep that opportunity open. Second only to the family in this respect is the small face-to-face friendship group where one's shortcomings can be occasionally overlooked and one may occupy a role as a very exceptional fellow, in certain respects, if in no other ways than in a demonstration of hospitality.

### Attack of Unemployment on Friendships.

It is not easy for these major requirements to be met when unemployment comes. Lack of money reduces the number of events and contacts. The telephone is retained not only to get jobs but to provide the wife with an opportunity to share experiences with her friends. But even a telephone conversation is dependent upon something to talk about, and inasmuch as the lack of funds has reduced the number of contacts there are relatively fewer events which can be shared. We do not need to quote many of our informants in order to convey the idea that the lack of money is a serious handicap in the maintenance of friendships or cliques. Says the wife of a former contractor:

Suppose you go to a friend's house and she gives you a cup of tea and something. You feel shamed. You think—now I got to do the same when she comes to my house. You know you can't so you stay home. If you walk a long way to see a friend you get thirsty and your friend will feel that she must at least give you a cup of coffee, and often she can ill afford to do this, so you don't go.

Another former ironworker said:

It's all right to talk about being friends, but, you know, there are certain things that go with having people to your house. For instance, you can't even have a card game without serving sandwiches and coffee, or pretzels and beer or something, but that all costs something. We had some people with whom we kept up our contacts, and by common agreement we decided that we wouldn't serve refreshments. Somehow it wasn't much fun any longer and very soon we broke up.

Furthermore, when there is entertaining to be done it costs more for heat and light. One riveter said:

You know, it's awful to have to keep up a front, but you have to do it. Now the other night some of our friends came and it cost me about $1.50 to heat the rest of the house. We've shut off some of the house, you know, and we're not using it, but I couldn't let the rest of the house be cold when these friends came because they'd go away and they'd say, "Gee, George's house was cold. Something's wrong. George is kind of slipping, isn't he?" So we had to spend that extra money to keep the house warm, but I tell you it was worth a million dollars to us because, you see, you have to keep some of your friends and you have to keep them thinking good of you.

Family events in particular are curtailed, so that husband and wife are thrown back upon their individual friendships more thoroughly than ever and the common friendships tend to disintegrate. But even the groups of which they are separately members require the expenditure of money and these consequently tend to be reduced also.

Furthermore, the friendships between those who hold jobs and those who do not tend to break up. Those who are unemployed are continually being reminded of the difference in their incomes. They are reminded of a difference in status, and as one man said:

You can't get any fun out of constantly being the unfortunate dog. You hate to feel that you are dependent, even in your mind, on your friends. And even though they don't say nothing you know they wonder what's wrong with you.

The way in which friendships tend to break up is vividly portrayed by the wife of a rubber worker:

This friend stood up with me when I was married. She was in the habit of bringing palms to me on Palm Sunday. Two years ago she came. At that time she saw that I needed new teeth. We were beginning to feel the depression and I had not gone to the dentist to get my teeth fixed. A year ago she came with her husband, and again she found me without my bridgework. She married a man who is fairly well-to-do, and I felt very much ashamed that I was still without my front teeth. My friend, I think she was ashamed too because this year she did not come to bring me the palm. I waited for her all afternoon. I thought of going to see her, but she lives out in Fair Haven and for such a long trip I would have to stay for a little visit, and that would mean taking off my coat and I did not have a suitable dress to put on.

It is not only the expense, however, which makes the continuance of friendship difficult. A part of the value of friendships is to give one a feeling of satisfaction and pleasantness as a contrast to many of the unpleasant experiences of the routine day. But, when a man is unemployed, friends are apt, in spite of the best intentions, to remind him of his difficult circumstances. Said a carpenter:

Every time I go to the home of one of my friends, they will say, "Well, how about it? Do you have a job yet?" and constantly I'm being reminded of the fact that I am out of work. I hate to go even to see my relatives because I know that they're thinking "So-and-so has a job; why can't Jim get one?" Perhaps this is only all in my own mind, but it keeps me from enjoying these relationships with them just the same.

Since one of the functions of friendship is to give a person an opportunity to display his standing and status, it is not surprising that when the appearance of the house begins to deteriorate one does not care to have friends there. One enjoys having friends in the house not only for their company but for their admiration of one's furnishings and household management; and since during unemployment it becomes difficult to care for things properly one no longer wishes to have the results observed. Mrs. Dillinger, the wife of a railroad worker, commented also on how badly her house looked outside:

It isn't so bad at night though; when only the street lights are on, it looks pretty good. And when Mr. Dillinger starts back to work again I'm going to start entertaining, but I'll do all my entertaining at night so that when my friends come the house will be looking its best.

Since "keeping up a front" is very difficult when one is unemployed, the general tendency is to withdraw from those contacts in which it is necessary. Even the reputation for hospitality can survive only by objective evidence, and objective evidence costs money.

For all these reasons, therefore, the normal friendships or cliques which set the standards by which individuals measure their own behavior and attitude tend to disintegrate during unemployment, and with their disappearance the constant checking of the standards of the individual by his group associations is reduced.

### Recreational Relations and Practices.

Statistical verification for these comments on disintegration of group associations is found in the results of our sample survey of two hundred unemployed families in New Haven. It may be well to have before us a table indicative of the proportions of these families who participated in the various types of recreational associations both prior to and during unemployment.

## TABLE 1. PROPORTION OF THE 200 UNEMPLOYED FAMILIES PARTICIPATING IN VARIOUS FORMS OF RECREATION BEFORE AND DURING UNEMPLOYMENT.

| Type of Recreation | Proportion Participating While Employed | | Proportion Participating During Unemployment | |
|---|---|---|---|---|
| | Number | Per Cent | Number | Per Cent |
| Visits with Family and Friends | 132 | 66.0 | 58 | 29.0 |
| Clubs | 119 | 59.5 | 61 | 30.5 |
| Movies | 111 | 55.5 | 32 | 16.0 |
| Trade Unions | 64 | 32.0 | 29 | 14.5 |
| Excursions | 47 | 23.5 | 4 | 2.0 |
| Parties | 40 | 20.0 | 6 | 3.0 |
| Auto Trips | 38 | 19.0 | 6 | 3.0 |
| Walking | 30 | 15.0 | 33 | 16.5 |
| Sitting around Home | 26 | 13.0 | 49 | 24.5 |
| Cards | 25 | 12.5 | 10 | 5.0 |
| Watching Athletics | 25 | 12.5 | 12 | 6.0 |
| Bathing | 24 | 12.0 | 4 | 2.0 |
| Reading | 18 | 9.0 | 17 | 8.5 |
| Dances | 17 | 8.5 | 4 | 2.0 |
| Participation in Athletics | 12 | 6.0 | 8 | 4.0 |
| Church | 10 | 5.0 | 6 | 3.0 |
| Gardening, Home Repair | 8 | 4.0 | 19 | 9.5 |
| Italian Shows | 8 | 4.0 | 0 | 0 |
| Picnics | 4 | 2.0 | 2 | 1.0 |
| Lecture and Discussion Groups | 4 | 2.0 | 4 | 2.0 |
| Singing | 3 | 1.5 | 0 | 0 |
| Saloons | 3 | 1.5 | 0 | 0 |
| Chatting and Gossiping at Corner Store, Gas Stations and on Street | 0 | 0 | 24 | 12.0 |
| Sleep (during the Daytime) | 0 | 0 | 8 | 4.0 |

### Effects of Unemployment on Recreation.

Several interesting conclusions can be drawn from this table. In the first place, while employment was normal the most frequent recreation reported was visiting with friends and family. Over half had discontinued these friendly contacts and the other half continued them on a much-reduced scale. Many workers indicated that this reduction in friendships would be a permanent matter since in the experience they had learned who their "fair-weather friends" were. Visiting with relatives did not decline as much as visiting with friends. The greatest change in activities occurs in those items where expenditures are most necessary. Movie attendance was cut down to two sevenths of its former importance. Our records indicate that the 56 per cent who regularly attend the movies when employed spent for the family an average of 83 c. per week. This same group after they were unemployed spent an average of 10 c. a week, usually for the children. Excursions, both the week-end variety and those to Savin Rock, were one twelfth as frequent as before. Automobile trips were reduced to one sixth; bathing to one sixth; and dances, although they did not figure prominently in the normal activities, to one fifth of their former proportions. Although, in contrast, participation in formal and informal clubs was reduced only by half, the average amount spent on them fell from $20.50 to $3.82 a year. The formal lodges and associations requiring dues tended to be dropped in favor of informal associations which cost less.

The only activities obviously to increase are those which require no expenditures. Walking increased slightly, sitting around the home and listening to the radio or reading the newspaper doubled, and gardening and puttering about the house, although they did not occupy an important position in the original activities, increased two-and-one-half times. An interesting new activity which did not appear at all in the normal list is chatting and gossiping at the corner grocery store, on the street, and at the gas station and other convenient places. Four per cent of the individuals indicated that sleeping was their chief recreation at the moment. There is a notable lack of any increase in cultural activities. Reading remained exactly the same, and it is to be noted that only 9 per cent in each case recorded this as a customary activity. Lecture and discussion groups also remained at 2 per cent for each period. A sprinkling of men indicated that they had taken up some handicraft or started going to the Y.M.C.A. since unemployment.

### Unemployment Is Not Leisure.

If the opportunity for making progress toward one's goals during hours of leisure were proportional to the number of hours, the unemployed would indeed be in a fortunate position. Several hours in every day have been transferred to the leisure account. But the transfer is made under circumstances that cancel many of the opportunities usually related to leisure. No social role is substituted for those gone with the job. The very chance to appear in any role before one's fellows is reduced by the curtailing of contacts. The furtherance of economic security possible through trade-union and club membership is given up or postponed. The indirect security of a well-integrated family is lessened by the reduction of recreational events which help to bind the members of the family together. The reality of citizenship has been reduced by the loss of contact with organizations which participate to some extent in the larger interests of the community. The formal clubs, lodges, and trade unions through whose programs and affairs a man learns something of the larger issues in the community and gets a training in democracy—all these have been curtailed. Moreover the excursions which at least bring the worker in contact with a larger world than his own neighborhood have been severely cut down. The activities through which he might broaden his understanding of his part in the life of the community, such as reading and lectures and discussion groups, seem not to have been increased. He spends more time at home, and frequently the newspaper has been stopped and the radio sold, so that even this source of contact with the larger world is reduced.

### Community-Sponsored Recreation.

The question has been frequently raised, "Why do not those who have had to forego leisure which costs money turn to community-provided leisure, why do they not make use of the meetings at the Y.M.C.A. and the Y.W.C.A., why do they not flock to the settlement houses, why do they not use the public libraries?" The first answer is that the workers apparently do use such community-provided leisure as is consistent with their ordinary leisure-time habits and equipment. The second answer is that if no renewed earning makes possible a renewal of normal activities, free opportunities will eventually be accepted if a man's training fits him for them at all. Free movies, for instance, are much in demand and could be more used; but what training do most laboring people have which would fit them for participation in a Wednesday night forum at the Y.W., or in a reading club, or in lecture and discussion groups? The plain fact is that these are not a normal part of their life; they have little or no experience with them; they have no normal incentive to make use of them. Moreover, the most frequently used forms of recreation are those in which one participates with his own family alone or with very intimate friends. When the small familiar party group cannot be sustained because of various costs, nothing which quite corresponds to it can be substituted by the community. The plain fact is that the decline in recreation results from a decline in income, and only an increased income will make it possible for the unemployed to use their ordinary experience and habits in restoring that leisure-time life to which they have been accustomed.

*Effect of Unemployment on Family-Centered Recreation.*

There is little question that unemployment throws the families, both as small families and as clans, back upon themselves. It is questionable, however, whether such retirement into the family circle has increased the stability of family life. The greater proportion of the leisure time spent at home and with the clan is not chosen but forced association. Visits out of town to relatives or friends, useful in relieving tensions in family life which had grown out of the monotony of daily routine, are now rarer. Moreover, just when more time is spent at home, the frustrations in keeping up the home are increasing. The replacements of home furnishings cannot be made, so that the home is not as satisfactory a place as it was before. We shall presently discuss the effect of unemployment on the institution of the family. One item may be anticipated, namely, that other members of the clan often give gifts of money to children for amusement purposes, so that they will not notice so much the change in routine due to unemployment. This unquestionably tends to strengthen the ties between children and donors. But having to depend upon other members of the clan frequently has quite the opposite effect upon the parents. For instance, the fact that the grandparents are now furnishing the children with their recreation is simply one more factor in making the father feel that he is not doing his proper job as head of the family.

One further effect of curtailing recreation should be noted. An incidental, or perhaps a major, value of recreation is in bringing together young people of marriageable age; it performs a very real function in their courtship. When these normal diversions have to be cut down, an activity which has a real social purpose has been reduced and the opportunities for contact with one's future mate, in which many adjustments of personality and personal idiosyncrasies can be made, have to be foregone.

## II

## RELIGIOUS RELATIONS AND PRACTICES

UNEMPLOYMENT places a severe strain upon the individual's ability to control his own destiny and to realize his ambitions. For the believer, religion presumably offers comfort and help in this situation, either through the furnishing of divine assistance in reaching what one is after or in so redefining one's goals that achievement is more nearly possible. We are in no way attempting to develop a comprehensive discussion of the place of religion in the contemporary life of American workers; nor are we attempting to make our observations on the religious belief and practices of the unemployed consistent with either church doctrines or the conception of the priests and pastors of the place of religion in the life of their communicants. Indeed, having had contacts with a representative sample of the Roman Catholic, Jewish, and Protestant clergy, we are well aware that some of these attitudes and practices on the part of unemployed are not consistent with that conception. We are attempting merely to present the comments by the unemployed workers with whom we have had contact as to the place of religion in their lives and as to the effect of unemployment upon their religious experience. Furthermore, our chief concern with the function of religion in the present study is its effect or lack of effect in gearing individuals into the society of which they are a part.

### Services of Religion to Workers.

From our contacts with New Haven workers we would summarize the ways religion performs these services as follows:

    1. It gives an explanation of the unknown sources of

difficulty and of good luck which in some cases diverts blame or praise from human agents.

2. It provides the assistance of the Divine in making social adjustments and in meeting problems.

3. It provides the assistance of an organized institution, the church, in the making of social adjustments and in the meeting of problems.

4. Through the clergy, help is provided in straightening out problems in social relations.

5. The church and religion provide a source of moral authority in defining the proper relationships between individuals.

6. Religious practices provide an interest and activity in common with many other members of one's family and with the members of the community.

7. The activities connected with the church provide an opportunity for group relation and the participation in those associations which give one an opportunity to have status and to function as a social being.

### Explanation of the Unknown.

We have noticed that workers desire an understanding of the multitude of difficulties and circumstances in the midst of which individuals live. The twentieth-century culture in New Haven provides secular explanations for many of these. The self-maintenance problems which workers (particularly industrial workers) face can be almost entirely explained in terms of the relations they have with human beings. Among the many forces which influence the success or the failure of the individual in his efforts to maintain himself and his family, those which are directly traceable to human beings and consequently are amenable to the influences which can be brought to bear on human beings are the most important. In contrast to the agricultural worker, the industrial worker might better greet his fellows in the morning with the salutation, "Good wages," or

"Good working conditions" rather than with the salutation, "Good morning." The forces which influence the winning of a mate and the successful carrying on of family relations and the rearing of children are not quite so clearly
dominated by human agents. Political activities very seldom involve the spiritual world. Recreation is primarily a
relationship to human beings. There are sufficient unac-
counted for frustrations, however, in all of these areas of
human interests, including economic life, so that a religious
explanation for these matters is still sought by a great
number of workers.

What explanations do we find being offered by the
churches which some workers believe have a bearing upon
these frustrations and in particular upon the problems of
unemployment? A very real difference exists here between
the Roman Catholic and the Protestant point of view. Most
frequently we found Catholics explaining their circumstances in some such terms as these:

I believe that God is good. I've had so many prayers answered
that I cannot help believing in His goodness. I think that you
have to take the bitter with the sweet. The more God loves you
the more you suffer, and nobody gets along without some suffering. The more you suffer the more welcome good experiences
are. If you have to go through your hell right here on earth then
you probably won't have to go through it after death.

The Catholic church teaches us that the more we suffer on earth
the greater will be our reward in heaven. Up in heaven somewhere there is a book where suffering is recorded, and the more
suffering recorded the happier will be your life in heaven.

Such explanations are very frequent, particularly among
the women. Other less frequent explanations found among
Catholics were the expectation that such affairs as are at
present dominating the world indicate an end of the world,
and an interesting and presumably unorthodox explanation that upon death one's soul enters that of a new-born

babe so that one has another opportunity to enjoy in another life what one has missed in this one. As proof of this, our informant noticed that usually when there was a death there was also a birth.

Another Catholic belief which is relevant to our present problem is the faith that sins can be erased by means of penance, that having thus been forgiven there is no need for further punishment after death, nor even in this life. Misfortune is not necessarily, therefore, a punishment for past sins or even mistakes.

In contrast to these relatively comforting doctrines, the Protestant emphasis seems to be upon the relationship of rewards and punishments on earth to one's actual past behavior. Anything that happens to one now may be a punishment for something one has done sometime previous to the misfortune. Far more emphasis is placed upon the justice than upon the mercy of God. While ministers tend to place a great deal of emphasis upon the latter quality of the Deity, there is little supporting arrangement in the church ritual save in the story of God's gift to the world of the redeeming Christ, and practically no emphasis in the actual religious practices for making such a faith symbolic. The Protestant worker of a religious turn of mind frequently suspects that present difficulties are punishment for past sins.

It will be noted that these explanations are generalized ones and that for purposes of explaining particular items of misfortune, like the inadequate income or the lack of a job, they are not particularly useful. Their chief function is to give a generalized comfort for or useful explanation of specific difficulties.

The church's explanation of these difficulties is not in terms of major social events or forces. They are chiefly in terms of the individual's relationship with the Deity. When, therefore, present misfortune is understood to be a result of the operation of economic or social forces, God is given

very little place in the scheme of causal events. This makes
religious help for those who believe that more realistic and
human causes are at the root of their troubles seem somewhat unreal, and is at the basis of a good deal of scorning
of religious by nonreligious people.

### Unemployment and Religious Explanations.

What is the effect of unemployment upon this understanding of the place of religion in giving an explanation of the
difficulties under which men live? The Catholic explanation fits in nicely and without any difficulty. The "suffer-
ing-here–reward-hereafter" formula is very nicely suited
to producing a more comfortable acceptance of one's lot.
The Protestant point of view on the other hand, if actually
related to Divine forces, is very likely to raise resentment
when it is felt that one's present misfortune is after all *not*
due to one's own shortcomings. On the whole, however,
secular forces are considered to be far more prominent
than Divine forces as causal agents of misfortune. God has
nothing to do with the big forces of social and economic
affairs which these workers vaguely understand to be at
the root of their problems. The only way in which the social forces are related to the functioning of God in the
world, according to many workers, is through the fact that
many of these conditions are the results of the greed of
employers and others. Since greed can only be removed,
according to them, by a change of heart, and only God can
do that, He may be neglecting His duty. But then He is
dealing with very resistant stuff. The net result of this attitude is that God is not blamed for their present condition.
If they are religious enough to seek a religious explanation,
they do not blame their troubles on God because that would
be disloyal. If they are not religious, of course, they do not
hold God to account, for their attention is directed toward
many secular forces which operate to produce the situation.
In any case God doesn't get blamed.

From conferences with Protestant ministers it seemed clear to us that the Protestant church was not reaching any large numbers of the unemployed workers who would be seeking an explanation for their problem through the church, and where they are reaching large numbers of workers the relationship is a social and secular rather than primarily a religious one. God is not involved, therefore, because God is not the center of interest in the church affairs of these particular workers; and as we have seen, although the Catholic church is reaching a great mass of Irish, Italian, and Polish, as well as native American workers, the Catholic explanation offered is one which discounts the causal relationship of God to harsh economic circumstances. We can summarize the attitude therefore of the workers in the words of a French Canadian:

It has never occurred to me that God had anything to do with unemployment. The jobs are in the hands of men, and God doesn't have anything to do with it. Go to church—or don't go to church; believe in God—or don't believe in God, you'll get jobs or lose them just the same.

### Institutional Assistance for the Unemployed.

Many of the practices of primitive religion are directed toward the increasing of one's success in self-maintenance. To a lesser degree this is true of contemporary religion. Jobs very definitely come under the category of those things which may be requested as a favor from God and for which, in the case of Catholics, one may request the saints to intercede. We have not noted any great difference in the extensiveness with which Protestants and Catholics made use of this possibility, but we do feel that Catholics have prayed with greater confidence in the efficacy of their prayers. Several priests told us that since the depression there has been a large increase in those attending novenas on Monday nights in their churches. Particularly they noticed an increase in the number of young girls of high-school age and above attending. Our contacts with young people of this age lead us to suspect that this increase is due to two factors: first, the fact that these young people were getting out of high school without prospects of jobs; and, second, that a number of them were having to postpone their marriages because of the fact that their prospective husbands did not have jobs, or if they did have, were having to spend a great deal of their income in caring for parents who were without the customary means of support. These young people were seeking help of God in this manner so that their lives might become more normal.

The contacts made in the church itself are of some value in securing jobs, according to the testimony of one or two of our men. In other words it is simply one more source of contact from which recommendations or influence may be secured. The church itself has frequently undertaken to be a clearinghouse for odd jobs which its members will have done by those members who are unemployed. This practice was only temporarily successful in the case of those churches we inquired about. The chief reason given by the pastors was that the unemployed themselves were "too picky and choosey" about the jobs they would do. They didn't "seem to appreciate the fact that people were putting themselves out to employ them." Some of the men who were members of unions refused to take jobs at wages below union rates for fear of losing their union status. The pastors felt that workers should be willing to take any job offered at any wage in order to get off relief and "regain their self-respect"—apparently not aware of the fact that self-respect involves more than getting off relief. They interpreted refusal as showing the deterioration of people through our relief methods. They said they had encouraged people to take jobs paying as low as $2 a week with board, to "save their self-respect." We do not wish to tar all jobs offered through the churches with the same brush,

but the comments we gathered from those who were offered
such jobs were too consistent to permit doubt that the idea
failed largely because the wages offered were substandard.
The comment of one electrician is typical of many others:

The church people you work for think they are doing you a favor. They never stop to think, "Well, maybe he has some regular price for these jobs." They ask you, "Well, how much do I
owe you?" but you know by the way that they ask that they expect you to say, "Whatever you want to give," so they give you
25 c. an hour or so. Those that are best able to pay are the ones
who think they are doing you the biggest favor and pay you the
least.

This attitude characteristic of most relief giving is mul-
tiplied many times in the case of that offered through the
church. Apparently those who make offers of help are
doubly anxious that those who receive such help should return gratitude for it. They are doing it as a benevolent act,
and benevolence calls for gratitude. We make no judgment
as to the justice of such an expectancy, but we do wish to
point out once again that such a situation is not consistent
with the requirements of self-respect, independence, and
control on the part of the worker.

Administration of relief through the churches has de-
clined in recent years. Both Catholics and Protestants indicated that their relief practice at the present time, which
differs from that of 1929 and before, is to carry the relief
client until he can be taken over by some government
agency. Seldom do they carry the church member completely through his period of dependency.

*Pastoral Service.*

Extremely important in contemporary church life is the
role of the pastor. Both Catholics and Protestants, although
the latter to a greater extent than the former, indicated
that the importance of the church in their lives was pro-

portional to the liking which they had for the particular pastor. Certain it is that pastoral work has become equally important with, if not more important than, the ministration of the sacraments in the case of the Protestants and is occupying an increasingly important position with the Catholics, although in the latter case it has not superseded the sacraments as of first importance. The Catholic priests indicated that their parishioners expected them to understand something about social and economic affairs and about the social and economic problems in addition to the religious ones which their parishioners faced. They tended to agree that their parishioners were right in this desire. Protestant ministers also noticed an increase in the amount of expectancy that they should be aware of the issues of a social and economic nature in the community. However, they felt that this was limited largely to the younger people and that the older people felt that they should "stick to the gospel." From our contacts we are inclined to think that it is the younger ministers also who are responding to this demand from the younger people.

A further verification of the comment which we have made above that God was not involved in the matter of unemployment is the fact that the ministers claim they have not been called upon extensively to explain unemployment, partly because individuals did not believe that God was involved in the causal forces and therefore His ministers had nothing to answer for, and second, because they looked upon the minister as the personal adviser rather than as an interpreter of social and economic events, in the latter of which they found most of the causes of unemployment. Protestant ministers especially are valued for their personal qualities rather than as a representative of the Deity. Again and again men and women indicated that they liked to go and talk with such-and-such a minister because he was fatherly and seemed to understand their problems and knew so many things which would give them practical help. There was very little indication from the workers that in their contacts with the minister they were seeking his intercession with God. More than one indicated that he was very fond of the priests and the preachers because they were among the few educated people with whom he was acquainted.

The effects of unemployment on this situation are just what one would expect. Every pastor indicates that increasing numbers were coming to him for secular advice as a substitute for that advice formerly given by the lawyer, the doctor, and the broker who charged for their services. They were even asking questions about health, the sale of real estate, court affairs, insurance, and the like. Although Catholic priests insist that the sacraments are the first and most important ministration, and Protestant ministers also contend that they are chiefly and primarily responsible for the souls of their parishioners, the increase in this secular pastoral service is notable.

An interesting commentary on the extent to which the several denominations are reaching the working class is involved in the fact that very few of the Protestant ministers with whom we had any contact, with the exception of three, two of whom had working-class churches, knew anything at all about unemployment since they hadn't had any experience with it in their groups. Some of them explained it on the grounds that they had the better-class workers and that religious discipline and philosophy tended to make better workers; therefore their members were not laid off. The more normal explanation, however, seems to be that the Protestant churches do not reach that great mass of workers among whom the unemployed are to be found. This is not true of the Roman Catholic church. The Catholic church, according to several priests in New Haven, has a membership comprised of about 70 per cent of skilled, semiskilled, and unskilled industrial workers. Possibly as a result of a necessity imposed by this fact, the Catholic priests were very intelligent and intelligible about the problems of their unemployed members. We do not wish to indicate that all Protestant ministers could be characterized by the statement that they knew very little about unemployment and the problems of unemployment. That is obviously not the case. But the fact remains that relative to the Catholic priests they were less acquainted with its problems. Moreover, Protestant ministers tended to share the middle-class attitude toward the unemployed worker characteristic of the period prior to 1929. They have not even changed their opinions as much as, we have reason to believe from our surveys, middle-class opinion has changed concerning the unemployed. Such pastoral comments as these lead to such a conclusion: "Anybody who really wants to can get a job"; "A really good man never lacks for work"; "These unemployed are crochety and incapable individuals anyway"; "If it weren't for the fact that I am in the service of God, I'd be feeling that it would be very human to take exactly the same attitude that I heard an employer take the other night when he said, 'Really, you know, the unemployed don't want to work.'" The issue here is not whether or not such comments about the unemployed are true. The point is that these attitudes shared by a large number of Protestant ministers are not on the whole designed to make them effective leaders in any attack on the problems of the unemployed. Anyone who believes that people on relief or who are unemployed are, by and large, lazy, inefficient people who would be in trouble or on charity even without the depression is not in that state of mind which would make possible an understanding of the problems of those individuals whose circumstances we have been reporting.

There are a number of notable exceptions to this point of view. A number of the pastors have shown interesting initiative in organizing job-clearance houses, although with the shortcomings we have already indicated. Some of them devised work-relief projects around the church for men. One of them took the initiative in organizing a work seekers' club. Several working-class church pastors showed a real and intimate knowledge of the problems faced by their parishioners. One is not suprised, however, to find that so far as job hunting is concerned the church does not play a very large role.

### Religious Sanctions for Morality.

Traditionally the church has stood as a source of moral authority giving Divine sanction to the mores, or, as declared by a good many proponents of religion, has become the source and the fountainhead from which moral ideals and ideas spring. The conversations which we have had with the unemployed on ethical matters lead to a far greater confidence in the first statement of the case than in the second. Morals tend to be just what the group with whom one associates believes is right or wrong, and very little difference is noted between those who are religious in their morality and those who make no appeal to religious sanctions for their ethics. We shall not attempt an outline of the code of ethics of these working people other than to indicate this fact about them. Such statements of morality as "being good," "never being mean," "being faithful to your husband," "telling him if you are unfaithful," "being honest," obviously do not characterize religious people alone. Indeed there is some indication, at least among the unemployed and in several cases among those who were on the lower economic rungs of the ladder but not unemployed, that loyalty to the church became secondary to their loyalty to their own secular responsibilities. A very interesting story was told by one Roman Catholic woman illustrating this point.

Sit down and let me tell you a story. Once there was a poor widow with a son. They were so poor that the child was almost starved. The widow had two hens that each laid an egg a day.

She saved the eggs until she had a dozen. These she sold, receiving 20 c. She gave this money to the son asking him to take it to the priest in the next village in order that he might say a prayer to help her departed husband's soul on his journey to heaven. One day as the boy went by a store he smelled macaroni. He was hungry so he went inside, and giving the 20 c. to the proprietor asked for all the macaroni it would buy. When he went home his mother asked him as usual if he had given the money to the priest. He said he had. That night her husband came to her in a dream. He said, "Mary, that was the finest Mass I have had yet. At last I am going into heaven because of it." She woke up and thought, "What a funny dream!" Then she went back to sleep and dreamed it again. This time she woke up her son and asked her son who the priest was who said the Mass for her husband. The son was frightened and began to cry. Finally he told her what he had done, and she realized that the lesson in this dream was that you must first feed your children, or in other words, "charity begins at home."

Perhaps a very brief note from one of our notebooks will indicate this situation more thoroughly than generalized description. The wife of a building contractor who had seen better days and who was now on relief was speaking:

If you give to the poor you will get reward in heaven, but you must always do it in a spirit of love. One day a poor man came to my door when I had only a dime with which I expected to buy fish for the children's dinner. Believe me dimes these days don't come any too easy, so I was torn between two desires. One was to help this poor man, and I know the teaching of the church is that we should always give alms to the poor. The other was to buy fish for my children because I had been taught that charity always begins at home, and besides it looked to me like it was sensible that charity should begin at home. I finally asked my mother, who advised me to buy fish for the children. Mother, you know [and then she turned to her mother], is kind of liberal in these things. Long ago she stopped going to church. So I bought the fish, and never in my life have I eaten such awful fish. If I had given the dime to the poor man it would have been better, and it was a definite warning to me when I discovered that the fish was not good.

Immediately, however, her mother spoke up and said in words, I think, which would be repeated by a majority of individuals in contemporary New Haven: "The trouble was, Maria, that you didn't pick out good fish."

It is noteworthy, we think, that in neither our conferences with Protestants nor those with Catholics did we find much reference to the Deity in connection with morality. Being good was its own reward, or was defined in terms of merely obeying the customary rules of one's society; it did not have its source in Divine command or its reward primarily in terms of Divine approbation. Dishonest or other apparently immoral acts encouraged by unemployment, therefore, do not challenge one's position as a religious person as much as they challenge his status with his community associates. For those who feel this way about their morality, necessity is a great determiner of what shall be considered right and wrong. For instance, those Catholics who indicated to us that they were not telling the agencies about work which they were doing on the side while receiving relief felt that this was a necessary method in order to get any amount of security for themselves and their family. They, therefore, did not feel that it was wrong; and although from the point of view of an outsider this might seem to be dishonest, they did not feel it such and therefore did not report it in confession to their priests.

### Religion a Source of Family Solidarity.

Religion offers assistance to members of families in gearing themselves more closely together. The moral training of their children, which baffles workers and without which they feel that family life is not solid and safe, is undertaken for many of them by their Sunday school and by the parochial schools. In this way religion performs a very real service in integrating this most important of social institutions, the family. We are inclined to think that the parochial school in particular has demonstrated its value especially to foreign communities, providing a form of education which stressed an important part of the cultural inheritance of the parents, namely, their religion, and which also made possible training in the language of the parents. This area of social maladjustment between the parents of the first and the second generation is a difficult one to solve, and we are inclined to think that the parochial schools by giving dignity and importance to the elements of culture held by the parents have eased this transition very materially.

Exercises held by Sunday schools and children's classes of various kinds which the parents attend also provide an event in which the family may jointly participate.

Religious ritual in the home is another element through which family solidarity may be increased, although in the case of liberal Jews it furnishes a barrier to association with the older folks who insist upon the observance of Jewish ceremonial. There is little question, however, that the possession in common of adherence to a ritual is a bond strengthening the ties of family life. The feast and the holy days are more than religious occasions. They are also opportunities for family gatherings. They may do no more than provide an excuse for such a gathering, but even such an excuse is important in providing an activity in which the family finds itself sharing a common event. Other customs rooted in the life of the church are equally important. The custom of taking palms about on Palm Sunday to members of the family contributes, be it ever so little, to making the bonds of the family closer and to showing that the family is a unit. The fact that, on the whole, there is a general lack of a tendency for individuals to marry across the religious line is another factor which would tend to strengthen the hold of the affection of each upon the other inasmuch as they would both be sharing at least a very large body of the culture in which each of them had been reared. That one cannot be too broad in his assumptions of this sort of a result, however, is indicated by the fact that so far as our working-people correspondents were concerned there was very little sharing of religious beliefs between the husband and the wife, between the parents and the children. Neither would risk speaking for the other in matters of religion, and apparently it was not customary to carry on discussion in a religious vein or to mention religion in the normal conversation that took place in the home.

Unemployment has had little effect upon this function of the church. The influence of the church upon family relations continues unabated, and the various ways in which religious matters bring families together are especially important in those families in which family irritations have grown up. Indeed it is very frequent that the religious forces, such as ritual and observance of holidays and feast days and the religious training of children, are one of the few remaining bonds which give a common interest and a common purpose to family life when the strain of unemployment is felt most severely. Even such ritual observances, however, must be curtailed in view of the reduced funds available during unemployment.

### Relations and Status in the Religious Community.

Finally, there is to be noted as a contribution of religious life to the gearing in of the worker to the community the fact that he is participating with others of the community in common activities, practices, and beliefs. Some of this is resultant upon a mere sharing of the activities with each other. The mere meeting with other members of the community is indicated by some as a big help in making them feel that they are not alone, although even here it is to be noted that the association must be with people of the right sort as defined by one's group culture. For instance, one

woman who enjoyed greatly a meeting at the City Mission
every Sunday afternoon was told finally by some of her
friends that the meetings were sponsored by Protestants,
whereupon, being a good Catholic, she felt that it was not
proper for her to continue to attend. The comments made
to us indicate, however, that the association which one has
in church is not with some mystical "community of God."
The chief association is with one's own friends, and individuals would not like to go into a church alone if that
church had none of their friends in its membership. There
is a satisfaction in doing the things required by religion
which many people are doing also—attending church, observing church festivals, those ceremonies surrounding the
departure of loved ones (mourning, the laying of wreaths
and the wearing of mourning clothes), as well as participation in the less clearly religious "activities" sponsored by
the church. The participation in the celebrations of the
feast days and the holiday services at the church are also
religious functions which give an opportunity for one to
realize that he is a member of a community. It is interesting to notice that the attendance at such important services as Easter and Christmas very frequently are the limit
of attendance at church services by workers with whom we
came in contact. In other words, apparently the value of
participation is increased by the universality of that participation. Here we find a form of communication. When
people participate in religious observances which they see
others participating in, they are saying to each other, "We
are of the same people."

The multiplicity of religious groups and the difference
in religious belief keep religion in a modern community
from being a dominant integrating force. When there are
so many lines of thought and types of practice it is difficult
for the religious institution to become the clue to the community life which it was in a good many medieval communities and in primitive and less civilized groups. Neverthe-

less, for one's own circle of acquaintances very frequently the church does become the chief common denominator of life among the group.

It would not be fair to complete the discussion of those contributions which religion makes to the integration of individuals in the life of the community without mentioning the numerous church activities which urban churches have undertaken in the service of their members. The numerous women's clubs, boys' clubs, young people's clubs, men's clubs, mothers' clubs, the organization of teams, of singing societies and of choirs provided for many of those who are religious in nature, and for many who are not primarily interested in the church for its religious purposes, an outlet for their leisure-time activity and energy. Moreover, we are inclined to think that where both sexes participate in these groups they perform an important part in acquainting young people with each other, which acquaintance is an important prelude to marriage. As we have already indicated in the chapter on recreation, however, unemployment tends to reduce the participation of individuals in these affairs. Most of them require some monetary contribution, or if they do not specifically require it it is assumed as one's "moral obligation," so that when one is unemployed or when one's chief breadwinner is unemployed there is less possibility that the associations can be freely and satisfactorily undertaken and continued.

Another contribution of these meetings to the social status and stability of the individual is the fact that through committee services and through services as officers of these institutions and through the representation of these groups at various district and even national meetings individuals secure an added prestige among their fellows.

### Bases of Continued Participation in Church Life.

As we look over these ways in which the church functions to bring workers into contact with others and to give them a consciousness that they are geared in, at least in this respect, with the other members of the community, what are the major premises of that association which most clearly affect the continued participation of the unemployed?

### Financial Expenditures.

One of the first, and we are inclined to think the most important, is that money is required to establish this association and to maintain it. The numerous ways in which money is necessary in order to maintain the association ought to be clear. Money is required in collections in church. In Roman Catholic churches it is customary to deposit 10 c. or 15 c. upon entering the church and an "offering" is taken during the Protestant service. Various assessments are made for particular purposes. The social activities of the church require that one shall contribute either money or the things which money can buy. When one belongs to a church which is some distance from his home, there is the problem of carfare. There are constant requests for money to support things which the church as a group is supporting—missions, educational projects, contributions to the larger church organizations, and the like. We cannot pass over this matter without realizing that clothes cost money and decent clothes are a prerequisite of attendance at church. Ministers are quite aware of this and have attempted to adjust their programs and their practices so that there would be less inclination on the part of workers to drop out on this account. Many ministers have abolished "offerings"; they have constantly made statements to their parishioners that after all it was their own attendance and participation that were desired and not the attendance and participation of their money. Some pastors have even told their parishioners if they didn't want to appear to be noncontributors to put in their envelopes without anything in them. Ministers have offered to supply their parishioners with clothes. With respect to the organizations connected with the church, dues have been constantly reduced and even abolished. Nevertheless, these devices seem not to satisfy the workers, at least not to create within them the impression that they are actually participating in the life of the church when they are not contributing money. Although Catholic priests indicate that they have never urged their members to continue the 10 c. or 15 c. contribution at the church door, workers say that they feel the priest expects them to do so, nevertheless. We have some indication of shifting of churches in order to get away from a priest who very obviously expected such contributions to a priest who was more lenient in this respect. Even the priest who most strenuously insisted that he had not made any such requirements of his parishioners said that he noted that some people who really could afford it had stopped putting in the 10 c. or 15 c. at the door, indicating that he had been standing there observing them. It is quite obvious that workers who pass the offering box without contributing would feel that he was directing his gaze at them. The attitude of workers toward going to church without contributing is well emphasized by the statement of one Catholic that:

Of course they don't absolutely require you to put your 15 c. in when you come in. They allow you to come in without it; but of course you feel sneaky not to do it, so most of the time you set up your image at home on the table and you know your prayers and you have your beads and you can do your praying just as well there. That's what I think.

A Protestant worker expressed the same feeling:

I go to church maybe once a month, but they always want money. You've got to put in a dime when the basket comes around, and if you don't put something in they look at you and then they look at the basket [he opened his eyes wide and craned his neck in a very surprised expression], and then you hear about it later. What's the use of going when it just makes you feel rather sneaking-like to do it?

One of our Protestant families gave an indication of one way out of this dilemma in the reduction of the contribution. She said that she and her husband attended church always on Easter Sunday, and that they were in the habit of putting in a five-dollar bill. This Sunday they felt that they could not afford it, so when the collection plate came around her husband pulled out a dollar bill. His wife whispered to him that 25 c. was sufficient and that he might need the rest for himself that week, so he grinned and pulled out a quarter and dropped it in the plate. Nevertheless, in spite of such adjustments, it remains true that people are dropping away from the church because of the necessity of financial contribution. Now this is not surprising when it is realized that a statement of relationship to the church which our culture approves of is the following: "I *support* the church."

Catholic priests indicate that there has been no decrease in church attendance, and Protestants say that only the marginal people are dropping away from church and that these were looking for some excuse, anyway. This is possibly true; but the comments that men have reduced their church attendance because of the necessity of contribution are too universal to verify this comforting assurance from the priests and the ministers.

### Class Status.

A second major premise of the participation in the community life as sponsored by the church is that one shall be not too distantly associated, so far as class status is concerned, with the other members of the church. Several of our members, after long-continued unemployment, indicated that they still continued to want the ministrations of the church. But they had transferred to a church in a section in which those who attended were more nearly of their own economic status. This usually meant a transfer from a "downtown" church. In spite of the doctrine of the churches which emphasizes the brotherhood of man, it still remains true that people feel more at home in that brotherhood which is composed of individuals whose economic status is not too far distant from their own. The damage which unemployment does to one's economic status is therefore a contributing factor in decreasing one's association with other church members who continue to retain some of their former economic resources.

### Training in Customary Faith and Practice.

A third major premise in establishing the degree to which the church is a satisfactory way of gearing into community life is that one shall be trained in the habitual practice and routine, and in the relationships, belief, and practice of the church. In this respect we think it is significant that early training and constant participation are more consistent and more habitual in the case of Catholic than of Protestant church members. It is not surprising therefore to find that Catholics continue to make use of their church in the midst of their difficulties more thoroughly than do Protestants. As one Catholic priest said:

The solution of most problems or decisions as to what to do is practical. Problems that are too great for them to grasp or solutions too difficult for individual action are looked upon as religious problems. Catholics have been trained during their youth for over fifteen years to turn to God for aid in difficulty. No matter how dormant this training may be, in times of distress the early teaching will assert itself. This accounts in large measure for the Catholic turning to the church in times of difficulty furnished by unemployment.

Protestants, on the other hand, instead of constant and habitual turning for Divine aid, have been accustomed to do so only in great emergencies; and in spite of the fact that unemployment does furnish such an emergency, the lack of continual practice and of habit asserts itself and does not suggest the turning to the church or the source of its religion for help.

## Acceptance of the Church's Authority.

A fourth major premise in making the church a valid help in promoting relationship to the community is that its authority in its own field shall be unchallenged. Here again the Catholic church has the advantage over the Protestant. Protestant pastors tend to describe their relations and the relations of their parishioners to the Divine in rather theological terms. Catholics retain such discussion chiefly for intellectual debate between the clergy. With respect to the people, the relationship to God is discussed in simple terms of human-divine association, and of the relationship to the Divine through the intercession of the immortals and the saints. There is little arguing with people about philosophy. According to the Catholic priests, the masses of people do not want to argue, they want to believe. The strange thing, they point out, is that "one would suppose with this attitude one would lose the intellectuals; but you don't." One Protestant pastor sees his job in winning respect for God's authority and as getting people to see a definite organization of the universe into which individual actions should fit. The people are on the whole not well enough educated, he says, to comprehend the universal view of things. That is very true, but from our contacts we cannot escape the conclusion that in many cases the Protestant church has catered to the intellectuals among its group who demand such a soundness of world view and has neglected the assistance to those people who, unable to understand or not caring for such a world view, find little help in the methods which the church and its pastors employ. The upshot of this is to leave the Protestant church with an authority which is not well understood, nor is it accepted as unchallenged. Furthermore, the numerous points of view represented in the several denominations tend to cause a conflict in the workers' minds as to just who is right. In spite of the fact that there is an inherent movement toward church unity in the Protestant church, such movement is not having an effect upon the present trust which Protestant workers have in the authority with which their church speaks. The major comment among the worker members of the church on this trend toward unity is that "One church is as good as another." That may be an indication that the Protestant church is on the way to a universal authority, but certainly only that it is on the way and not that it has arrived.

### Consistency of Religious with Secular Philosophy and Practice.

Another major influence on the willingness with which individuals participate in religious relationships is the degree to which the church and its doctrine and its requirements are consistent with contemporary secular philosophy and practices. This influence exists both among Catholics and Protestants and is to be seen in their insistence that "Charity begins at home," that their first responsibilities are to maintain themselves and their families, and to make a place for themselves in the culture of which they are a part. If the church helps with this, so much the better; if it does not, so much the worse for the church. If one were making a survey entirely of church members, this point of view might not be so evident, but our contacts have been with a large number of people who do not participate in the church and with another large number who have withdrawn from church membership under the stress of unemployment. We are speaking, therefore, not of the position of the church, so far as its own members are concerned, but of the place of the church in the life of the working-class and in particular of the unemployed groups in the community.

### Human Qualities of Pastor.

Another major premise of participation in church activities is that the priest or pastor shall be a likable, service-giving, and friendly individual on a purely human basis in addition to his position as a representative of the Deity. Although this is less true in Catholic groups than in Protestant groups, it is nevertheless obvious in all denominations. In other words, if this observation is indicative of a present and continuing condition, more and more the relationship of the unemployed to the church will be determined by the personal attitude and understanding of the pastor or priest in charge.

### No More Obvious Secular Solution.

A final major premise is that there shall be no more obvious secular solution or explanation or help available. As we have already indicated, the dominant methods used for solution of economic difficulties at least in our contemporary culture are secular. Far more prevalent than the appeal to God is the appeal to human ingenuity and organization in the endeavor to solve one's economic difficulties. The obvious usefulness of the techniques which we have discussed in the chapters on economic adjustments frequently seems self-evident as superior to those involved in the participation in religious exercises or practice.

### Summary: The Unemployed and the Church.

In summary it may be said that the general attitude of the unemployed toward the church is one which neither praises nor blames, which neither neglects nor embraces the church as a help in the present difficulties. This generalization is particularly true of the Protestant church members. The attitude can be described among those of all denominations, however, as that of maintaining a nominal contact with the church just in case there should be validity in its help and assistance in times of stress. The continued presence of images and religious pictures, of crosses over the beds in the families when there was practically no realistic participation of the members of the family in church services is an indication of this. The normal type of church attendance is an occasional one, particularly on the festival days, and in particular on Easter and at Christmas time. Participation in social church festivals and in the ritual of the church which furnishes occasion for family and community relationships does not emphasize primarily the religious nature of the relationship.

The chief indication of turning to the church is not for the religious or the primarily religious succor which it is always supposed to give, but for the personal help and advice of those representatives of the Deity, the clergy, whose personal intelligence and integrity and spirit are appreciated by those who are in difficulty.

There were few strong negative reactions to the church, and these only in the case where the individual held a strong conviction about the secular nature of the causes which determined men's destiny. When we say that those who had such a positive conviction were opposed to, we do not mean that they were concerned about destroying, the religion of other people, but simply that their steadfast conviction in, let us say, a socialist or communist analysis of life's affairs was such that they just could find no place for religion. And their attitude emphasizes the point we have just made that religion is desired when there is no more substantial and no more promising solution to life's difficulties. Those who held to a socialist faith were most frequently found to put all their hopes in this. It might be that if the socialist analysis were correct, they contended, exploitation was really at the basis of all of it and then something could be done about it; whereas if it were all dependent upon an unknown God, the contact with whom was never certain or sure, it is questionable whether anything could be done about it. Their demand and desire for action were such that they did not care to spend their efforts where there was little promise of success. Only occasionally did we find, however, that this attitude on the part of the radical thinker put him in bitter opposition to the services of religion. One such may speak for all of the very few who took this attitude:

I tell you, my friend, the workingman is blind. He goes to his church and he prays, "Oh God, feed us for we are hungry! Give us bread for we are starving!" [At this point he actually got down on his knees to make a pantomime.] Fool! The only God is science. Where did we come from? Out of the ground, from the trees and the animals. No man gave and no God gave Mr. Rockefeller or Mr. Morgan the right to control this land which is for us all; and there is no God to hear prayer and give people bread as long as Mr. Rockefeller and Mr. Morgan control it all. Maybe the priests and the preachers can do some good, but they will do some good because they are men—strong men with intelligence and open eyes and courage—here [and he touched his breast]. They are good men—priests and ministers. Not because they are members of the clergy, but because they are men.

The only comment that we would make upon this statement is that this man is quite in error in ascribing the attitude he does to the great masses of workers. Religious activity among them seems more a matter of retaining a nominal contact with a possible source of well-being than a matter of sharing intimately and constantly in the ministrations of the church or the comfort and convictions of religion.

## III

## POLITICAL RELATIONS AND PRACTICES

POLITICAL group action does not rank high among the tactics adopted by the unemployed as a means for solving their problems. In view of the limited part played by politics in the life of employed workers this is not surprising. The worker's conception of government and of his practical relations to it is not such that political action, beyond the regular visit to the polls, appears to be an appropriate method for dealing with the problems raised by the lack of a job.

His customary political practices are limited to voting. No characteristic form of political practice has been developed to meet the recurring problems of working-class life as such. For the great majority of workers, government of the people, by the people, and for the people means primarily a periodic right to kick. He is not very clear about the process by which his vote is interpreted as the "will of the people." He is, in a more or less confused manner, aware that the politicians for whom he casts his vote are employees of a political machine, and he feels a certain contradiction between this reality and the political theory that these men "represent" him. These politicians make their living by working for the party just as he does by working for a particular firm. Their job is to carry on the "business" of the city, the state, or the nation just as his is to make locks, or bird cages, or guns. His taxes, or those of his landlord, pay their salaries, which they supplement by graft or by good contracts or fees which their prestige makes available. But what he thinks about what the laws should be or the way in which they are administered counts for little until election day when he can register a "kick" or approval about the way these officials have done their job.

This identification of political action with periodic voting for or against employees of a political party is strongly ingrained in the folkways of the workers. It does not suggest to him that he is an integral part of "the government." The government is a thing apart from him. It is not an agency of which all are a part, engaged in a coöperative doing of jobs of common interest to all. The technique of politics for him does not include practical ways other than voting by which he might participate.

Nor is government a fulcrum by which power might be exercised in the interests of his particular class. Even if he understood what certain of the more radical of those who occasionally speak to him from soapboxes meant by the word "fulcrum," he could not see clearly enough the technique and processes which gave objective meaning to that term to visualize his own place in such political activity. Aside from the claims of soapbox speakers he has little direct evidence that "interests bring pressure to bear on government officials and legislators." He may have his suspicions when the foreman drops a hint as to the man he is voting for, or when a printed message from the boss appears on his pay envelope. They apparently have some interest in getting the "right" man elected. Since they cannot control the worker's vote, however, he is apt to dismiss this evidence from his mind. If he is a member of a trade union, he knows that his state and national federations have lobbies. Union leaders are frequently "party men" and have "axes to grind" with the support of union members. Political issues are discussed at union and Trades Council meetings. But men must be organized to share in such practices and a minority of New Haven workers are organized. On every day of the year save election day the government tells the worker what to do and what he may not do. He takes orders; he does not give them.

He has enough contact with the game of politics to know that the game is not a free-for-all. He has enough contacts

with those who do play the leading roles to know that they
are primarily job holders or hangers-on working in self-
interest, that their first concern is to keep the machine
they serve in power. He does not resent that; "they have
their living to make too, you know." But the knowledge
does not stimulate confidence that government is "of the
people, by the people, and for the people."

### Worker's Experience with Government and Politics.

It is not difficult for the worker to arrive at such conclusions about politics. Any thinking he does on the subject
will have to find a place for such typical comments as the
following, heard in conversations among workers during
our study. Such comments are the raw data of his convictions about political processes:

Look, Jim, you know what politics is in this ward, don't you?
5,000 people live here. 2,500 are men old enough to vote;
women and children do not vote. Only about 25 per cent or a
little better are citizens. A fair proportion of these are professional and business people who never take sides for business
reasons—so about 300 people are the total active party members. There are two families controlling between them 87 votes.
The Democrats give to the leader of one family (who runs a
grocery store) all grocery orders from the Charity Department.
The leader of the other family gets a job driving trucks or in-
specting trucks, and half the necessary votes are in the bag.
This ward is, politically, no better off than the podestas in Italy
when 151 people can control the political life of 5,000.

Truck Driver.

Of course I'm a politician, and you want to know what that
means? The idea in politics is to put yourself in a place where
you can do other people favors, to always make a friend wherever you can. The other part of the game is to always do what
you are told by the man who put you where you are. By the
first policy you get votes. Take my cousin, Jim. During the Republican administration he wanted a Public Works Department

job because here he had the power to give out about a thousand jobs during his term in office. But if it was now, Jim would take the Charities Department because, even if it's only a two-dollar grocery order, you're giving out something to somebody, and if he was in the Public Works, they haven't got any money. And everybody would be calling him an s.o.b. because he was so tight with the jobs. Munitions Worker.

By doing what the party leader tells you, you are piling up credits for yourself which can be cashed in on good jobs or big favors when the opportunity comes along. The greatest crime for a politician is to become independent of the party once he has been elected to an office. If it takes a lifetime, the party leaders will get you. Why I even know of a boss who gave a police job to a Republican because the Democrat who was in line for the job had crossed him up in a primary election ten years before. Laborer.

I wish you could come around some afternoon between four and six and sit in my parlor and listen to the fellows that come to see me. "How about a little more on my grocery order?" "Jesus, Paul, you got to get me a job." "Can't you fix me up on this W.P.A., Paul?" Another wants me to get his mother a widow's pension and him and three brothers working and owning their own home at the same time. Somebody else wants a little off his tax bill. God, it's terrible. If I could get my old job at the Eastern Machine Screw Co. back again, I'd give this racket up tomorrow. But you can't give it up. It's like football or baseball—you swear you're not going to waste time playing any more, but when the boys get the ball out and begin kicking it around, before you know it you're out. I swear off politics, but when they start having meetings in the fall and speeches, somebody comes around to the house and says: "What's the matter, Paul, ain't you coming around?" And the first thing you know you're out telling the public what a hell of a good man your candidate is. Printer.

Some of the people that come around to see me are unreasonable. It's all right to ask about getting out of a court scrape or even fixing up city contracts; but the way these fellows expect you to get them jobs! There's a fellow who came around last fall, every day, *every day!* Wanted me to get him a job on the F.E.R.A. as painter. What could I do with all the F.E.R.A. fellows in the city Republicans? I told him I couldn't do anything, but he kept pestering me. "Didn't I vote for the party last year? You gotta do something for me." I said: "Geez, Al, you voted last year for the first time; there are fellows out of jobs that have been voting straight Democrat for twenty years." But he wouldn't listen, so finally I called up the Charity Department and had him put on the list for a three-dollar order, milk and federal food. That didn't go so well because the investigator had to come to his house. Then one day one of my friends came around and told me he got appointed to the State Employment Bureau. God, did I grab him! I said, "Put this s.o.b. into a job the first thing you do and put him on as a laborer." Well, he did first thing, and the fellow hasn't been around to see me since.                     Toolmaker.

There are only two reasons for going into politics—it's either to get something for yourself or to be able to get something for somebody else—usually it's the first. You fellows today are turning to politics more than to anything else just because there's a better chance to get jobs. You have to make a living somehow.                     Carpenter.

Politics is just like the Masons or the K. of C. If you're on the inside there is always somebody around who will do you a favor. If you want a job, you go to the ward leader. Well, maybe he got a little knocked off the taxes for the fellow who owns the X Co. So he calls up and says, "I've got a friend who is looking for a job. Is there anything at your plant?" And the fellow at X finds a place for him even if it means letting somebody else go. Same thing in the Masons—you get hobnobbing around and if you need work, there will be somebody there who knows somebody who can fix you up. Politics looks after its own if you play the game right.          Machine Operator.

Before the depression you used to be able to make pretty good money in the political racket, but not any more. When times was good, a fellow who wanted a building permit to put a store

in front of his house would come over. I'd get it, and he would
slip me twenty-five bucks. Another fellow gets in a court jam.
He would pay me ten bucks to get him off rather than get a
five-dollar fine from the court and have his name on the record.
Now if they come to you, it's only because they haven't got
money enough to get it through the proper channel, and as far
as I'm concerned, it's a charity job.                 Painter.

Paul has been a grand juryman and notary public for fifteen years. He says he has never charged a person for any
of the jobs. "Why should I charge 50 c. for putting my
name on a piece of paper when I can let the fellow keep
the 50 c. and make a friend?"

From such casually acquired details as these grows the
worker's conception of politics and government as a business pursued by the few in the interests of the few. To be
sure, those who make a business of politics do favors for
humble people like himself in the hope of getting his vote.
Yet he is not a real participator in all of this elaborate
business which appears to him much more likely to influence the course of events than can his occasional journey
to the ballot box.

Moreover, the two-party system does not encourage the
practice of reliance upon political action for the solution of
the worker's problems as an individual or as a member of
the working class. Each political party apparently carries
a full stock of goods and services intended to win the support of all economic classes in the community. Aside from
the Socialist and Communist parties which are mistrusted
on other grounds, the major parties do not pretend to
serve the working class alone. The worker assumes that
promises to workingmen are placed in the party plat-
forms primarily to catch his votes and not because party
leaders have an understanding of the importance of working-class welfare to community well-being. In this assumption he displays a crude but realistic political wisdom. The
realization of this fact, however, does not cause him to

seek new avenues of political expression. It leads to a distrust of all politicians rather than to political activity in behalf of a more consistent working-class party.

It should be remembered also that New Haven is not a strongly organized town. The political activities of trade unions have not therefore stimulated in any large number of workers the awareness that such techniques are available as alternative ways of improving their lot.

Such a limited conception and practice of political life do not, on the other hand, characterize the "party workers." They have ample evidence that their relation to the machine can be used to improve their personal fortune. But this group of loyal supporters of a particular party, who think that in voting for a mayor or alderman they are voting for an employment office with a bias in favor of their application, is not large enough so that their practice and ideas can be declared characteristic of working-class folkways and mores.

A tendency may have existed early in the depression of 1929 and immediately after the inauguration of the W.P.A. for the rank-and-file workers to look to politically influential persons for help. That tendency was reduced by experience. It was usually "the other fellow" to whom favors were given. Only the few party members who qualified by virtue of effective party service could be placed in the "gravy jobs." The degree to which politicians' recommendations could alter the relief check was limited. A practice does not become customary unless it is consistently successful.

### Recent Changes in Relations to Government.

The past few years have seen two changes in this basic pattern of the workers' relation to government and politics. Workers employed and unemployed have begun to distinguish between the national government on the one hand and state and local governments on the other. The second change is an apparently growing conviction that Roosevelt honestly has the interest of the workers at the basis of his policies. In both of these changes the importance of the national government has been emphasized. Indeed, it stands out as *the* government in contrast to the political maneuverings and horse-trading and machine politics which pass for government in the local community and the state. To many of the workers this involves no difficult readjustment of political ideas. The Federal Government is simply a new entrant into their calculations. Formerly it had been a hazy symbol connected with the flag and the Fourth of July and wars and presidential campaigns. The *real* government was a composite of local and state political arrangements. The Federal Government was not involved in their day-by-day experience. They seldom talked with anybody who knew much about it. Now it began to appear in very realistic ways in their everyday life. Closer acquaintance with the processes of national politics might dissipate the judgment that they are not identical with those of local politics, but at the moment the national government is beginning to assume importance as a trustworthy channel of adjustment of workers' problems. As yet that conception is unclouded by the belief that "government means the politicians and the politicians mean graft." The faith that one's vote actually accomplishes results in better wages and working conditions while on the job, and more adequate security when earning power is interrupted has been carefully cultivated by national politicians and by certain of the organizers for the newer unions. On the whole the cultivation has yielded a good crop of increasing conviction that voting for national officials is a positive technique for increasing working-class security. Such a conviction has increased the awareness of participation in the processes of government, and it has given a bit more reality to the idea that government can be used as a fulcrum to raise the standards of living of one's class.

Particularly have those men employed on W.P.A. developed this attitude. The national government is their employer. The fact enhances the reality of the government's relation to them. The connection between their own well-being and government has become as vivid for them as for the large taxpayer or for management subject to government regulation. Those workers now employed upon W.P.A. are participating in a project sponsored by the national government. Heretofore, their employer had been a private corporation. As citizens they were related to their national government periodically through the activities of an election campaign. Their personal interest in national affairs was considerably limited and was outlined by the party propaganda placed in their hands by the local political leaders. Employment with W.P.A. changes that pattern of relationships. They are now directly interested in at least one major activity of the Federal Government. It takes no malicious planning on the part of party leadership to establish this pattern and to make the unemployed realize that their daily bread is directly affected by national politics. Since the channel of improving their status in that relationship is political, voting has taken on a new significance. It is noteworthy, however, that even with this increase in political consciousness, the political techniques used by the vast majority are still limited to the traditional one of voting. Organized political pressure urged by energetic leaders has not appealed to any large numbers as a feasible and desirable avenue of political activity.

### The Unemployed and Radical Political Action.

These basic political conceptions, folkways, and trends influence the reaction of workers to suggestions of radical political action. The observation is unavoidable that such suggestions have not obtained a large following among the unemployed. Such a result could have been anticipated by anyone acquainted with the political realities of working-class life.

### The Hold of Custom.

Trained only to vote periodically, the appeal to the tactics of pressure politics was not in the habit equipment of the average worker. The intricacies of machine politics he did not understand and, moreover, he looked upon them with suspicion. He had not been personally involved in the subtle types of pressure politics understood and used by other interest groups. When the reality of a new possibility for using his political power to better his position dawned upon him it was still a possibility to be exploited through voting for a party and more particularly for a person whom he believed had his own interest more at heart than that of other classes. The attack of members of the administration upon "economic royalists" and "America's sixty families" was effective in breaking down the customary observation that political promises were extended to *all* economic classes primarily to get votes. The concern of Mr. Roosevelt for the "forgotten man" he interpreted as concern for his own welfare. He could use his only traditional political technique with more confidence. His increased confidence in traditional techniques reduced his inclination to try new and untried methods led by men whom he distrusted on other grounds. The radical political technicians attracted only a small following from among those beginning to see a new hope in the use of old ways. In this field of folk practice also it is evident that men turn slowly to new methods as long as there is a ray of hope that the old can be made to produce satisfactory results. For the time being at least the new hope in what could be accomplished through the national government shone through the clouds of disillusionment with the politics of city and state with which he was more intimately acquainted. Other reasons, however, account for the lack of success on the part of the radical political leaders and the organizers of the unemployed for direct political pressure. Let me set down a list of the reasons which inhibit any marked tend-

encies toward radical action by workers as they stand revealed in the conversations we have had with the unemployed of New Haven.

### Lack of Reinforcement for the Radical's Clichés.

At first glance the appeals made by radical agitators would
seem to be admirably designed for stirring up an enthusiastic response among workers so unfortunate as to have no
opportunity to work. Here is a page from my notebook
written after attending a May Day meeting on the Green
in 1934:

There is no sullen grimness about the expressions on the faces of
those listening to the speeches. The John Reed Club enacts a
tragic drama—the sale of an American worker. He is auctioned
off. His qualifications are announced; bids come from the audi-
ence—starvation wages, Fascism, paternalistic soft soap, wage
cuts, etc. He is sold to the N.R.A. for a New Deal. A tragedy in
its implications, but it is taken by the crowd in holiday spirit.
It is good fun. "Better than a movie," one man remarked.

No one is paying very much attention to what the speakers are
saying. They have heard it all before. I am talking with two;
we cannot hear the speaker. One of his remarks is applauded.
All three of us join in the clapping and cheering.

A better-than-average speaker gets a better-than-average
hearing:
"You men and women are not fundamentally revolutionists.
You are human beings to whom 'things as they are' promise very
little. You are fighting for what you need. Nail down this
point: You have been denied a self-respecting place in capi-
talistically organized industry and business. One door after another has been slammed in your faces; but here in this movement you can accomplish something. If you can make your demands loud enough and forceful enough the bloody capitalists
will have to give in. Industry has said to you, 'There is no
achievement here for you. You are inferior to the ruling class—
if you weren't you would have enough money to get into that

class. You have no power to make decisions. We who rule industry know best and will make them for you, and in some cases, of course, that means that we decide we can't use you. You have no real ability to manage your own affairs. You ought to be glad when industry can find a place for you and not be outraged when it doesn't.' To all of this communism opposes a tremendous 'No.' The sort of a 'No' that makes you hold your chin up and realize that you amount to something; you count; you are important. The sort of a 'No' which says that every worker has a place, a place that takes him out of the category of tools in the service of capitalist overlords, and grants him status as a man in serving the common good. What does it matter that recognized economists call you a fanatic? They would. Their prosaic and sensible world, their orthodox system, has cast you off. What are you going to do about it, bow your head and take it? Prove yourself the mere tool they think you to be? Or are you going to be a 'man' and assert your human dignity and your own self-respect?"

Every word of this speech rang true to the experiences men had had. Yet when he called for volunteers to stage a march on the City Hall, only a few followed him.

No one can deny the realism of the cases cited by radical agitators in their appeals to the workers and the unemployed. They are as vivid as the sight of a mother evicted from a dilapidated tenement house sitting in the street on a broken chair, trying to shelter her baby from the icy winds with a ragged blanket. If such word pictures can't whip up in unfortunate men the spirit of revolt, an explanation must be found. The fact is that such pictures shouted from the soapbox were not sufficiently verified by experience to arouse confidence in their universality. Experience with "the government," with supervisors, with landlords, and bosses just didn't universally fit the agitator's picture. Even if some verification existed in his own case, the worker had enough associates who had contrary experiences so that the charges were too watered down to stimulate action.

*Familiarity with Capitalistic Institutions and Ways.*

Equally important as a damper on radical tendencies is the experience of living in the midst of a culture whose beneficial aspects apparently are dependent upon capitalistic arrangements. Workers have a vague feeling that "it all hangs together." "Smash the bad, and you smash the good," would be their phrase. Those who wonder at the inertia (or patience, according to the point of view) of the working class and their lack of revolutionary fervor forget how thoroughly all the foundation stones of the worker's life are held together by capitalistic mortar. His job, his wages, his insurance, his chances for achievement as a productive worker have grown out of a capitalistic system. They would all be better and more secure in utopia. Granted. (But who is to manage this utopia? The soapbox speakers? The workers know what is required of a good industrial manager.) The memory of the prosperous '20's under present management is not completely dead. Home building and managing, the education of one's children, recreation, political activity, the stores laden with more kinds of goods than one can ever hope to buy, one's social status, all are keyed to and have grown out of the present capitalistic arrangements. It is in part because man lives in these other areas quite as much as in the area of economic affairs that he says to the arguments about industrial injustice, "Yes, *but* . . ." And then follows consciously, or unconsciously, the realization that all he has, little as it is, and all he can hope to have is bound closely to things as they are. Life is lived as a unit not in departments. As long as other than self-maintenance interests are not too thoroughly frustrated and self-maintenance is not "too bad," that *but* in the "Yes, but . . ." will be a large obstacle to revolutionary activity. Any "swing toward the left" will merely mean that the "Yes" is growing a bit stronger and the "but" a bit weaker. The change in emphasis is not apt to be rapid as long as the cultural stability and daily habits of men are intricately bound up with the arrangements and products of a capitalistic system. A period of rapid institutional disintegration would hasten the process, but such was not the condition of society in the 1930's.

### Suspicion of "Foreign" Ways.

The characteristics of *his own* world define for the worker a way of living which is his conception of the "American way." That radical solutions for his problems would deviate from this American way is enough to damn them in the minds of many workers, even those whose place of birth was on foreign soil. Let some of them speak for themselves:

I'm American citizen now. Thirty-three years I been here. Let us look to America, make her good country. We no need bring from where I come from what I left. It's no different. I know those people. What if they do call it Socialism. I know it can be no different than what I left.                              Laborer.

You know what good American citizens are like. They don't want to riot; they want to go straight. They don't carry guns. They don't make damn fool speeches. They don't ask advice from foreigners and, by God, they *don't take orders* from foreigners. Why should we listen to these birds that get their orders from Moscow?                              Carpenter.

Now suppose they could set us up in that kind of a heaven they tell about. *Suppose* they could I say, because one look, and you know they couldn't. But if they could, would it be America—or would it be Russia? And who the hell wants to live in Russia?                              Boilermaker.

This identification of all radical ideas with Russia is all but universal. From listening to New Haven workers one would never suspect that any brand of radicalism could spring, native-born, from American soil.

One afternoon after talking with three or four groups of workers and finding the same general spirit of dissatisfaction dominating the conversation, I joined a group outside a cigar store at State and Grand Avenue. For no good reason I asked where the Communist office was. The antagonistic reaction was instantaneous. A Greek (thirty years in the United States) said, "Take my advice and stay away from there. It's dangerous." When I questioned him as to what he meant by "dangerous," he replied: "Somebody will hit you over the head, them foreigners will. This is what happens. If you are working in a restaurant, dishwashing, and somebody sees you, they will go and say to your boss, 'He's a Communist.' " A very effective gesture indicated that you would be let go immediately.

In order to draw them out I took up and defended the Communist cause—not one of the men would give ground on the subject. Two reactions to Communism were constantly reiterated:

1. Anyone who thought that the slavery in Russia was desirable, not only was crazy but ought to be shipped back immediately. One of the men put it this way, "If I want to take a boat ride tomorrow, there is nobody who can stop me as long as I have money to pay, but in Russia I'd have to go to some fellow and get a permit to go to Savin Rock."[1] Furthermore he insisted that if I thought conditions were so good I ought to go there and live—he offered to take my name and said someone would call on me and send me back there. A member of the Communist party, meanwhile, had joined the group. After he left, one of the group said, "We don't want fellows like that in this country. We don't need them."

2. To be a Communist is similar to being a representative of a foreign power attacking our shores. Regardless of how badly one is treated, how much he despises his own work and employers, when a Communist is around, it is the American worker's duty to uphold America and American conditions. For example, two of the fellows said with

1. New Haven amusement park.

pride that they were working for anywhere from twelve to eighteen hours a day at wages of ten–fifteen–twenty dollars a week. Their point was that there was work for any decent American who had energy enough to work or get out and look for a job. In the face of Communism the most insecure American workman becomes a hero by defending American conditions.

I assumed the role of one who was out of work and had become a Communist because I couldn't get a job. I was told frankly and with great emotion that I could get work if I wanted it; that I was simply lazy and wanted a handout from people who had energy enough and ambition enough to work for a living, even though it meant twelve to sixteen hours per day. The Greek in the crowd offered to get me a job at a restaurant on Church Street washing dishes twelve hours per day for $8 a week and meals. When I asked him where and how much, he got angry and said, "That's always the way. Where? How much? You don't really want a job."

The "un-American" judgment is emphasized by the fact that many of the radical speakers are members of race and nationality groups which are not trusted and frequently are despised. A reamer in a munitions plant put the matter this way:

There is a decided swing toward more socialized feeling among factory workers. If capital with all its wealth can't supply men with a living, the workers will demand something else. But the men won't join up with anything that's organized by foreigners. *If the Socialist party had a few honest-to-goodness American leaders, it would be O.K., but you can't put in with something run by fellows with names like Topletsky or some such. They may be American-born and all that, but you can't get away from the name.*

Another former munitions worker stressed the fact that the associations one would have in any radical working-class movement would not be "with our own kind."

Why don't men riot in this country? I'll tell you why they don't riot. There's no one to start it, and who wants to follow the foreigners that would? And besides that, there are too many languages. We all speak different languages, and you can't feel like joining with men in doing something like that when they don't speak the same language as you do, can you, now? Even if you could trust them what would your own bunch think of you?

He apparently saw no inconsistency in the opposition to "foreign" leaders on the part of Americans who could not understand each other's speech. But the testimony of many of his fellows among the unemployed leaves little doubt that the polyglot character of our population raises solid barriers to any acceptance of working-class solidarity so essential to radical mass action. When workers use the word "foreign" to describe the radical, they mean more than that he was born on a foreign shore. Likely as not he was born here. Nor do they mean that he speaks a foreign tongue or uses a foreign accent. Anyone who has attended union meetings is aware that a multitude of accents betrays a multitude of foreign origins. What they mean is that the radical uses ideas which are not customary among their associates, his terms are not in their familiar idiom. They do not know the implications of these terms. Like the primitive savage who visits another tribe, the radical is under suspicion because his hosts do not know how to interpret his signs, they do not know what to expect. The signs may mean good or ill intentions, but they are different. Radical speakers and organizers are labeled as "foreign" because that is the handy designation for an outgrouper, one who speaks and acts out of harmony with one's familiar ways of speech and practice.

### Negative Character of Radical Emphasis.

An almost universal criticism one hears of the Communists is that "they are not constructive." Said a laborer in a clock factory:

They'll give you some mighty perty pictures of what they'd do if they just could run things. But what have they ever done to show they could run things? When it comes down to what to do, why it's always a plan to bust something up.

The reminiscences of trade-union members were filled with testimony similar to that of a former linotype operator:

As far as the theory of Communism is concerned, I think it's all right, but the Communists in this country have not done one constructive thing. They want to tear down but never build anything. I've seen too many strikes come to a point where a real settlement was possible with some benefit to the workers, only to have some of these birds come in and wreck it.

A boxmaker held this point of view:

Why, yes, they've got some plans, and some of them sound O.K. so far as I can see. Maybe the government ought to run the railroads. Maybe the workers should have a lot more to say. Maybe Uncle Sam ought to run the banks. But so far as I can see about how they're going to do it—looks like they aim to shoot Uncle Sam first. Now what kind of sense does that make?

Among Catholics in particular the conviction was that:

Socialists and Communists for sure are going to destroy religion.

I've heard say that Thomas used to be a preacher. Well, all I can say is he's keeping mighty strange company.

I'm not a religious man, but I believe in letting men who are alone. It means a lot to some of them. Why smash it like the Russians have?

Unite against the present system, that's what they say. And they say it so loud and so often that you can't hear what plans they've got for another system. Now uniting against some system ain't what has made this country what it is.

Perhaps it is expecting a great deal of men who have spent a lifetime making positive constructive adjustments to their personal problems to follow leaders even to a utopia through a period of what seems to them to be a tearing down of what securities they have.

Even among men who admitted they had strong inclinations toward Socialism, there was a frequent criticism of the effectiveness of the Socialist political tactics:

They won't elect a president in a hundred years. They don't know the first thing about organizing a political party. They should take lessons from Davy Fitzgerald and Jim Farley, then maybe they would get some place.                    Toolmaker.

I tell you my reason for steering clear of any radical party. And it's as selfish as hell. But here it is: There's one place where I can belong to a goin' concern. I fought enough losin' battles in my life, and, by God, in politics I'm goin' to play a winner if I can. A man can be a Democrat or a Republican and be able to get drunk once in a while on election night because he won. But the Socialists—when do you think they're going to have the chance to get drunk?                    Rubber Worker.

This rubber worker was the only one of our informants who voiced such a sentiment, but one wonders as he looks over the reported frustrations on more than one front of the workers' life if this desire "to belong to a going concern" is not an unspoken but nevertheless important motivation warning men from association with any political party that is bound to lose.

### Differences in Radical and Conservative Politics.

A major obstacle to the winning of adherents for radical political action is the fact that such action calls upon men to do more than political action normally involves, i.e., choosing and checking up on government officials. Socialism and Communism are not really politics, thus defined in terms of the workers' folkways. Both involve comprehension of and working for a reorganization of society. That goes beyond "politics" and involves passing judgment not on an officeholder but on a change in the social system to which the worker has become accustomed. Even if the blueprints of the new order could be understood, the habits of political action are not geared to such effort. Being a Socialist or a Communist involves the adoption of a larger than customary conception of "political action." When supporting Socialism can be defined as "voting for a Socialist who has demonstrated his ability," a larger following can be secured. That is politics as the worker understands the term.

Not only does radical political action involve judgment on a change of social system, but it requires a greater degree of hope and confidence in the future than many unemployed can muster. Those qualities among many workers and particularly among the unemployed have been severely curtailed. Even when hope has not been completely crushed by the impact of insecurity and misfortune, the goal of that hope is likely to be not collectivism but individual achievement.

### Fear of Consequences.

Moreover, fear of the consequences of being known as a radical must always reduce the rate of conversion and the number of converts. The realistic judgment of the worker is that radicalism is a "sure fire demoter." He has observed this fact in his working days. He cannot forget it now. The warnings of administration officials about what will happen to "dissatisfied radicals" do not fall on deaf ears. Such warnings cause no surprise. He may know some of the men who "lost what little they did have" because they "wouldn't listen to reason." Call it foresight. Call it fear. By either name it is equally a discouragement to any radical activity which would go further than voting Socialist. Certainly the appeals to direct action would hit this snag:

There will be no riots as long as there is charity enough left to support the men. If that were not there, there might be trouble, but the men are afraid, in the first place, to riot because they might lose what little they have left of security.    Laborer.

Well, who's going to start it? That's the point. You all stand around and you talk and you say, "Of course we're going to do something if we don't get relief, and you get darn mad and you feel like throwing stones in windows, but nobody's going to start it. I tell you, we don't have anybody who dares to start the thing, and until we do, nobody's going to do anything about it. Riots won't happen in this country as long as there's a little bit of relief left. As long as there's an iota of security, men will not risk the thing by rioting. And then, too, what's there to riot for? You don't have any confidence that if you did riot it would do any good. How would you get anything any better than what you have? If you're going to riot, normally you ought to have something ahead that you can look forward to. You are rioting *for* something as well as *against* something. My philosophy is to hang on to what you have.                Textile Worker.

### Influence of Alternative Adjustments.

After close observation of the adjustments made by the unemployed to their problems, however, I am inclined to lay at the door of that adjustment process itself the primary responsibility for any apparent inertia. Once again we must record the fact that the most constant occupation of working people throughout their lives has been the adjustment of their goals to the actual possibilities of a worker's insecure existence. Radical action in the face of unusual problems is certainly one alternative solution. But it must compete for allegiance with a way of meeting difficulties which is much more deeply implanted in social habits, namely, "put up with it, grin and bear it, and use the common sense and experience you have to pull out." That way may not promise much, but it is implanted in men's reactions by the training of a lifetime. One brassworker put the matter in a short sentence, "The poor are

used to being poor." Our examination of the objective content of the goals of workers has indicated the effect of
"getting used to being poor" on the level of satisfactions,
failure to achieve which might arouse active resentment.
The world of labor to which the worker has become accustomed offers a minimum of satisfactions measured against
the standards of more favored economic groups. But these
latter are not the standards he uses.

This process of adjustment to the inevitable is even more
necessary during unemployment. Prior to that point in unemployment at which radical proposals might seem the
only path left open, a gradual modification of normal goals
has been taking place. A slow readjustment of relationships
and activities adapted to the new circumstances has been
effected. Substitute efforts have replaced the old as ways
of securing a livelihood and satisfactions. The unemployed
worker and his family have rationalized their new status
and the worker has even derived a degree of satisfaction
from his ability to meet the ultimate test of a "real man"
as defined by our culture, "the ability to grin and bear it."
All customary avenues of readjustment will be explored
before he turns to a radically novel alternative. And in this
exploration and the development of new practices for
achieving his modified goals he has gone through a process
which has reduced the aggressiveness which might have
been anticipated if one were merely to compare his status
as an employed worker and his condition as an unemployed
man, say six months or a year later. One cannot measure
the force of his aggressiveness by a direct estimate of what
he has lost, for the losing has been accompanied by a readjustment which has left him a different man.·

Offer this man the alternative of radical action early in
his period of misfortunes, and he will turn away from it as
inconsistent with the customary folkways of his group and
as unnecessary until the paths suggested by them have
been explored. Nor is his loss sufficient at this point to jus-

tify so novel a gamble. Offer it to him when customary ways have failed to restore to him his normal status, when his loss has been great, and the adaptive activities of the intervening period will have weakened his power to accept effectively such a positive and effort-demanding alternative. It is not surprising that firm opposition by the authorities cancels what remaining willingness he might have for such action.

Until radical thought becomes ingrained in the worker's culture as a normally accepted analysis of his problems, and radical action as a normal program for dealing with everyday needs, one would anticipate little change. For the efforts of the readjustment period are conducted on the premises of customary ways considered appropriate in the worker's world. Perhaps the Communist who was deploring to me the inertia of the unemployed spoke a truth which he had not meant to imply when he said: "They don't take to it, that's sure. The American worker is so patient and dumb that you've got to hit him on the head to open his eyes."

### Experience of Misfortune Not Simultaneous.

Closely related to the last reason for the failure of workers to respond en masse to the challenge to radical action is their failure to arrive at a point simultaneously at which the radical alternative seems attractive. A, B, and C are thrown out of work in 1937. For some time they try to make the customary techniques meet their new problem. A succeeds sufficiently so that he retains his confidence in them. B and C eventually are attracted to radical action, but B after a short time makes adjustments which renew his confidence in the efficacy of the more customary ways to make progress toward his goals. About this time D, E, and F become unemployed, but, before any one of them is ready for radical action, a time period must elapse and by this time none of the original potential recruits may be associated with the radical movement.

So the process goes, with the result that at any one time only a small minority are in the stage at which radical action seems appropriate, and of this minority only a few overcome the inhibitions to taking that step. The reinforcement for individual action which might come from the awareness that many others were simultaneously at the same point in their problems and were simultaneously undertaking the same action is missing.

This explanation is an obvious simplification of a dynamic situation. Many factors might counteract the tendencies named—mass layoffs, particularly in isolated communities or among a majority of members of a narrowly bounded community, the complete breakdown of forms of maintenance alternative to wages, a realistic, comprehensive radical program focused on the immediate needs of the long-time unemployed coupled with a long-continued depression. Any of these factors might cause permanent recruits to radical movements to be more numerous. But as long as the unemployed are a changing group, it is probable that a relatively small number at any one time will reach the stage at which they will respond to the call to radical action. For this reason, among the others, radical movements among the unemployed are likely to remain minority movements in a society which does not suffer a complete breakdown of its customary ways of self-maintenance.

It should be obvious that the foregoing discussion has attempted to offer no explanations of why some—comparatively few—men do turn to radical political activity and direct action. That is another problem. For it has been our task to explain in terms of the evidence we secured the predominant reactions of the large majority of the unemployed in New Haven. In this field the predominant reaction was to decline the bid of the radical spokesman. No doubt an intensive investigation of the circumstances and personalities of the minority who responded favorably would disclose forces and factors which overcame the influence of those we have mentioned. Probably the acceptance of radical action was an adjustment to *their* problem. But that question must remain for further investigation. As we surveyed our cases, what needed an explanation was not why men said "Yes" but why they said "No" to the appeal from the soapbox.

## IV

## *THE UNEMPLOYED ORGANIZE*

THE experience of the unemployed with the donors of public assistance is not such that it creates confidence that every man can rely on these agencies for fair treatment and adequate maintenance. This implies no moral judgment upon the work of these agencies. It is too much to expect that arrangements to fill in the gaps left by private employment and wages should be more effective than the latter in creating any such confidence. The frustration to the workers' basic goals when "self-maintenance" involves an application for relief is more severe, the undermining of self-respect is more marked. If the decisions made and rewards for service paid by employers do not jibe with a man's conception of his own worth, how can the decisions made and the allowances distributed by relief officials be expected to do so? At least for a large number of the unemployed whose belief in their own worth and dignity has not been completely shattered, faith that the dispensers of relief will "do the right thing" would be a most unusual phenomenon. This lack of confidence may be expressed in mere "belly-aching" or it may take the form of organization for pressure upon the new sources of self-maintenance.

If the bargaining power of individuals is weak on regular jobs on which the worker at least has some chance to demonstrate his worth, it is practically nonexistent at the relief office where his qualification is a demonstration of need. That relief clients and project workers show as little tendency as they do to organize for collective pressure is a challenge to the theory that weakness in bargaining power automatically stimulates organization. Yet organization among the unemployed did develop and the outline of economic and social adjustments made is not complete with-

out considering the forces which stimulated such organization, the degree of strength they developed, the methods
they used, and the help they gave to workers in getting
what they wanted.

### Stimulators of Organization.

Stimulus to protective organization of the unemployed
came from three sources: (1) existing working-class pressure groups who saw in the unemployed a possible body
of support, (2) liberal and radical individuals outside the
ranks of the unemployed who wished to "do something for
them," (3) a minority of thinking and ambitious individuals among the unemployed who were restless under
the circumstances in the midst of which they lived. I would
rate the activity and effectiveness of these stimuli in the
order named. There was little evidence of a spontaneous
grouping of the unemployed for their own protection in
spite of the common lot of distress which was theirs. Indeed the testimony of the organizers indicates a discouraging inertia among the masses and a constant demand from
the converts that the balance of reward and group effort
be struck almost immediately. Working upon this mass inertia are the stimulating forces indicated.

Earliest and most consistently in the field was the Communist party. Early in the depression individuals alleged
to be Communist party members organized the Unemployed Protective Association nominally as a nonpartisan
organization. It was so presented to the unemployed and
to citizens who were asked for support. After an initial
successful demand for a betterment of single men's relief,
an occasional demonstration at eviction proceedings, and
agitation at mass meetings, this group gradually lost its
effectiveness. Its efforts had more and more the flavor of
Communistic propaganda, and, partly as a result of this
emphasis (focused, it is reported, in a motion to have members affiliate with the Communist party), a group of officers

seceded to set up their own organization. This secession was almost simultaneous with the appearance in New Haven of an organizer for the National Unemployed League invited to the city by the Workers' party, a "Trotskyite" organization. Around the seceding anti-Communist group he built the New Haven Chapter of the League. There is no anomaly in this situation since the Communist influence was "Stalinist" and much deprecated by the "Trotskyites."

With the organization they had sponsored practically defunct, the more radical leaders turned to other tactics. They made advances to the League for coöperation and even membership. Communist (Stalinist) representatives made continued attempts to secure a hearing before the latter group, but without marked success. They at last apparently left off efforts to obtain a foothold in the League, and turned their attention to the F.E.R.A. Union. A group was organized around one project which gave promise of growth but eventually it affiliated with a union organized on the airport project by Mr. Hanson.[1] For the time being Communist influence seems to have been overshadowed, partly because the city administration gave evidence of possible coöperation with Hanson, partly because the workers were not sympathetic toward the Communists. But their consistent understanding of the workers' problems, and their familiarity with organization technique, together with the conviction of many workers that the radicals were sincere representatives of the working class soon became apparent. Eventually one of them succeeded in being elected business agent of the F.E.R.A. Union. His efforts now were directed toward securing the close affiliation of the Unemployed League with the F.E.R.A. Union. The Unemployed League had meanwhile become primarily an organization of single men on direct relief. There was more than interest in the lot of the unemployed in this attempted amalgamation. The Stalinists were trying to get the Trotskyites'

1. All names are fictitious.

child away from them. They did not succeed. The child died. When the F.E.R.A. work projects were absorbed by the W.P.A., the Communists were active in helping to organize the Project Workers' Union.

The second New Haven group backing and stimulating association among the unemployed was the Workers' party already mentioned as the backers of the Unemployed League. This group was composed of keen-minded individuals whose philosophy and interest were revolutionary, who conceived of their job as the preparation of leadership for the coming revolution. They as "Trotskyites" were in opposition to the regular "Stalinist" Communist party line. Their apparent technique was to appeal to the few competent to lead. Consequently their interest in the unemployed was biased by this search for leadership. A student and an instructor in a local school furnished consistent help to the Unemployed League in an advisory and money-raising capacity and practically dominated its program and policy. The Workers' party paid the rent on the hall used by the League.

The attitude of the Socialist party might be described as that of benevolent interest. Whatever their efforts may have been in securing legislation helpful to the unemployed, they made little effort as a party to organize that group of citizens, save through the efforts of individuals who happen to be members of the party. A leader of the Building Laborers' Union in 1935 (much concerned about its unemployed members) was an active Socialist, and Mr. Hanson of the F.E.R.A. Union joined the party. The F.E. R.A. Union originally met at the Socialist headquarters.

At the invitation of the local organizer of the Socialist party, David Lasser, organizer for the Workers' Alliance, came to town for a mass meeting. Heads of the Project Workers' Union and the Trades Council spoke. Only twelve, all single men on relief, signed up. Meetings were held under the leadership of the Socialist organizer for a while and then discontinued.

Another force continually active outside spontaneous efforts of the local unemployed was the national office of the Unemployed League and of the Workers' Alliance, the latter of which seeks to unite all organizations of the unemployed. These national organizations on two occasions sent organizers into New Haven. They maintain national offices and newspapers. They contributed to the local organization by suggesting tactics of mass demonstration on relief issues, symbolization of any injustices, and like activities, and by creating at times a feeling of participation in the mass attack upon large national issues.

Prominent among the individuals giving personal support to unemployed organizations, particularly the Unemployed League, were a former assistant pastor of a leading downtown church and three persons prominent in the educational institutions of the city.

Very little spontaneous combustion can be noted among the unemployed themselves, with the exception of the airport-project explosion on the issues of a particular job. During our visits to the unemployed in 1934 we occasionally ran across small social groups of F.E.R.A. workers. Even these tended to disappear in the succeeding years. While they lasted, they were largely based on former associations and had no ambitions beyond the spending of leisure time. The support of the unemployed has been given sporadically to the several organizations stimulated by such groups and individuals. Very few if any initiators of action have risen unsponsored from the ranks. None have challenged their mates with a definite program of their own.

To summarize the lines of stimulus and support behind the four unemployed organizations:

1. *Unemployed Protective Association* (now defunct). Stimulated by Communist party members.

2. *Unemployed League.* National Unemployed League with the support of the Workers' party. Liberal New Haven nonworking-class individuals.

3. *F.E.R.A. Union.* Predominantly personal influence of leaders one of whom in the early days was, the other was not, Communist. Later infiltration of Communist emphasis.

4. *Project Workers' Union.* Personal influence of leaders with Communist and Workers' Alliance encouragement.

5. *Workers' Alliance.* Sponsored by local organizer for the Socialist party and encouraged by the national office of the Workers' Alliance.

### Strength of Organizations.

It is impossible to get accurate figures on membership and still more difficult to estimate the active strength of the membership of these organizations during a period in which the unemployed in New Haven fluctuated between 13,000 and 18,000.

The Unemployed League claimed a membership of 125. Meetings were held weekly and drew from 40 to 50, normally the same persons. The rank and file took active part in the meetings for a few months. A canvass of the membership revealed that about half were single men, most of whom had moved from the address originally given. Other members were not clear as to purposes and possibilities of the organization. Certainly one found no indication of a militant, hard-headed group of men demanding their rights. Their bewilderment and lack of active interest contrasted sharply with the tone of their national paper, *Mass Action.* My judgment is that there were few action possibilities in this group, that its activities furnished action outlets and status-giving effort to only a small leadership group. There was difficulty in obtaining men competent for leadership. Although the group claimed to represent the families on home relief, it appears not to have served as the recognized voice of any large section of such recipients. Leaders were

faced with the dilemma of trying to get the relief administration to recognize them as representatives of this group
on the basis of a small membership roll, and of winning
members when they could not promise them definite representation before the relief administration.

The F.E.R.A. Union and its successor, the Project
Workers' Union, claimed a membership of 800 and had a
varying group of from 30 to 40 at weekly meetings. In
spite of this small attendance, the large registered membership plus the militant activity of its leaders apparently
furnished it with enough strength for several victories.
Regular opportunity was given by relief administrators for
complaints and sufficient adjustments were obtained to
create the impression among the rank and file that membership was useful. The men who joined regarded the small
dues (50 c. a month) as insurance against unjust layoffs.
Until September, 1935, they had not responded in great
numbers to the call to mass protest against the proposed new
W.P.A. wage scales. Yet potential strength was there if the
leadership could make the chances of protest seem greater
than the danger that protest might bring down the enmity
of the relief administration upon their heads. Eventually
the protests became strong enough to get a revision of
hours and rates. After that victory, the temper of the rank
and file was focused on security. I should expect the task
of organizing any large-scale protest to be difficult unless
the relief administration were to create unnecessary enmity by unsympathetic actions. This group and its successor, the Project Workers' Union, came closest to any of the
unemployed associations to being a powder keg. Directors
of labor management did well to coöperate with it rather
than to produce any unnecessary friction productive of
sparks. The capitulation of the W.P.A. administrator to
the Project Workers' wage-and-hour demands strengthened
the hold of the leadership upon the rank and file, but it
simultaneously removed a potential rallying point for ac-

tivity without which continued loyalty and strength suffered. That its claimed membership of 800 did not represent its true numerical strength is evident from the fact that only 300 signed the request for an A.F. of L. charter and two months later only 165 had paid-up memberships.

The Workers' Alliance local never had more than 24 active workers, primarily single men on relief.

### Program and Methods of Organizations.

The Unemployed Protective Association can be dismissed with the brief comment that insofar as it had a program and technique it was at one with the Communist party. The general impression among the unemployed was that it was a recruiting organization for that party.

The program of the National Unemployed League, as announced in its official paper *Mass Action,* was committee action before the authorities on complaints of members backed by mass demonstrations outside the doors "threatening to enter and do some educating." The local chapter made little headway with this program, the dominant attitude of the membership being to "let the leaders do something for us if they can." Aside from the outside organizers and the "advisers" from the Workers' party, I found none among the leaders who was educated to the theory and technique of mass action.

Items discussed at the meetings were the injustices of single men's relief, the inadequacies of home relief, and the desperate plight of some of the members. Efforts were made to get recognition from city officials for a grievance committee but they were, in their language, "given the run-around."

The Unemployed League obtained a copy of the budget used as a guide for investigators in determining relief allowances, mimeographed the maximum items (so labeled), and distributed it to their members. The chief result of this was a bit of dissatisfaction among a few who didn't realize the budget wasn't mandatory but merely suggestive.

Members of the League coöperated on two occasions to maintain picketlines for workers in regular unions who were on strike. They participated twice in May Day parades. Never did their activities promise sufficient benefit to members so that any large increase in numbers occurred.

The F.E.R.A. Union and its successor, the Project Workers' Union, conceived its function as one of protection for its members, "to see that no man is laid off on a job without just cause, that no boss fires a man for political reasons or for 'Union' activities and to see that working conditions and wages are satisfactory." Their technique was to put complaints into the hands of their leaders and let them "do battle with city hall," or confer with the W.P.A. authorities. They backed them on important issues by a threat to strike. The leaders of the groups expressed no fear whatever that the city would undermine its credit by stepping up its relief costs. Said one:

They have plenty of money. It's just a question of how they are going to spend it. For instance, the other day they paid out $80,000 in interest to bondholders. Now, they didn't need to do that. During the last three years, they have paid out $3,000,000 to bondholders. Now, they don't need to do that. The community ought to come first and the bondholders ought to be able to wait for their money. It isn't a case of life or death with them, and it is with us. They can wait. We can't. I am perfectly confident that the city can find the money if they want to, and the way to make them want to is to instill fear into their hearts so that they will get busy and scurry around and get it.

The Project Workers had ambitions of being a regular union and to that end sought affiliation with the Building Laborers' and Hod Carriers' Union, an A.F. of L. group. One of the reasons back of the failure of unemployment to produce a class-conscious labor movement is revealed in their experience. The Building Laborers' Union was very

weak, fighting for survival, its leader fighting for his job.
Some of the Project Workers felt they were out of jobs because as former members of the Building Laborers they
had fought their leader and had tried unsuccessfully to
oust him. Union jobs didn't come their way after that. As a
result of this feud the Project Workers sought affiliation
directly with the national union. A charter was granted.
Then began the conflict over jurdisdiction. The increase in
government construction on which union labor was to be
favored offered a chance to build up union strength. Both
locals wanted that chance. National officers were called in
to mediate, and a compromise was effected by which the
Building Laborers received jurisdiction over buildings and
bridges, the Project Workers over roads. In effect this
meant that the Project Workers were limited in operation
to relief work.

After the protest on wages and hours, mentioned above,
the activities of the union have been practically limited to
minor complaints presented to the Director of Labor Management. Even this activity was undermined by the Democratic party officials in a very interesting manner. A leader
of the party in one of the wards served in the W.P.A. office
as a receiver of complaints for the unemployed on projects.
At first the representative of the union received and trans-
mitted these complaints to this official. It soon became
common knowledge, however, that complaints made in this
way received less attention than those made directly to
the official by individuals. Although men were aware that
the official was building party strength at the expense of the
union, they went where action was direct.

Miscellaneous activities are to be credited to the Project
Workers. Representatives were sent to the Washington
conference for all organizations of the unemployed. Education lectures were given during one spring by Yale in-
structors and others at the weekly meetings. The meetings

held with or without education programs gave the members a place to which they could go, a forum for letting off the steam of discontent.

### Values of the Organizations.

All organizations of the unemployed perform important functions of attempting to increase the "security" provided by relief, the most significant of which is of course protection of the minimum allowances or security wages. But there are other functions. They offer activities through which a small group of men can retain their confidence that all roads to their goals are not blocked. With normal routes to satisfaction cut off, with one door after another to status-giving activity closed in their faces, they are by this activity proving to themselves that *effort is not useless,* that their *influence does count,* that what they do is of *some importance.* The organizations have in the past had just enough success to give some substance to their belief. Being a few, they tell themselves that they are of the minority who "are not licked," who "still have the guts to fight," who "won't knuckle under to the bosses."

For the few hundred members of the union, this association, these activities, this awareness of unity with similar organizations in all parts of the country have acted as a stabilizing factor in preventing a complete disintegration of their conception of their own worth and dignity. For men who in numerous ways have slowly been eliminated from the varied relations of community life, this is no small contribution. Men who are becoming social atoms are unquestionably made more socially secure in the larger meaning of that phrase by being geared in in this way to the life of the community. Their own role has increased in importance, to some degree their economic security is enhanced, they have obtained at least a measure of control over their conditions of work, they are associated with a national organization which through its correspondence and press is giving one explanation of the difficulties they face as workers.

In all of the organizations the meetings supplied for those who attended a much-needed outlet for complaints suppressed during contact with relief officials.

Not in the program, not in the technique, however, are these organizations symbolic of unstimulated spontaneous reactions of the unemployed. That they have obtained any converts does suggest that *on work-relief projects* the conditions of work and the possibility of remedying them are such that militant leaders meet a degree of support. Their analysis of difficulties appears correct to at least some of the men; their program of action seems to be the only alternative, to a minority at least. Work relief furnishes experienced organizers with the sort of situation with which they are acquainted, regular association of the men with a common purpose, a set of conditions to which the whole group is simultaneously and equally subject.

### *Reasons for Lack of Response to the Organizations.*

That the organizations have had such hesitating support may be traced to several causes. The personnel of the W.P.A. and relief agencies is constantly shifting. In spite of individual exceptions, we found little evidence that the unemployed considered their status in any sense permanent. Those intellectuals who suggest a permanent government works' program with a permanent labor force are not supported by any large numbers of the Project Workers. They still think of themselves as a reserve of labor available for private jobs. The draining off of the union leadership into private jobs is a serious handicap to continuing effectiveness of the union.

When the Institute of Human Relations study of human reactions to relief was made in 1935, the reactions to relief status in general and to the loss of a job gave major emphasis to the action-inhibiting rather than to the action-stimulating effects of employment and relief. Anxiety, restlessness, depression preceded anger in the order of declared subjective reactions.

A basic reason for failure to join the union is that many men feel that participation in union activities brands them to the community as a "reliefer." They resist anything which increases the apparent reality of that role.

It must be remembered also that New Haven is an open-shop town and that workers who become unemployed save those in a few occupations have had little experience with organized action which would suggest such an alternative for increased security on relief work.

The distaste for the suspected radicalism of the leaders is clearly evident in talks with nonmembers (seven eighths of those eligible). On the other hand, the lack of response may indicate that forces tending to suppress active support—fear of complete removal of all assistance, mistrust of other racial and nationality groups among the unemployed, suspicion that action typical of Communists must be stimulated by Communists, the inertia growing out of having tried and failed—that all these negative forces still dampen the powder so that sparks will not set it off. My judgment is that the latter is the case. Yet powder has been known to dry out.

The leadership of every one of these organizations was and is subject to radical influence. That influence has been counteracted by several forces: (1) conservatives among the underexecutives of the organizations chosen by the rank and file; (2) the conservatism and inertia of the rank and file; (3) distrust of the Communists; (4) the knowledge that no coöperation could be expected from relief officials if the Red flag were waved. I would not care to predict a continuation of this situation even though relief officials have opened up successfully functioning channels for the adjudication of complaints. The essential conditions and wage rates under which relief work is carried on are not productive of those satisfactions and incentives which normally deter regularly employed workers from radical action. Nor is such relief free either from symbols of disregard by officials of public interest through primary concern with political advantage, or from those irritants which constantly give point and frequently proof to the agitator's message. The deterrent factors named above still operate. Conservatism and inertia of the rank and file are the strongest factors. They will be removed if at all not by the agitator's challenge, but by the accumulation of circumstances proving to relief workers that the agitator is right.

# V

## A WORKING CLASS

A MAJOR theme of this book and of the companion volume, *The Unemployed Worker*, is that the goals the worker strives for and the practices and attitudes he develops in the striving are shaped and modified by his own experience. They bear the mark of their origin in the world of labor. Social and economic security means to the worker a gearing in with the institutions of his own community and the successful manipulation of the resources, techniques, and helps available to working-class people. The worker's reactions and adjustments to unemployment have been interpreted in the light of this assumption which we have supported by the evidence available.

The readers who do not normally think of themselves as members of the working class must have observed that at many points the difference between their points of view and activity and those of workers is very marked. They must also have sensed the author's implication that for the great numbers of workers the distinctive goals, problems, practices, and institutions of the workingman's world must be the basis for whatever economic and social security they can hope to obtain, and that mobility toward a more substantial economic and social status is not a possibility available to the great majority.

The current assumption of most individuals who have thought about the structure of American societal life is that the cultural heritage in this country was one in which all members of the community shared, that the tendency toward a *class* culture was of relative insignificance in determining the practices and reactions of American workers to their problems.

The present study has not attempted a comparison of

the goals and ways of living of workers with other economic groups in American society. Yet the question inevitably arises whether working-class culture and behavior are such that a distinctive "workers' world" is beginning to emerge within the American community and whether those who are citizens of that "world" are tending to become more conscious of that fact and govern themselves accordingly. If that is the case—if a distinctive working class, moving toward working-class goals by means of working-class techniques, is appearing—the significance for industrial, social, and political relations is great. If the social security which we have emphasized to be a product of a "gearing in" with community institutions is being accomplished through a gearing in with distinctive working-class institutions, then we must revise many of the fundamental assumptions of democratic procedure. We may expect the alternative adjustments which workers will attempt in critical situations such as unemployment to be influenced by this association with such a subculture.

Conditions which are favorable to a group becoming aware of its common interest need not necessarily result in such awareness. The causal relations between the two are difficult to establish. It has been one of the weaknesses of Socialist theory that it has counted too heavily upon the assumption that the effect must inevitably follow the cause regardless of interfering factors. I cannot demonstrate the existence in New Haven of any degree of class consciousness, if by that term is implied a tendency to depend on working-class philosophy and leadership in the adjustments to workers' problems. One can observe, however, a number of factors which might very well encourage that tendency. What are they?

*Favorable Conditions: Tradition of Industrial Work.*

Sixty-two out of every one hundred of those unemployed men upon whom we depended for information had fathers

who were engaged in industrial work. This means that a
majority have lived in an industrial environment, breathed
the air of the shop from childhood. True, 23 per cent were
the sons of farmers and the remaining 15 per cent were
sons of professional or businessmen. Whatever may be the
cumulative effect of family traditions, that factor would
operate in the case of 62 per cent to ingrain customary re-
sort to working-class practices in dealing with problems of
living. That is far from a universal tradition which might
be expected to encourage a sense of continuing working-
class status; but it is a positive influence in that direction.

### Common Goals and Frustrations.

There is no reason to suspect that the goals toward which
we have found workers directing their efforts are basically
different in kind from those desired by other groups in society. We have noticed, however, a very realistic limiting
of the objective content of those goals by the necessary circumstances of working-class experience. What workers
mean by a socially respected role, economic security, control of their own destinies, understanding of their own situation, is to be defined in the humble terms of possible
achievement in working-class life.

We have found, moreover, a common theme of dissatisfaction running through conversations with our informants,
a set of dissatisfactions which was monotonously similar
for all workers. Workers cannot be unaware that the essential frustrations of each are the problems of all.

Furthermore, many of these problems are primarily
characteristic of the working group. The growing recognition of control by impersonal forces and by nonworking-
class individuals is one such problem. The obvious fact
that these latter individuals are frequently opponents of adjustments, legislation, and regulation which to any worker
seem a sensible attempt to improve his status, emphasizes
a difference in point of view which encourages a recogni-

tion that there are at least two classes in society, workers and others. Every pronouncement of the Manufacturers' Association in opposition to labor legislation increases this conviction, and the preamble to such opposition statements declaring the essential oneness of interest between employers and workers does not dispel it.

## Awareness of Outgroupers.

Every day of his life the worker sees men and women whose activities are not his activities, whose ways are not his ways, whose clothes differ from his, whose manners and speech are not his own. He has a car, but it is parked on the lot instead of in a reserved space or the company garage (to be simonized on company time). He eats in the company restaurant on benches and wooden tables and occasionally catches a glimpse of the "officers' mess." On his way to the movies he is passed by a car in which he catches a glimpse of the boss dressed in evening clothes. He notices the difference in appearance of his own mates and others higher on the economic ladder. He feels there are distinct differences between the executive and professional group and factory workers. His analysis of the difference is not very penetrating; he just knows it exists and he is likely to put it this way, in the words of an American machinist:

You can tell the difference when you meet them on the street. You can tell the difference by the way they look. The professional men, the businessmen have more confidence in their eyes; the workers' faces are drawn more, perhaps it's from worry, perhaps it's from working harder; I don't know, but at any rate you can tell the difference. Then when you come to the factory worker, you certainly can tell him every time. He doesn't have any hope in his eye at all or any spring in his step. His cheeks are all faded out because he works inside all the time and he doesn't look as if he hoped to ever be any better than he is right now.

He also pointed out a difference in the methods by which professional people and trades people are paid, declaring that the way in which trades people are paid is more honest than the way in which professional people obtain their income. He pointed out that doctors would charge for the same job $75 and $150 from different people according to the size of their respective pocketbooks. That, he says, is not fair. Jobs ought to be paid for on the basis of the value of the job, not upon what people are able to pay. A trade will have a definite price for a definite job. "I don't know what you think, but to me that looks a bit more honest than the other way." He knows that the sins of the bankers and stockbrokers and high-salaried executives are not the sins of the workers. He is aware that he has standards which these others do not share. Even when he declares he has no class feeling he is apt to admit with the man who called himself "the best gun assembler in the whole damned country":

It's funny how some guys feel they are working class and some don't. But I guess we all recognize it—all of us, when someone from the office waves to us. We sort of feel honored.

### Specialization of Functions.

Moreover, he can see that in a rough way there are different functions performed by individuals that create a like-mindedness and common interests.

You know it's hard to tell just what class divisions there are in America, and I don't know just how to say it. It seems to me it's something like this, that when you've a job where there's some call for planning, some call for figuring out things—I think that's the word, figuring out things—in your head, you feel that you're in a different class from the fellow who handles things. Now that fellow, I'll tell you right now, that fellow feels that he is just about next to the top notch, even though he is paid a salary just like the others are paid wages, but just the same, he feels that he is important, and he doesn't feel out of place when he's associating with men like professors, lawyers, and doctors—and oh say—bankers. He doesn't feel that he's out of place. He associates with them and he's sure of himself. Now, sometimes, you know, a man who's a real skilled artisan will be getting more money than that fellow, but it isn't always the money that makes the difference; it's the fact that you're figuring out things, or you ain't, and that's a matter of your training. If you've had a long experience of doing that sort of thing, you get a confidence and an assurance that just naturally makes you feel a bit superior. Some men get that by going to college. Sometimes it ain't so; sometimes they don't do much figuring out in college, but they at least think that they've done it; but it isn't necessary to have gone to college if your training has been that of figuring out things. You feel pretty much the same way. Now, I think that's the big class division in America, a division that comes right in the experience of men, something that's real, something that they see every day. And it usually works out that the "figuring-things-out" group is the same as the bosses and employers and the ones who tell you what to do. Now, of course, within the *figuring-out* group, and in the *handling-things* group, there's a lot of divisions too, but those aren't real class divisions.                                          Mechanic.

### Differences in Authority and Control.

Another indication of class status revealed in the statements of a relatively few men is the degree of control one is able to muster in managing his own affairs. The importance given to the fact of control in discussions about the workers' goals and their problems in reaching them leads us to assess such statements as a vocalization of an idea which is more prominent than would be indicated by the number who put it into words.

Of course there are classes in America. But when you ask me to point to what makes that true, well, that's a tough one. Suppose you have what you need to make what *you* want to do mean something. Then you're in one class. Now, suppose you

*don't* have enough, so that you have to give up trying to believe
that what *you* decided makes any difference. Then you're in another class. Does that make sense?                    Toolmaker.

I thought a lot about the difference between me and my boss.
We're both men, and have families, and work eight hours a day,
and try to be decent citizens and all that. But he's different just
the same, I know that, in lots of ways. But I envy him only one
thing. That is when he decides to do something, he can carry it
through. He has the authority to do it, and if he thinks he'd be
better off by making some change in where he lives or where he
works or where he sends his kids to school, why he has the
dough to do it with.                             Metal Worker.

There's no two ways about it. Some birds have got enough and
stand high enough so that what they say goes whether it is
about what they aim to do or what they tell other guys to do.
And anybody who can do that won't be found very often to be
what you might call a worker.                      Truck Driver.

"If I had *my* way." How many times have you heard a chap
say that? "If I had my way," they says. And when you hear
them say it, you know they're talkin' big to cover up the fact
that they never will. There's nothin' that shows up where a fellow's got to in this world more than the number of times he says
that. Anybody as can have his own way don't say "if," he says,
"We'll do it this way." But you have to look somewheres else
than among workingmen for birds that can talk that way.
                                                   Machinist.

Both of these status indicators, "figuring out things as
opposed to handling things" and ability to control as opposed to the absence of that ability, are present of course
within the group called workers. They mark off hierarchies
within that group as well as between this group and others.
Yet the difference in function and in the possession of tools
for control between those who work for daily or weekly
wages with no or few supervisory responsibilities, and
others, is likely to be more marked than any differences
within the group. Any foundation which this realization

furnishes for a class alignment is negative rather than positive. He knows that he *does not* belong to the "figuring-out group" or the "bossing" group or the group whose decisions count.

True, the recognition of a definite out-group is normally an added whip to the recognition of an in-group; but this is not necessarily a strong and deciding factor unless a positive set of unifying factors establishes the reality of that in-group association.

### *Limited Chance for "Getting Ahead."*

There are definite evidences that such factors exist in New Haven and that workers realize they are sharing in numerous ways a common fate and a common way of life. One of the most powerful of these factors is the awareness that life's possibilities do not extend onward and upward in the social and economic scale for the worker. The success stories have been written by the successful; they do not furnish workers with a philosophy and a hope. Workers have not succumbed to the American success philosophy. More unrealistic assumptions have been made in this matter than in the discussion of almost any other set of workers' motives. We would have to assume millions of people living under the circumstances we have described, observing the experience of those about them, listening to the conversation of fathers and grandfathers whose lives had been spent on the comparatively dead level of work for wages, knowing the sort of meager opportunities for advancement offered their mates, and still, in spite of the wisdom of experience, believing that the success stories held the clue to their own possibilities. That is an evaluation of working-class common sense that has little basis in fact. A few individuals with ambitions to be world beaters had the superb audacity to hope that they could overcome the almost impossible obstacles? Yes. But the working masses motivated by the same hope? No.

I want to emphasize the result of premature old age among workers in this connection. It is common knowledge that in business, industrial executive, and professional occupations, the level of productive usefulness and social status is on a slowly rising plane from, say, age eighteen to sixty-five or beyond. It is equally common knowledge that the workers' cycle of productive usefulness and any accompanying social status begins at age sixteen, rises rapidly to about twenty-five, remains on a plateau until forty-five, and then begins to decline. This means that almost before children leave home they are sharing the ideas of fathers reconciled to a life at a fixed level of achievement and usefulness, and that in many homes they are imbibing the point of view of grandfathers old, in terms of industrial usefulness, before their time. Their minds would have to be very inactive to miss the point and to generate the degree of unbounded individualistic hope frequently and indiscriminately used to characterize the workers' point of view.

### Common Practices.

Workers not only share a common limitation of the possibility of advancement, but they participate in a great body of practices designed to meet problems common to all workers. Since the problems are essentially the same—unemployment, irregular and insufficient income, the pressure and speed of work, the control by others of their opportunities to earn a living, a struggle for self-respect in the midst of almost identical social and economic environments, one would anticipate a similarity in those practices which experience had selected for survival as the ways of the folk. The large body of practices we have described, a residue of all but universal adjustments remaining after the obviously individual ones had been eliminated from the practices we observed and about which we were told—these bear testimony to the sharing, consciously or unconsciously, of folkways to which the modifier "workers" can be fairly attached. Customary association with workers in the routine activities of shop and home and community necessarily emphasizes the similarity of this way of living.

When we turned to the other than economic institutions we found again such emphasis. A possibility exists in New Haven for satisfying the noneconomic as well as the economic wants of workers through participation in institutions and relations which are largely working-class in character. The possibility, if not the reality, of class lines develops when a measure of success in the drive toward these goals can be achieved by remaining a worker instead of getting out of the working class. It is no secret that the latter road has been the accepted path in the past. That is a circumstance which has necessarily left many a man frustrated in the attempt to do what in the very nature of the case only a few could do, namely, change one's class.

*Barriers to Class Formation: Divisions as to Function.*

These positive factors which encourage or at least make possible a consciousness of class interest and association do not, of course, operate freely and without restriction on their power. Barriers to the end result are present in New Haven society.

First among these barriers is the fact that face-to-face associations on the job are not with "workers" but with "workers doing a particular job." Job consciousness rather than class consciousness is likely to result. The putting of the matter by our informants differed; the idea was essentially the same. One may speak for all:

The point is just this—you work with your own type of worker; all you know about is trucking. You don't have any feeling that you belong with the rest of the workers of the country. That's what I understand there is in foreign countries, a feeling that men belong to a working class; but here you don't particularly feel that you are in one class or another. I suppose maybe it's because everyone thinks that some day he'll be a capitalist. Funny, you know you never will, but at the same time you never think of putting people in another class from yourself. So the only time that you ever hear of there being classes in this country is when you see an agitator up on the corner, and of course you don't have time to listen to him. You're too busy doing your job.

This feeling was particularly strong in the building trades. A carpenter expressed the matter in these words:

Class lines? There ain't no class lines among American workers. There's only job lines; but believe me those are mighty strong. Why on one construction job you've got about five lines that are recognized by the men—from the laborer up to the general superintendent. Now let me tell you; you don't cross those lines either, when you think of the group you belong to. Why, you're closer to the boss if you happen to have the job that I did than you are to the fellow that's wheeling the cement in a wheelbarrow. You don't think of him as being a member of your class. That's one reason why the American labor movement ain't never going to get any place, because the big boys, the fellows who ought to be the leaders, don't think that they're in the same class with the fellows who use the pick and shovel. It's funny what makes you feel that way—the wages you get plus the responsibility that you have. You know right well that there isn't any real barrier to you getting that boss's position except that there aren't very many such positions. But if you should be lucky and get it there ain't any real barrier to you having it, and when you get that way he's gonna associate with you just like he does with all his other associates right now, so you point yourself ahead instead of looking down at the rest of the men who might be thought of as belonging to the working class.

There is a strong barrier; yet one finds among New Haven workers two factors which are tending to reduce it. The variety of occupations and industries in which all but the craftsmen have worked has broadened workers' acquaintance with other occupational groups. A tandem job consciousness might well be a step toward a realization of broader class interests. The second tendency is the large number of semiskilled and unskilled jobs in which there are no particular qualifications upon which one worker has a semimonopoly. To realize that one is an interchangeable unit in the industrial organization is to possess a less powerful stimulus to job consciousness.

Closely associated with this job consciousness is the appropriate realization of status which goes with the possession of a particular skill:

The skilled class have definite attitudes just like the unskilled class have. They live in different worlds, them two do, and you'll find the skilled men will criticize the unskilled for their laziness, their lack of incentive, and all that sort of thing just like—oh say—a banker will criticize all workmen in general. Only, of course, the skilled man's criticism is a lot more sensible because he has seen these fellows at work beside him. Why, you take unskilled men—if you had anything like unemployment insurance, don't you believe that they would try to get by on it just as much as they could? If you got down to the place where wages was pretty near what they would get on the unemployment insurance, don't you suppose they'd rather get the insurance than work? Of course they would. You can't tell me they wouldn't. No, I'll tell you, the skilled man's attitudes and his feelings and his thoughts is lots closer to the employer's than you would imagine. Particularly when you get to be not only a skilled workman but a supervisor. Why then of course you're just like the boss; you're one of them of course.

Such a barrier might of course be reduced if the philosophy of opportunity for unlimited advancement were replaced, as we have indicated it is being replaced, by a philosophy of adaptation to a plateau of achievement. Skill as a symbol of advancement may have created quite a different frame of mind from skill productive of sufficient prestige to offer an opportunity for working-class leadership.

*Lack of Easily Recognized and Constant Opponent.*

Another barrier to class consciousness is the lack of an easily recognized opponent in other social groups in American society. Were it possible to picture American employers, bankers, clergy, professional people, or any one of these as consistently making their way to wealth and power on the backs of workers, the integration of class for a recognized conflict might proceed more rapidly. One cannot deny that attempts have been made to compose such a picture, or that the actions of individuals in these groups have given it plausibility. As we have indicated, such actions have furthered the class consciousness of which we are speaking; but on the whole the present judgment of New Haven workers has not been shaped so much by such factors as by the recognition that the division of labor in society is a coöperative arrangement, with the work of each unit important to the work of every other. The unquestioning assumption that employers and bankers have interests which are eternally opposed to those of workers is not sufficiently widespread to be an active factor in integrating workers' interests and relations in opposition to what might be termed exploitation. The more general point of view can be summarized in the words of an Irish welder:

I feel no particular unity with workers any more than with any other respectable citizen. Everybody has his work to do. Everybody can do his work better than anybody else, so what's the object in feeling that you belong to one group more than another? These people who agitate for a class struggle represent nobody. They represent nobody but themselves. The average American worker is a mighty sensible person and he knows that he is not the only pebble on the beach and that his own work is not the only work that needs to be done in society. He doesn't always understand how it is that the people who own bank accounts and bonds and industrial stock are useful, but he knows that they have some kind of relationship to his own job and he supposes that that relationship is an important one.

*Lack of Analysis and Dogma Consistent with Experience.*
Another barrier to class consciousness is the lack of a definite pattern of analysis furnished by thinkers or agitators
with whom the workers are acquainted, the lack of any
dogma emphasizing the importance of class unity, which
fits the daily experience of the worker. A dogma or a philosophy which was consistent with and could be verified by
daily experience might furnish a rallying point for practice
and organization. The dogmas presented for the American
workers' approval which emphasize class conflict have not
been consistent with the facts of his work-a-day world.[1]
Experience, not philosophy, is the foundation for conviction and action. That experience may be tending in the direction of the verification of the dogmas of class interest or
even of class conflict. At the moment the tendency has not
progressed sufficiently to make class conflict a realistic alternative of action. It has proceeded far enough to make
organization on class lines an acceptable alternative to
class desertion. A particularly thoughtful worker expressed
this idea:

When you see the kinds of jobs that have to be done in order
that things can keep on going, you see that there isn't really
anything in those jobs that would make men pull together and
make them think that they're a class, a working class, say.
There has to be something outside of them; something, say,
like the kind of dogmatic and definite pictures that socialist
agitators give of society, something like the dogmatic picture
that a fellow by the name of Karl Marx gives to society. You
see, it has to be something outside of your job itself. Any idea
of classes doesn't grow out of your job. When you see that picture and then your job experience kinda fits into that, why then
you really begin to think that maybe there are some class divisions. But you see that's just the trouble; in America our job
experiences haven't fitted into that picture, and so consequently
we haven't put much stock in it. We haven't needed to listen to

1. See chap. iii, p. 56 f.

it except as a kind of diversion like. That may not always be the case though, you know.

### Variety of Nationalities.

We may mention, finally, among the barriers to class consciousness and action the presence of many nationalities whose ways differ from each other. Among men past middle age the awareness of nationality differences among New Haven workers was very real and buttressed by suspicion and distrust of each other which must for them continue to make the idea of united action with other nationality groups unpleasant, if not dangerous. We have seen evidences of this throughout the foregoing discussion. With the retirement from the labor market of men born on foreign soil, this barrier may be expected to be reduced. It is not low enough yet to be an insignificant factor in dividing men socially who have common economic interests.

### Evidences of Class Consciousness.

In spite of these barriers, however, and in spite of the numerous comments indicating little realization of the extent to which customary sharing in primarily working-class ways was contributing to the actuality of a class culture, evidence was not lacking that the most thoughtful among the workers accepted the trend and could see real values in it. Their comments, though few, are an essential part of the evidence on this matter. The following are representative:

Look here, young man, don't put too much stock in what guys like myself say. [He had started as a mill hand in Massachusetts and climbed the occupational ladder for fifteen years in working-class jobs. He is at present general manager of a small firm.] We made the grade, see? But how many of us did? That's the big point. How many of the gang I started with in Massachusetts? I'll bet not more than two or three. Now that's swell for us, and we're inclined to say, "Ain't America grand?

No class lines get in the way of a good man gettin' to the top, to hell with class lines." Because you see we couldn't have got where we are if they had been too fixed. But that isn't the only place to get by a long shot. How about the rest of those birds? Haven't they got some rights? Don't they want somethin' out of life too? Of course they do. But we've been so all-fired set on keepin' the ladder open that we've forgot the fellows who never get even one foot on it. Do you think my satisfaction balances out all that disappointment? I wonder. Sometimes I get disgusted with these damned union men I have to wrastle with, but then I think they are doin' more for the workingmen than I've done. I'm vain enough to think that I've showed them what is possible in America. But those birds are actually workin' out means that all workers can use to get on. And how many can do what I've done? And, hell, even if they did work as hard and studied and connived like I have, where would all of them find jobs like this?                                    Boilermaker.

Let me tell you, mate, what's wrong with this country. Now, most of us are going to be workers all our lives. Right? Well then, if that's the story, we've got to get any kick we get out of life by getting ahead as workers. Right? Now suppose the only way to really be a big shot is to not be a worker. Get what I mean?                                    Molder.

I've sometimes thought—and I don't think very often and not very straight when I do, but I think this idea is better than some—I've sometimes thought that workers would be happier if we stopped harpin' on how to get ahead far enough to move in the bosses' society. Not many of us have such highfalutin ideas for long, mind you. But we don't have any others about how to get ahead, either. Now suppose we said to ourselves, "You damn fool, you, and the likes of you, is never goin' to be anything but a worker." But what the hell—that ain't so bad. You can get together with other guys like yourself and you can work out some perty damn good ways of making your lot better. And when them ways work, by God there'll be a hell of a lot of satisfaction knowin' that you and the likes of you done it.
                                    Welder.

What's eatin' on a lot of these birds, anyway? Why don't they accept what has to be for most of us? Once they do that they're goin' to find plenty of chances to make good because they know how to get for workers what they need, not because they walk off and leave most of us to stew in our own juice.      Laborer.

Hell, brother, you don't have to look far to know that there's a workin' class. We may not say so. But look at what we do. Work. Look at who we run around with and bull with. Workers. Look at where we live. If you can find anybody but workers in my block, I'll eat 'em. Look at how we get along. Just like every other damned worker. Hell's bells, of course there's a workin' class, and it's gettin' more so every day. What we need to do is to work out ways to make bein' a worker amount to something. And when you look around, you see that some things have been done along that line. But there'll be a lot more when some of the guys that's really got brains start workin' on that job instead of hopin' that someday they'll be bosses.                          Machine Operator.

I've lived a good many years, son, and I'm about through. But take this from an old man. There ain't so many chances nowadays for a youngster to ever stop bein' a worker. I used to worry about that. You can see it anywheres you look. I've got two boys, and I used to hope they wouldn't have to break their backs all their days in the shop. They're thirty and thirty-two now, and I know they'll always be just what I am. But I've stopped worryin' about that any more. There's a lot of things workers can do for themselves that no one else can do for them. And Jim and Jerry are smart lads. They're workin' every minute they're off the job on clubs for workin'-class boys, and their union, and some sort of plan for cleanin' out them rickety old shacks across the street. God, but I'm proud of them. Just as much as if they had been doctors or lawyers. It's no shame to be a worker when you do what them boys are doin'.
                    Laborer in a Rubber Factory.

Now you take Phil Murray, or Mike Golden, or Feinmark, or Walter Davis. What has any of your boys way up in business got that those boys hasn't got? More money, maybe. But I'll bet there ain't more men that looks up to them and thinks they're damned good. And they didn't get where they are by desertin' the working class, did they? You bet your boots they didn't.                                    Printer.

Some day in this country, mate, just like in England where I come from, a man's going to be president because he stuck with the workers. Only in England you know we don't call him president. But the idea's the same. The working class in this country or any country is damned important and one of these days they're going to know it. I may not live to see it, but it'll be a great day. And the reason's just this. You can't forever stir men up to big ambitions by holding out hopes that only a few can have. But if you get the workers together and give a man a chance to work right up to the top by being a worker—why that is something. And it'll be a damned sight more honorable than lickin' the boots of the gentry so as they'll let you be one of them. Workers for workers I says and before very long that'll mean that a man'll hold his head up and say, "To hell with your black coats and white collars, I'm a workingman and proud of it. Look at what we've done for ourselves. Can you show me anything else that's more important?"    Mechanic.

### Cultural Requirements for Class Consciousness.

The culture of any economic group normally provides for a set of relationships, for a set of alternative socially respected roles, for participation in associations, or for avenues of activity giving some control over the problems of living. In a society with rigid class lines the boundaries of one's field of participation are set by these class lines. A working-class culture, as such, develops, offering a practically complete set of functions and codes which one may share without stepping out of his class.

This development has not reached its peak in New Haven. Achievement is measured not by reference to a working-class standard alone, avenues of achievement are not completely within the working-class community, socially sanctioned roles (even within the working group) frequently make necessary breaking contacts with one's working-class associates. There is, of course, a body of practices and relationships which make up what might be called a working-class culture. But they do not furnish a complete home for the worker. The more ambitious find it a poor cultural home. They must part company with their former mates and seek roles and relationships reserved for nonworking-class people.

This is possible for a few. It is not possible for the many. The many must find their cultural home in working-class life. The opportunities for escape are not many. The response to this situation leads to the formation of workers' institutions frequently robbed of the leadership which would help to adapt them more perfectly to working-class needs. The open ladder may have been of inestimable service to the few who wish to climb and can find room on the ladder. It has left the many, with a reduced number of leaders, participating in the formation of stable working-class institutions adapted to the needs of millions who must toil with hands and brain for a remuneration which makes hope for a radical change in the standard of living futile and life as a worker an inevitable fate.

### Results To Be Anticipated.

Two fairly obvious results may be anticipated from the tendency for a growing body of working-class relations and institutions to provide an avenue of achievement for workers. Class consciousness will increase and social stability will be encouraged, social unrest reduced, by the existence of opportunities supplied by a working-class culture. The two results may seem paradoxical. They are not. For the majority of workers, security, social status, control, and understanding are most real and satisfying when extensively possible through institutions and relations in which all may share. In a society in which the majority of the population must always be workers, subject to the limitations we have described, it is useless to hope for social stability from the restriction of satisfying achievement to those who are able to shake off the practices upon which the masses must continue to depend. Class consciousness—if it can be realistically described as an awareness that satisfying achievement is possible through the practices and institutions upon which workers on the whole must depend —can, and has become in other nations the very foundation for social stability. In a society in which attempts are made to retard the growth and restrict the function of working-class institutions, and to relegate them to an inferior level of social importance and usefulness, class consciousness could, however, furnish a dynamic force of another sort. Aware that the adjustments evolved in the community of workers were assigned to a place of secondary importance and that first-rate men could not realize their ambitions through and by the support of second-rate institutions, such group feeling might be used to create the morale for an attack upon the ways of other groups who stubbornly held to their conviction that they were the chosen people and that their ways must be adopted ere the mark of social importance and usefulness could be placed upon an individual.

This is to say no more and no less than this. Workers, as we have seen, have certain goals toward which they are striving. The society into which they are born is a body of practices and institutions developed out of experience in this effort. These bear the class mark of the people they serve. In America the greatest amount of success and satisfaction has been reserved for those workers who deserted the class into which they were born and won their way into another class. This road by its very nature was closed to the majority of workers. Satisfactory for the few, it left the creation of working-class institutions to those unable to make the transfer from one way of life to another. The shutting off of this road to class mobility and the other fac-

tors we have mentioned may result in a growing class consciousness, but it will also result in a concentration of the
best brains and abilities in developing more satisfactory
social instruments for the use of workers. Whatever may
be true in the professions and in business, leaders of labor
in this day can go little faster than their ability to lift the
level of living for the whole working class. It is not beyond
the range of conservative prediction to estimate that when
men may achieve a reasonable measure of success in reaching their goals by remaining workers, the stability of our
social institutions will increase and the attack on them
from the ranks of labor will decrease.

The weight of evidence in the observations we have made
in New Haven is that the solidification of a working class
is well on the way. This fact has an important bearing on
social and economic policy. It means that the satisfaction
of human demands will be undertaken by the development
of practices and institutions which have a class character
and that economic and political arrangements must take
account of the fact of class stratification. Security will be
increasingly sought through bargaining between groups.
Working-class groups will continue the process perfected
by other social groups to use government as a lever toward
greater security. This increasing reliance on organization
and government is no indication of the decay of self-reliance. It is a form of self-reliance which substitutes collective for individual skills. Class organization and class pressure become the developed means for escaping dependence
and providing self-maintenance. The development here
charted is not one from self-reliance to dependence, it is
from individual to collective self-reliance.

We cannot continue to assume that working-class goals
and judgments and reactions are traditional business-class
goals, judgments, and reactions. They will have to be understood as the product of their own peculiar environment
and accepted as adjustments to it.

Successful managers of industry, in relations with workers, will accomplish less through proclaiming the unity of interest of all partners in industry, or through assuming that the march to management positions is the motivating stimulus for all workers, or assuming that workers are pleased with free gifts from benevolent employers. They will accomplish more by accepting the necessity of bargaining honestly with unions representing a class of people becoming conscious of their distinctive interests and the desire for self-respect in terms of the possibilities of their own environment, led by an increasing number bent on finding within the world of labor an equivalent achievement heretofore denied to all save those who might desert that world.

It means that all of us will become aware that working-class life and conditions are not something which the majority can escape, that the majority will have to make the best of such life and conditions. Social stability will be increased if what they must make the best of is not too frustrating to human wants, and if institutional arrangements provide an avenue for satisfying solutions to the major problems of living in the world of labor.

# SECTION II

## THE UNEMPLOYED WORKER AND HIS FAMILY

## VI

## *THE FAMILY CONFRONTS UNEMPLOYMENT*

THE impact of unemployment upon the recreational, religious, political, and familial affairs of workers is a subject which, if thoroughly explored, must be studied with far more adequate knowledge and techniques than I have been able to bring to the task. Comment upon such matters is undertaken in full recognition of my own shortcomings in these respects. Yet any attempt to see more clearly how and why workers react as they do to unemployment and unemployment relief cannot ignore this subject. The worker with his dependents in each of these fields of human activity and relationship has developed interests and practices which are influenced by the loss of his job and which in turn affect the adjustments he makes to that problem. He is a member of a community, not an atom. Through these fields of activity that fact is made real. Self-maintenance adjustments are so closely bound up with his relations to the community that explanation of his economic behavior in economic terms alone is inaccurate.

The family is of particular importance. The family is not only the primary social unit but also the basic economic institution in our culture. It is of equal significance to the work place as an arena in which the problems of economic security are faced and solved. Upon the family is placed the obligation of transmuting a wage into a living. Within this institution are initiated and nurtured the habits and practices which spell self-maintenance for its members. Out of its life arise incentives and satisfactions which are important answers to the question, "Why do men work?" Within its councils are formulated the strategies by which attack is made on the hazards to economic security which are the lot of all men and the particular burden of workers.

When we inquire therefore what effect unemployment has
had on the stability of the family and what adjustments
unemployment has made necessary in family organization
and practice, we are asking about the fate of an institution
whose importance in the economy of the community is very
great. What answers to those questions are suggested by
our evidence?

A first reading of the eight-year records we gathered
concerning the twenty-four families brought out one clear
fact. Each of these families had an individuality of its
own. In the midst of many indications of similarity in the
type of adjustments they made, it was evident that each
came to the period of unemployment from a background
and with characteristics distinctly individual. Moreover,
usually some dominant fact of family life influenced the
particular way in which each family met its problems, although this fact did not destroy a general conformity by
each to the trends in adjustment displayed by all families.
This conclusion will become clearer if considered in the
light of brief case histories of five of the most interesting
of our families.

## COHEN

### *A Professional Family Loses Its Social Status.*

If one were to piece together from the literature concerning the effects of unemployment on family life a "typical"
family history, the account would serve up to a point as a
pattern for the record of the Cohens. Man and wife and
two children are living happily together. The man loses his
job. Savings are soon gone. Job hunting is fruitless. Discipline problems with the children become difficult. Health is
impaired for all by reduced expenditures for food. Debts
pile up. Tempers become worn. Arguments increase. Discouragement gets the upper hand. The man, realizing his
failure, wishes he could die and contemplates suicide. In a
wave of despair the wife, losing patience with her husband,

takes the children and goes back to her mother. All of this
and much more happened to the Cohens. But such a record
does not present an accurate picture of what unemployment did to their family. It gives only superficial and sometimes misleading indications of the changes taking place in
the institution of the family and of its struggle to survive.

Several characteristic features of the Cohen family appear to have played a deciding part in determining the
course of adjustment to unemployment. In the first place,
they thought of themselves as a professional family. Mrs.
Cohen had in 1924 accepted her husband's proposal in
preference to that of a skilled cabinetmaker, whom she declared she really loved, because Mr. Cohen was a professional musician with his own orchestra and a reputation as
a good violin teacher. Her family encouraged her in this
choice. Both her father and mother were music teachers
and felt she would be "marrying beneath herself" if she
accepted life with a cabinetmaker. Soon after they were
married Mr. Cohen came back to New Haven to take a job
with a well-known orchestra at a salary which surpassed
his combined income from his own orchestra and from his
teaching. Up to the time of his unemployment he had been
making about $50 to $60 a week. That was enough to support his wife and two boys on a plane of living satisfactory
to all concerned and in a fashion appropriate to "professional people." Their home, a duplex house, was in a
middle-class neighborhood. It was attractively furnished.
They had a car. A woman came daily to "do up" the house
and care for the children. Mrs. Cohen was active in club
life. She was satisfied that she had made a good choice. She
was the wife of a successful professional man. Her family
was also proud of the match she had made.

The second important fact about the Cohen family was
that the children, age five and seven, were partial to their
father and responded more readily to his discipline than to
their mother's. They were hard for Mrs. Cohen to handle.

She left them very much to the care of the woman who helped her. When she was at home she tried various methods, ranging from excessive affection to irritated scolding and threats, to secure their obedience and respect. She had little success. Mr. Cohen remarked that "she always had to go off some place before she could carry anything through." The children, however, showed great affection and respect for their father and through his efforts the friction between mother and children was kept at a minimum.

The third relevant fact about the Cohen family was a lack of mutual activities by husband and wife outside the home. In part this was due to the fact that Mr. Cohen's orchestra responsibilities kept him away from the home most evenings. His chief friends were in the musicians' union. He spent much of his spare time with them and at the union hall. His only other associations were with his mother, sisters, and brothers. Mrs. Cohen did not share to any extent in these latter contacts. She had an intimate circle of "girl friends" in whose company she spent many pleasant hours at cards or at shows or on picnics. The Cohens had only a few common acquaintances outside of the larger family and no mutual intimate friends. Each had developed a set of companions satisfactory to himself but knew the friends of the other chiefly from conversation and snapshots. Mrs. Cohen's interests were centered in her "girl friends'" affairs, and when not in their company she kept in touch with them by telephone.

The chief occasions of common life for the family were meals and the prayers which followed the evening meal. Neither parents nor children attended religious services or took part in any activities in connection with religious institutions. Mr. and Mrs. Cohen occasionally attended a school program in which their older son took part. The children's birthdays each year were celebrated by a family dinner to which Mr. Cohen's relatives were invited. Mrs. Cohen's parents living in Massachusetts were never invited. Once a year she and the children would visit her parents for a week or so.

The Cohens had a well-defined division of labor in economic matters. The husband earned the money and gave his wife what she asked for to supply the household with necessities and an allowance of $4 a week to spend as she pleased. She never knew how much he earned or what he did with the amount beyond what he gave her. She understood that he was helping support his mother and that he occasionally assisted his brothers, but of the extent of such help she had no knowledge.

The final fact of importance in determining events during the unemployment of Mr. Cohen was the difference in type of associations with the two larger families. Mr. Cohen's widowed mother and several sisters and brothers lived in New Haven. He was very much attached to them and spent much time in their company and was prone to listen to their advice much more readily than to that of his wife. No love was lost between these relatives and Mrs. Cohen. She resented their interference and their influence over her husband. Save for the annual visit, she saw very little of her own family in Massachusetts, and still looked back with pleasant memory to her early life with them. She found many occasions to contrast them favorably with her husband's family.

As long as Mr. Cohen was earning $50 to $60 a week by his playing, this pattern of life was not disturbed. The arrangements were generally accepted as satisfactory and to an outside observer the family would have appeared as a normal stable institution. For three months after the orchestra disbanded the routine and organization of family affairs were supported by the savings that Mr. Cohen had laid aside. The only economies undertaken were in food expenditures. To the outside world and to her circle of "girl friends" Mrs. Cohen kept her position as the mistress of a professional-class home. Her club life went on much as before; she retained her maid. She still drove the family car. She did not discuss the fact that her husband no longer had a job. He continued to supply her with the money she required although now its source was a dwindling savings account. At the end of three months this was exhausted and the postponed adjustments had to be faced. The car was sold. The maid was told her services were no longer required. Insurance loans were asked for and one large policy was cashed in.

The greatest difficulties revolved around the loss of the maid's services. Not only was this a sign that a necessary feature of a professional status had been surrendered, but it imposed upon Mrs. Cohen the necessity of spending more time on housework, which meant a sacrifice of some of the time normally spent with "the girls." These contacts were now limited to evening affairs. Moreover, she was more constantly with her children and her inadequacies as a disciplinarian became more apparent. Mr. Cohen's mother did not help matters by coming over to give her advice on housekeeping and the training of children. Even when she took the children to her home occasionally, she reported how well they behaved and how helpful the older boy was in little household tasks. The mother-in-law couldn't understand "why Daisy has so much trouble with the children." That was not a peacemaking comment.

Her new difficulties stimulated resentment against her husband for losing his job and destroying the fairly comfortable routine to which she had become accustomed. Mrs. Cohen was the sort of person who reacted emotionally to problems rather than solved them. Why had he put her in this position? Why couldn't he get a job? His report that the theaters weren't using musicians any more, that even rich people weren't having so many dances and were cutting down on the size of the orchestra at weddings and special affairs, that musicians were a drug on the market made little impression. That was his problem to solve in some way so that he could support her properly. Criticisms long withheld came to the fore. Why had he been so foolish as to quit high school instead of going on to college as his mother had desired in order that he might become a lawyer? Lawyers were still supporting their wives. Now take the case of two of her girl friends. Why had she married him anyway, he would respond. Why didn't she marry that cabinetmaker she was really in love with? Then, by heaven, she would have had to do her own work right from the beginning instead of having nine years of luxury! She was spoiled. A little work would be good for her. So, his mother had been talking to him again, had she? So the argument went. But not for long. Unaccustomed to mutual discussion of economic problems, each built up his own stock of resentment at the "unfairness" of the other. Getting no results or satisfaction from her nagging, Mrs. Cohen became stubbornly silent. Finding his wife unable or unwilling to understand his predicament, Mr. Cohen also stopped talking to her and stayed away from home, frequently even failing to turn up for meals. She became more irritated and resentful; he more discouraged and despondent. He wished a car or a trolley would run over him. Neither could sleep at night. He set up a cot in the kitchen. Both lost their appetites, partly no doubt because their food was less varied and Mrs. Cohen was inexperienced in cooking.

Obviously up to this point, affairs in the Cohen family were going as one familiar with their nine years of married life would expect; a separation seemed imminent. Unless Mr. Cohen could find a job as a musician which would once more enable him to support his family on a standard appropriate to professional families, what chance was there for renewed stability? But the family is an adjustable institution, and soon the processes of reorganization began to assert themselves.

The conspiracy of silence was unbearable for two people habitually voluble in their reactions to circumstances. As time passed, Mrs. Cohen became more expert in her house management and cooking and even began to take pride in her new accomplishments. Mr. Cohen expressed his pleasure with results occasionally. He began to spend more time with the children, and his success in discipline not only relieved his wife in this respect but gave her, she declared, a renewed appreciation of his abilities. The father even succeeded in getting the older boy to understand a bit the problems his mother was facing and encouraged him to help in minor ways with the care of the house. Two months after their savings had been exhausted we find Mrs. Cohen's complaints about the children supplemented by such statements as, "But they are our only ray of hope, you know." Mr. Cohen's family, in spite of their interference, had assisted them financially, a fact which Mrs. Cohen appreciated as a return for the help her husband had given them when they needed it. Occasionally the Cohens even discussed without quarreling such questions as getting the landlord to reduce the rent, the size of their mounting debts, whether or not they needed a telephone, matters upon which they had never consulted before. They talked over the desirability of Mrs. Cohen taking the children for a visit to their grandparents in Massachusetts until Mr. Cohen found a job.

This is not to say that friction between them was eliminated. Yet these adjustments demonstrate the capacity of the family disturbed in its customary ways to renew its progress toward stability. New practices were being developed, a new division of labor and new relationships were being established, on the basis of which the family's job was getting done. Yet these positive steps were taken in the expectancy that before long some orchestra job would turn up and the Cohens would once more regain their former status. How thoroughly Mrs. Cohen held to this hope is indicated by her reaction to a suggestion her husband made at this point.

He had heard of a job unloading trucks at a department store. Possibly he ought to take it instead of waiting for a job as a musician. At this suggestion the pent-up fury of Mrs. Cohen was turned loose. Never, she said, never would she remain the wife of a common laborer. Didn't he know why she had married him? What would her friends say? What would her family think? This and much more she said before she packed her things and took the children to their maternal grandparents. When he got a job that would support them decently he could send for them—not before. Apparently the new coöperative practices had not taken deep enough root. They could not survive the withering possibility that they led to a downward readjustment of family status.

Nevertheless, Mr. Cohen took the job and soon became foreman of the night shift, earning $25 a week. He found much personal satisfaction in his ability to make good on this job. He learned that his workmates had wagered on his power to stick to it. For three months Mrs. Cohen remained with her parents, refusing obstinately to come home until he got a "decent" job. Mr. Cohen told us that he understood his wife's position, but even if he was an ordinary workman instead of a professional man he was making his own way and could support his family.

What thoughts went through Mrs. Cohen's mind during this time we can only imagine from her reports after she returned. For return she did. At some point in that experience away from home she gave up the hope that she was to continue to be the wife of a professional man and determined to return to the task of building her home on the basis of the actual possibilities. Four facts supported her in this decision. In the first place the memories of her girlhood status in her parents' home were inconsistent with the actualities of her present life there. She had looked forward to returning to old times. Short annual visits had not dimmed her memories. It was one thing, however, to be a marriageable daughter of twenty-five with parents at the peak of their professional careers. It was quite another to be a potential grass widow with two children living on the bounty of parents past their prime and partially retired from active life. The destruction of this illusion of a possible satisfactory alternative to life with her husband was a necessary and important step in their reunion.

The second fact which encouraged her return was the difficulty of controlling the children without her husband's assistance. Thrown into a new environment, the children enjoyed themselves. But the problems of making them acceptable members of the household were even greater than the problems of control she had faced at home. The grandparents had lost their skill in such matters. Mrs. Cohen came to appreciate the real need of her children for their father. Her own ineptness emphasized this conclusion.

The third fact was the loss of her "girl friends'" companionship. She had never realized how much her interests were bound up with theirs and how much her pleasure depended upon them. She missed these friends more than she missed her husband, she declared.

In the fourth place she realized that even if a comfortable routine could be worked out in the new surroundings this would not be a home of her own.

The beginnings she and her husband had made toward coöperative action seemed more important as the weeks passed, and after three months she wrote him that she was returning. Seven years have passed since that day. Mr. Cohen is still a foreman in the unloading room. His wages have never gone above $25 a week. We shall not detail the slow process by which the Cohens have reorganized their home so that its activities and status are typically working-class rather than professional. Now and again an offer of an orchestra job has presented itself to plague them with the memories of bygone days. But they have resisted the temptation, knowing the likelihood of failure in such a break with the security offered by the present job. When the W.P.A. musicians' project was organized the temptation was nearly compelling. But Mrs. Cohen would not accept a renewal of her husband's occupation on relief terms even though the wages were nearly as much as her husband received for unloading trucks. Joining in that project would probably have interrupted the steady progress toward the new structure of family life.

New mutual friends have been made through the contacts in a parent-teacher organization. These have taken the place of the "girl friend" circle with which Mrs. Cohen gradually lost contact. The circle had served her well as a support for her former status. It no longer served that purpose. Mrs. Cohen speaks admiringly of the ability her husband has shown in his new job and of the position he occupies with his firm. She is proud of the fact that he is "willing to do anything" to keep his family together—a complete reversal of her former position which indicates how variously different points of view may affect the same situation. Mr. Cohen in turn has found many qualities in his wife to appreciate as she manages a working-class home.

As long as the dominant goal for the Cohens was maintaining a professional status and the activities and relations and symbols which characterize that status, their problem was insoluble. Had that goal not been modified it is altogether probable that the home would have been destroyed. Once that obstacle was removed the members of the family were able to go to work developing the practices and relationships, the attack on family problems, the customs and procedures which constitute the realistic pattern of institutional life. Unemployment did not destroy this family because the human beings who constituted it were able to modify their objectives in line with possibilities. The practical development of techniques to get the family's job done is an absorbing and demanding task. When these techniques are developed and consistent with the family's conception of its own status, they become the basis of family stability, the activities through which the mutual respect and regard of the members can be expressed and by which they can be tested. The family is a family as long as it continues to function in doing the economic and social tasks assigned to this basic institution in our society.

## MILANO

### A Patriarchal Family Changes Its Form.

For a quarter of a century the Milanos had labored toward one end, to provide a living for a large family of children. Every two or three years a new child was born. Three did not survive their first year, but when we first knew the family in 1932, it was providing a home for six children ranging in ages from four to twenty-two, and another was on the way. To feed, clothe, and furnish shelter for this family, to give them an education and to get them safely and comfortably married had been the one all-absorbing objective of Mr. Milano, a factory laborer, born in Italy fifty years ago, and his wife, ten years his junior and also a native of Italy. To all appearances they had succeeded in this primary task to a degree favorably comparable to the achievements of other working-class families in their neighborhood. The children appeared healthy and had no record of serious illness. Their clothes were presentable. All but $1,800 of a $6,500 mortgage on their duplex house had been paid off. Educational opportunities for the two oldest children, Jim, age twenty-two, and Celeste, age nineteen, had ended at the eighth grade. But progress was being made in this matter. Another daughter was finishing high school in 1932, and all agreed that the other children should finish high school also.

There were weaknesses, however, in the apparently stable structure of family affairs which the Milanos presented to the outside world. The most important one was the inconsistency between the hierarchy of family roles assumed desirable in the Italian culture from which the parents came and the actual pattern of authority and importance in the family. Both Mr. and Mrs. Milano strove to keep up the outward appearance of a father-centered family. But the relative abilities of the two did not permit this cultural expectancy to be realized in fact. The twenty-five years of effort to appear "normal" in the Italian community had left its marks on all concerned and had built up a deposit of resentment and mutual lack of respect between husband and wife. The children did not of course feel the need for living up to the cultural norm, but they knew who ruled the family and were mildly amused at the attempts to keep up an appearance of a different situation. Throughout their married life Mr. Milano had performed but one function of the head of the family; he had provided a weekly income of $20 to $25. But in all other respects Mrs. Milano was boss. She was the chancellor of the exchequer. She schemed and planned how to stretch the income to meet expenditures. At her orders her husband and son made repairs about the house. She planted and supervised the labor on the family garden. When the children came it was her agile mind which made decisions about their well-being, she who decided what clothes they should wear, how long they should stay out at night, what recreation they could have. It was she who worried about and disciplined the children, and arbitrated in disputes between them. She determined whether they were to quit or continue in school, and if they continued, what course they would take. In fact she was legislator, administrator, and judge. The father's part in such affairs was to rubber-stamp her decisions and to obey when they concerned him.

Their married life had not begun in this way. Mrs. Milano had entered into the relationship definitely expecting that she was getting a good provider and a capable father for her children. All omens were favorable. Mr.

Milano's father owned a saloon and his own home. The bridegroom had a job in that saloon and would inherit the business when his father died. He was ten years older than she. Her parents, in their wisdom in such matters, advised her to accept. She was in love with a "nice young man" with no family and no prospects, but she gave him up in favor of Mr. Milano. The economic advantages seemed clear.

A year later she was to wish she had never married him. He had no initiative, no "fight," no sense of his own rights, no very great ability as a worker. She soon learned that if anyone were to take the responsibility for making a home, she would have to be that person. She began her campaign. She fought her husband's parents for a fairer wage. She got out from under their roof as soon as she could push her husband into another job. This done, she reconciled herself to playing the role of a silent manager while he stood before the world as the head of the family. She never doubted who was the real boss, but in the Italian culture of which she was a part the community regarded the man as head in all things. Yet the realistic lines of authority proceeded from her and bound the family together in a functioning unit.

This fiction was not maintained without the sacrifice of mutual regard and respect for each other. Quite openly to our visitor (non-Italian and from a different social stratum) the wife showed her scorn for and displeasure with her husband. Within a year of her marriage she had realized his shortcomings. He was a "Mr. Milquetoast." He "got underfoot." He was "no-account about the house and with the kids." He "didn't show any fight" either on his job, or later in looking for work or in standing up for his rights. He was "no father at all." He "paid her no attention." She wished she had never married him. Clearly their relations were antagonistic coöperation with the emphasis on the adjective.

Mr. Milano, unable to demonstrate by works his status as head of the family, assumed a self-conscious air of superiority based on the fact that he was a northern, while she was a southern, Italian. The fact that Mr. Milano and his people were northern Italians and hence felt themselves superior to Mrs. Milano irritated her. She pondered over the obvious irreconcilability between their assumption of superiority and the facts. Evidences of their inferiority, her husband's lack of ability, the slovenliness of his father, the fact that one of his sisters was sent to Niantic for keeping a house of ill fame, his mother's anger when Mrs. Milano proposed a cash register in the saloon to make sure that all receipts were recorded, these all verified her conviction of her own superiority and intensified her scorn for her husband's family and for him when he no longer could even pretend to be the head of the family by providing it with a weekly income.

The marriage held together as an economic arrangement, as a means of providing a home and proper social status for all concerned. But the inconsistency between what the culture assumed in the way of paternal authority and function and the realistic pattern of arrangements gave a distinct color to the relationship. Indeed it might be said that this inconsistency was one of the chief objects about which family adjustments centered. Mr. Milano early recognized his comparative lack of ability to manage the family, took comfort in his confidence in the superiority of the northern Italians, sought his satisfactory status outside the home in his benefit association. Mrs. Milano's attention was focused on making good through her own efforts the gap thus left in family management. The children accepted her leadership as proper, her discipline as final, although after she had settled matters her husband's nominal approval must be given. Thus was peace kept in the family.

It cannot be said that in economic maintenance and family management the family was not a unit. But the sort

of integration achieved was inconsistent with the expectancies of the culture in the midst of which they lived.

In other respects the family was definitely not unified.
Each member had his own friends, and the home was not a
center for their entertainment. The older children faced
the conflict, particularly in their relations with the opposite sex, between the normal free association permitted by
the American culture—the ideas about which they acquired
in school—and the restrictions on such contacts in the
Italian home. Once a friend of the opposite sex was brought
into the home several times, it was supposed that there
was "something serious" between them. The younger children "ran wild" and no parental-planned recreation in-
hibited their freedom of the streets. Although the children
had all attended parochial school, the church and its ministrations were not a common focus of interest or satisfaction. One girl and a younger boy who attended regularly
declared that the rest of the family were "heathens." All
attended the movies once a week but, save for the young-
est children, never in company of other members of the
family. Mr. and Mrs. Milano each visited his own people,
but neither would have anything to do with the relatives of
the other. The children were ashamed of their parents'
poor English and openly made fun of them before our
visitors. They were ashamed of their parents' adherence to
Italian customs and in particular of their superstitions.
While Mrs. Milano was giving us the following information, two of the children threw down books they were
reading and went out of the house. Mrs. Milano was speaking of her distrust of doctors. She showed great pride in her
own treatment of herself and gave as an example her treatment of pains following the birth of one of her children.
She diagnosed this ailment as "the result of the dampness
from the out-of-doors having got inside me." She steamed
this dampness out by swallowing a hot solution of salt and
water and by the application of hot pads to the abdomen

and hot-water bottles to her feet. "And it didn't cost me anything, either," she said. Both Mr. and Mrs. Milano had contact in their childhood in Italy with witches as a source of treatment, and less frequently with the same source of treatment in America. Mr. Milano was cured of a rash in early childhood by a witch who drew out the hairs of his head one by one. Mrs. Milano's aunt in Italy had smallpox and no one would go near her except her sister who, taking a bottle of medicine which the doctor had prescribed, poured it upon a flower in the garden. Immediately the flower withered, and Mrs. Milano's mother decided that the doctors were trying to poison her sister. She threw the medicine out, thus saving her sister's life, and called upon a witch who accomplished a much more effective cure —at least the sister got well.

Absorbed in the task of self-maintenance and puzzled by the moral problems of their children in the new world with whose culture they were not familiar, the Milanos turned over the task of moral training to the parochial school. Aside from the normal Italian strictness with respect to the activities of the girls in the family, little moral discipline was exercised by the parents. The children had a reputation for dishonesty and the mother and father themselves connived in an attempt to get insurance on the latter by fraud soon before his death. (In this of course they had the coöperation of a dishonest agent and medical examiner.)

It is difficult to escape the conclusion that this family was primarily functioning as an economic institution and that it was held together by the practices and procedures necessary to such functioning. Yet weaknesses were already beginning to appear before Mr. Milano lost his job. The two older children were beginning to think of their own homes and resented the necessity of turning over most of their earnings to their mother. Her ability to keep her hands on this source of income was being weakened by

their increasing irritation at the sacrifice of their own future for the sake of the younger children.

Then Mr. Milano lost his job.

The loss of $20 a week was a serious blow to the family
pocketbook. Mrs. Milano faced the most difficult problem
of her career. From what source was the gap in income to
be filled? The older children must contribute *all* their earnings. The next two children in high school must earn after
school hours. Mr. Milano must be forced to look for work
instead of waiting confidently for a call from his late employer. Expenditures must be curtailed involving the denial to the children of customary allowances for recreation
and clothes. She herself could not go to work, for another
child was on the way, but she could wash and iron curtains.

She needed authority for this, and authority she got
from the sheer admiration her children showed for her
pluck and courage and ability in contrast to the listless and
futile efforts of their father. The last vestige of his claim
to authority removed by his failure to provide a weekly income, the mother took over the reins in earnest, not even
showing her husband the deference of a nominal consulta-
tion. The continued hold of cultural standards on Mrs.
Milano was demonstrated, however, by her refusal to ask
her husband's help in housework. Her tasks were multi-
plied and made even more difficult by her pregnancy. But
any rearrangement of functions in which her husband
might relieve her of some of her domestic duties was for-
bidden by the mores of her Italian group. That would
mean "bossing" him and seeing him in activities which their
culture's division of labor did not permit. She was torn at
times between the need for assistance in the routine duties
of the home and the realization that the last shred of her
respect for him would vanish if she put an apron on him.
Her self-respect depended on maintaining the cultural
standards, and by those standards their respective spheres
of influence and function were clearly marked out. If he

failed to perform his duties, she had no choice but to continue in hers and assume his as well.

Only twice in the next four years preceding his death was Mr. Milano able to play any role superior to that of a hanger-on in his own family. During C.W.A. days he obtained work for three months as a part of the nonrelief quota. Eight months before his death he was taken back by his old firm. But by this time the family had been so thoroughly organized around the authority of the mother that his position even as nominal head of the family was not reëstablished.

The first three months of the campaign to save the economic life of the family were filled with increasingly bitter criticism of the father by both wife and children. This criticism he avoided as much as possible by staying out of the home except for meals and at bedtime. But criticisms eventually decreased—they became old and lost their satisfaction for the critics. Moreover, the mother was doing wonders in her organization of the economic activities of her children. She succeeded in creating a morale and coöperative eagerness to contribute to the common effort which absorbed their attention and interest. With canny foresight she saw the morale-building possibilities of focusing the ambition of the two older children on helping the younger girl to become a nurse and on assisting the younger brother to go to trade school. She played upon their family pride in the effort to give the younger children a chance they had not had. She played on Jim's satisfaction at becoming "head" of the family after his father's death. She frankly admits that she has probably sacrificed the chances of her two older children to make good marriages by keeping them within the family circle so long, but she feels that the opportunity she and they have given the younger children justifies the methods used. Strangely enough, Jim and Celeste agree with her, at least vocally. They declare they will not marry until the children are raised. Since the last child will leave home from eight to twelve years hence, if they hold to their decision that probably means they will not marry at all. The younger daughter who became a nurse is now married. The son who finished trade school has a good job and is contributing to the family finances. He was married in the spring of 1940. Another daughter finished Commercial High School at the same time and had the promise of a job from a man whose son "had been paying her some attention." Two children are still to be "raised."

It is difficult to isolate unemployment as a definite causal agent in the affairs of this family. It is even more difficult to picture what would have been the course of family life had Mr. Milano retained his job. Certainly this is true, that his removal as an earner clarified the situation by relegating the husband to a position which, but for his weekly pay check, he already occupied. To be sure, unemployment brought to this family an irritant which increased the problem of righting a maladjustment already evident in the inconsistency between cultural expectancies and the actual structure of family relations. Yet it also presented a necessity so great that the issue could no longer be avoided, a necessity which freed the mother from the bondage to cultural standards which heretofore had held some of her abilities in check. Mr. Milano, pushed aside in the dynamic processes of family functioning, was a sorry figure. But he was a sorry figure in the midst of family affairs long before he lost his job. His unemployment pushed into the position of open leadership in the family's affairs the one person competent to fulfill the obligations of leadership and to organize the earning capacities of the older children around the major objective of this family's life, the raising of a large family.

Whether the opportunities for the younger children would have been as great had Mr. Milano retained his job we can only surmise. Certainly the opportunity for Jim and Celeste to establish their own families would have been greater. The only certain conclusion we can draw from this period in the Milanos' story is that the family has within itself great resources for overcoming difficult problems and for recovering from the impact of unfavorable circumstances.

## ROSINA

### A Family Resolves Its Cross-Cultural Conflicts.

Anyone becoming acquainted with the Rosinas six months after Mr. Rosina was laid off as salesman for a bottling works would have found Mrs. Rosina contemplating a divorce, and her husband thinking of giving up the effort to keep his home together. Unless one looked into the history of this particular family he would be inclined to set down this situation as a "result" of unemployment. Every evidence points to the fact that if Mr. Rosina had found a job at this moment which would have made it possible for the family to continue living in New Haven, the separation almost certainly would have taken place. As it was, lacking a job, the Rosinas went to New York State to live for a period with Mrs. Rosina's grandparents, and escaped for a time the factors increasing the tension between them. Upon their return to New Haven they had seen the source of their difficulties and had made adjustments which stabilized their family relations. Continued unemployment making necessary their removal to another set of influences was in this case the salvation of the family.

Mr. Rosina came from Italian Catholic stock, Mrs. Rosina from a Yankee Protestant family. Living in the Italian community, surrounded by his own family, depending for his prestige upon occupying the position as head of the family characteristic of the Italian home, Mr. Rosina insisted that his wife take a subordinate position, yield to his own wishes and decisions, and forego any rights which she might believe she ought to have. Their six-year-old daughter must be raised a Catholic. Mrs. Rosina, although possessing a high-school education as compared to his eighth-grade education, was not permitted to share in political activities or attend lectures with her husband. Her ideas with respect to insurance and other expenditures were pushed aside as of no account although these expenditures were leading the family into large debts. They must live in an Italian neighborhood and Mrs. Rosina must observe the Italian customs. In these and other ways Mr. Rosina strove to demonstrate to his parents and brothers and friends that he had not made a mistake by marrying outside the group.

For the first few years Mrs. Rosina had adjusted her own desires and interests to this situation, considering it a small price to pay for her escape from the insecurity of an orphan's existence, first in orphan asylums, later in a home with a disagreeable stepmother, and finally in an unsuccessful attempt at an independent livelihood. But for the past three years her resentment had been increasing, and she stated that long before Mr. Rosina lost his job she had contemplated leaving him. She submitted passively on fewer occasions to her husband's attempts to dominate and was held in check in her desire to be free only by the thought of what would happen to her child.

It cannot be denied that unemployment increased this tension. Her husband's family aided them financially and apparently felt that this help gave them increased right to interfere in family affairs. The one bond, the provision of economic security, which held her to her husband was weakened. Yet the fact remains that the stability of their relationship depending on this one factor was never very great, and that the other stresses were exerting severe strain even on this one bond. If Mr. Rosina had returned to a job which offered a steady income at this point, the union might have been maintained for a time, but there is every chance that the process of disintegration would have continued.

Mrs. Rosina finally decided to go to New York State to stay with her grandparents. Mr. Rosina, his confidence in his ability to support his family shaken by six months of unemployment, asked if he might accompany her. It was the first experience during their married life, she declared, in which he had submitted to her decision. She consented to his going along. The first step in reconstruction was taken with that decision. He had admitted that her decision, not his, was a controlling one.

Fortunately, the grandparents were kindly people who were much interested in the welfare of their granddaughter and her family. The grandfather in particular had considerable wisdom in the problems of human relationships. For six months the Rosinas lived in the grandparents' home, Mr. Rosina helping on the farm. This was his first experience outside of the culture of his boyhood. In this New York community wives shared in family decisions on a more equalitarian basis than in the community with which he was familiar. Grandmother was very active in community affairs and was the president of a literary society which met periodically in the home. It was his turn to be an "outgrouper," a Catholic in a Protestant community. Mr. Rosina's comment on this situation is interesting: "It was a hard lesson, lad, and I kicked like the devil against it at first, but eventually I saw what the Mrs. had been up against." After six months Mr. Rosina obtained work in a factory in a near-by city. For a year he held this job, paying board and rent to the grandparents out of his earnings. During the whole period he was slowly finding a basis for companionship with his wife in coöperation in decisions on expenditures and matters connected with the training of their child.

I learned she had ideas and good ones at that. She joined that literary circle her grandmother ran and got quite a reputation up there in a kind of a political club on labor legislation her grandmother belonged to. She made a speech one night, and it was a honey, darned near as good as I could make.

When the plant at which he was working closed down, the family returned to New Haven, but not before Mrs. Rosina had exacted from her husband a promise that they would not live in the neighborhood which had been the scene of their marital difficulties. He failed to find work in New Haven and eventually got work on W.P.A. where he has been ever since. But the coöperative relationship with his wife has not ceased. Possibly it is a fortunate circumstance for them that Mr. Rosina's father and mother had died in the meantime and that one brother had left town. The other brother began to interfere when Mrs. Rosina refused to wear the customary mourning black, but Mr. Rosina, comfortable in the new-found relations with his wife, told him in no uncertain terms to "keep hands off." Since that day, he and his brother have had nothing to do with one another.

The Rosinas have adjusted their standard of living to their new income level and, freed from the social pressures which impelled Mr. Rosina to assume and maintain a role incompatible with harmony, give every evidence of forming a stable family unit. The daughter, although confirmed a Catholic, is not regular in her religious devotions. The Rosinas have agreed to have nothing to do with any church. Both are now active workers in a Democratic political club and are finding many common objects for effort in such activities. The daughter, now reaching adolescence, is presenting them with more common problems to the solution of which they devote coöperative energies.

The conclusion from this story is not that unemployment does not destroy family harmony. It is that it merely acts as an irritant on whatever tendencies are already present. In this case at least the lack of a job opened an opportunity for the Rosinas to escape from a set of circumstances that for six years had been pushing them toward separation and to live for a year and a half in an atmosphere in which they could reëxamine the bases of their relationships. In that

period they found the source of their difficulties and undertook the readjustments which have resulted in the building
of a more stable family institution.

## RAPARKA

### *A Polish Mother Becomes Head of the Family.*

The impact of unemployment did not destroy the Raparka
family, but the adjustments made necessary did lead to a
complete reorganization of the structure of family relationships. When Mr. Raparka lost his job in the fall of 1933 he
dominated the family. Two years later it was Mrs. Raparka
who was the center of authority. She was ably supported in
her task by a nineteen-year-old son earning $25 a week.
When in the summer of 1938 Mr. Raparka left his family,
he had long since become a parasite, and his departure
caused little disturbance in the pattern of family living.
The story of how this came about is at once evidence of the
way the structure of family relations depends upon the
relative functions of its members and of the sources of stability of the family institution residing in the ability of its
members to develop new tactics in the face of disturbing
problems such as unemployment. The institution survives
though its pattern is altered.

When Mr. Raparka's job as a molder's helper ended in
1933, the pattern of family life was adapted to the possibilities of supporting two adults and four children on an
average wage of $15 a week. A higher income until 1927
had provided them with comfortable home furnishings.
Rent in a five-room "box car" tenement in a Polish neighborhood took a quarter of their income. Out of what remained they expected to give all the children a good education. A son, age seventeen, had been supported through
trade school; a daughter, age fifteen, had been sent to high
school; a son, age thirteen, was finishing eighth grade in a
parochial school. A new son had been added to the family
circle less than a year before. Regular expenditures were

made for presentable clothes, for a weekly family party at the movies, and for church. The children earned extra money for personal expenditures by work after school hours. Enough was spent on food so that no record of dietary deficiency diseases appears in the family history, and all members were apparently in good health.

Mr. Raparka as the chief breadwinner dominated this situation. His rule was stern and strict. He was not above putting down any dissension from his decisions, either on the part of the children or his wife, by force. On one occasion ten years previously his wife had left him for five days when he knocked her downstairs during an argument. The children received frequent whippings which only he was permitted to administer. All requests for money were made to him. He never told his wife how much he earned or how much he saved. She knew only that on payday she would receive her weekly allowance for household expenses, that he gave her and the children money for clothes and extras when he agreed that their requests were reasonable.

Both husband and wife had been born into Polish peasant families fifty years ago. They had lived in a Polish-American community in New Haven since 1911 and had been married in 1915. Apparently experience in this culture had led them to expect nothing different from this father-centered family life. Certainly no signs of revolt were evident. Since Mrs. Raparka's return from her weekend desertion of ten years ago, friends and in-laws reported that there had been no open signs of serious dissension. Mrs. Raparka described her married life as hard but never wanting in the basic necessities. Her husband, she said, was a hard master, but never unjust. Even when he beat her, she was aware that she had been foolish and unfair in her demands. She had learned when and how to ask him for money and took considerable pride in her knowledge of such tactics. The children declared that they feared their father, but that they respected him for his efforts to give them more education than many of their Polish-American companions could have. The eldest son was disappointed that his father insisted on trade school instead of an academic course, but he saw the wisdom in his decision and was overjoyed when he was permitted to go to night school to acquire a knowledge of history and literature after his day's work at the trade school was finished.

An observer could find many superficial evidences of family solidarity. The basic one of course was this submission of individual independence to paternal control. Apparently the evenings at home involved a mutual sharing of individual activities and interests. All members were regular at religious service and church activities. The weekly family party at the movies was the chief form of recreation. All were interested and nearly equally concerned about the welfare of the baby and shared a pride in every sign of his development. Polish was spoken in the home, and even when schoolmates were present the shame at the parents' language handicap, so frequent in the children of immigrants, did not appear on the surface. The children spoke freely to their parents in Polish. The division of labor within the home provided for a sharing of duties between mother and daughter only, but father and sons were proud of the immaculate and well-kept home and contributed occasionally small items of home decoration from their earnings.

How thoroughly this institutional structure depended on the father continuing his function as the chief breadwinner, however, became evident within two weeks after he lost his job. Earnings of $15 a week had provided no margin of safety, no savings. At best the plane of living had been supported in a hand-to-mouth fashion. The unemployment coincided with the need for new clothes for school. The food for the baby could not wait. A change from fresh to canned milk resulted in convulsions which alarmed the whole family. Mrs. Raparka's pains in the back, present since the birth of the child, suddenly became worse. Her husband, with no money to pay for a doctor, refused to call one either for the mother or child for two weeks. This decision was resented by the whole family. Finally he borrowed money from an aunt without telling his wife. She discovered the loan when the aunt, having suffered an accident, asked for the money back to meet her own expenses. He cashed his insurance policy to pay the aunt, again without telling his wife. He had exhausted his available resources and one day pawned his overcoat. Hunting for work in an early snowstorm, he caught a cold which rapidly developed into a serious illness.

At this point Mrs. Raparka took the initiative. She went to the Catholic Social Service Bureau and asked for help. She received medical attention for her husband and milk for her baby. From this moment the shift in family organization began. When Mr. Raparka regained his feet in about ten days he was furious at this move. He sullenly told his wife to mind her own business when she suggested that he go to the Department of Public Charities where the Catholic society had suggested there might be additional aid. He undertook a desperate search for work and finished a two weeks' job hunt a thoroughly beaten man. The change wrought in him by this experience is evidenced by the fact that for the first time in his life he submitted to his wife's insistence that he help with scrubbing the floors and doing the washing (though he still refused to hang out clothes, in which activity "he would be seen"). The notes of our visitor who arrived several times while he was engaged in domestic duties indicates his sullen resentment at this change in status. The notes also indicate that the wife was gaining a new position of authority in her supervision of her husband's efforts. On several occasions she insisted he do over again what he had not done well. His response to this request made in the presence of the visitor was to grab his coat from the hook and flee from the house, slamming the door behind him. At this juncture Mrs. Raparka would remark, "He'll be back. He say he look for work. But then why not find? He no look. He can help here." Then she would go into a long criticism of her husband. She could not understand why he couldn't find work; he always had before. He must be getting lazy. Maybe if she made him work at home he would find a job in self-defense.

We do not know the course this readjustment would have taken had it not been for two facts. The first was that Mrs. Raparka decided to look for a job herself. After a futile search of ten days, she learned that jobs cannot be had for the asking. The stories her husband told of "No Help Wanted" signs, company police who wouldn't even let one apply, blunt refusals, and vague promises were true. She declared she was filled with shame at making her husband work at home.

At about the same time Mr. Raparka got a job on C.W.A., and later under F.E.R.A., for the same wages he had formerly received as a molder's helper—$15 a week. Once more the normal pattern of family affairs was on the way to being reëstablished. It was noticed, however, that children and wife did not recognize his authority with the same passive submission as before. Possibly an adolescent assertion of independence was overdue. In any case the two older children argued frequently with their father when his decisions crossed their own desires. Mrs. Raparka also insisted that he turn over his work relief wages to her in full. This he refused to do, but his refusal had to be repeatedly made. Nor did he close the issue once and for all as he would have done a year before. He was less belligerent in the enforcement of his authority, and the renewal of the former pattern of relationships appears to have been the result of restored habits rather than of any dogmatic assertion of his own position as head of the family. This situation continued until the fall of 1934. The elder son, now graduated from trade school, obtained work as a mechanic and was soon earning $25 a week. The importance of this change lies in two facts. In the first place, since the F.E.R.A. wages were based on a budgetary deficiency estimate, added family resources of $25 a week automatically cut Mr. Raparka off work relief. Once more he became "unemployed," and a noncontributor to the support of the family. His status, dependent on his economic contribution, was once more under attack. In the second place, the earnings of the children in foreign-American families are customarily handed over to the mother. The son followed this procedure. Mrs. Raparka now had in her possession $10 a week more than the family resources had amounted to for some time, and *she* controlled the purse strings. It was her husband's turn now to ask her for money for his personal needs. She did not give him an allowance. Each request was judged on its own merits. She now decided how much would go for current expenses and how much would go to pay back bills, what clothes she and the children would have, whether the dentist would be consulted, and whether the daughter could go to the high-school ball. To this shift in roles the husband could offer no objection outside of sullen resentment, since his privilege in the control of expenditures depended on his provision of the income. He was not even called on to share in such decisions. The mother and the older son talked over the matter and shared that responsibility. When the daughter graduated from high school two years later and began earning, she also was taken into the family councils. When the younger son finished the eighth grade, the mother and older son disagreed as to whether he should go to trade school or to Hillhouse.[1] The son, in true paternal fashion, insisted that his younger brother should have the opportunity he had missed. But the mother eventually carried the day, by the use of the identical arguments the father had used to send the elder son to trade school.

1. College preparatory high school.

The consolidation of the mother's position was aided for a four-month period during which the father took a job on a farm as laborer for $20 a month and his keep. This occurred in the summer of 1935. With him absent from home, the organization of family life around the mother's authority proceeded without interruption even from Mr. Raparka's sullen dissent. When he returned to the family circle it was as a beneficiary not as a partner. One day while our visitor was present he went out saying he thought he would commit suicide. Mrs. Raparka remarked, "He won't, you know. But if he did, maybe I could get widow's aid and my boy, he could get married."

In the summer of 1938, Mr. Raparka asked for money to go to New York in search of a job. He has not been heard of since. But his departure caused little change in the routine or structure of family life. He long since had ceased to be an integral part of the major business of family activities.

So far as the present is concerned, the Raparka family is carrying on the economic and social obligations imposed on the family by society in nearly as adequate a fashion as it was in 1933 when Mr. Raparka was its unquestioned head. As a group the members have faced the problems of readjustment and devised new methods involving a new division of labor for carrying on the essential tasks of family life. Yet one major weakness is evident, a weakness which would not have been so obvious had the readjustments not involved the elimination of the father as an integral earning member of the institution. The economic support of the family rests on the earnings of the elder son and daughter. The former is now twenty-seven, the latter twenty-five. Both want to get married and establish families of their own. A major obstacle is the continued need of the mother and her young child for their earnings. Such is the new problem raised in many families in which the unemployment of the father has shifted the responsibility for support to earning children. The present institution faces the task and maintains its integrity and fulfills its obligations save this one, of offering its children the maximum opportunity to continue the process of building homes of their own.

## CASSELLA

*A Disintegrating Family Is Restored.*

Anyone observing the Cassellas in 1933 would not have been inclined to list them among the more successful families of New Haven. They had, however, contributed their share to the perpetuation of the race. At the age of twenty Mr. Cassella, American-born son of Italian parents, had married a girl of sixteen and in the next twelve years they had added eight souls to the city's population. Seven of these were still living when we first became acquainted with the family. The home was a place of dirt and smells. Housekeeping was an annual event which succeeded in arranging furniture, bedding, clothes, foodstuffs, fuel, dishes, cooking utensils, oil, and newspapers in some semblance of order during the entire week just before Easter. During the rest of the year the place resembled a not-too-well-kept blacksmith shop. Partly consumed food, dirty dishes, diapers, tin cans were abandoned where last used. Our visitor, pressed to accept the hospitality of a cup of tea from one of the obviously dirty cups, entered this footnote to her report, "If I get sick from this, I'm going to bill the University for medical attention." Overturned chairs remained overturned until someone wanted to sit down. The baby crawled about over the littered floor or lay crying on a ragged and unmade bed. One day while our visitor was present Mrs. Cassella handed the baby a spool, which had been on the floor, to pacify her. When that was unsuccessful, the eleven-year-old girl took a crust away from the cat, who had climbed on the table in search of food, and stuck it in the baby's mouth. This reduced the baby's contribu-

tion to the confusion for a few minutes. The family, with
the exception of Mrs. Cassella, stayed out of the house as
much as possible, returning there only for meals and to
sleep.

The four children who were able to walk ran wild on the
streets when they were not in school. No one paid much attention to the time they left home for school, and no one
except the truant officer was much concerned as to whether
they arrived at their destination. It is practically impossible to suggest what the reaction of the children to discipline would be since so little attempt was made to exercise
any sort of control. Meal times were bedlam, as might well
be imagined with nine people gathered in one kitchen. The
two bedrooms were filled with beds and clothes and were
unlighted.

With the exception of Mr. Cassella's repeatedly expressed affection for his two-year-old daughter, Maria,
there was little demonstration of mutual regard and respect. Quite the opposite. Statements of husband and wife
and of parents and children about each other indicated
little fondness for each other's company. Quarrels, bicker-
ings, and name-calling even in the presence of outsiders
showed a lack of restraint that boded ill for successful adjustment to the intensified problems of unemployment.

Mrs. Cassella's chief complaint about her husband was
that he spent all his time when not at work at a local
Democratic club. Certainly he was not among the most
needed workers in the New Haven labor market. He had
started work at the age of thirteen as a machine worker in
the National Folding Box Company. In the succeeding
twenty years he had held a variety of jobs including semiskilled work making auto parts for five years, reed work on
baby carriages for three and a half years, shipping clerk
at Winchester's for four years, and plumber's helper for
two years, as well as a number of odd jobs as a laborer.
During this twenty years a cumulative total of nearly four

years had been spent between jobs or in slack seasons, unemployed. His record shows frequent layoffs and recalls indicating that he was a marginal worker. Since the fall of 1929 he had never earned more than $22 a week and even at the height of his earning power as a shipping clerk he never earned more than $28 a week. When these maximums are reduced by the factor of short time and the extensive periods of unemployment, a very meager income was provided to cover the costs of raising this large family.

When we first came into contact with this family in 1932 soon after Mr. Cassella had lost his job, we could not but wonder whether unemployment could possibly reduce them to living standards lower and a degree of disorganization greater than their status at the time. It did not. In fact during the next seven years this family was gradually pulled together, was integrated into a working unit, became conscious of itself as a family, was reorganized in the management of the home, and developed a satisfactory technique of self-maintenance yielding a higher standard of living. Their source of maintenance for the past seven years has been work done for, and benefits derived from, federal and local government. During all of this time Mr. Cassella has not returned to private employment. The story of this process is an interesting revelation of the unexpected sources of family stability and the dynamic character of that institution. The seeds of reconstruction were present when we first stepped across the threshold of this disorganized home, but it is only in retrospect that this conclusion is made.

This was not the first time the Cassellas had faced unemployment. They knew what was in store for them. They cashed in their insurance policies as they had done twice before in the thirteen years of their married life. "We're getting used to that now. Only this time we tried to hold onto John's, for we know he hasn't long for this earth. But that finally went, too." They reduced their meals to two a day, going without breakfast until a visiting teacher complained that the children had no energy in the morning. After that they went without lunch and had an early supper. They reduced their normal diet to bread and beans. They let their rent go. They exhausted their credit at the corner grocery. They stopped spending money on movies and church. They pawned a clock which had been a wedding present. They finally applied for relief. All these things save the last they had done before. These were minor problems and experience had taught them what to do. But new problems kept arising which ordinarily, with the possession of even a small income, would have been easily solved.

One day the baby had convulsions. They owed the doctor so much money that Mrs. Cassella was ashamed to call him. She rushed the baby to a drugstore and bought camphor oil which she applied to its chest with hot cloths. She also put a few drops in his nose to help him breathe more easily. Her mother had done "something like this." She pinned an amulet on the baby's shirt. The baby became even more ill. When the relief visitor came a week later the baby was nearly dead. A city doctor was rushed to the scene and scolded her roundly for not calling him sooner. "Imagine it, he bawled me out for not asking for relief." A visiting nurse was provided. This was the family's first introduction to free medical service. "Believe me, now, whenever anything is wrong, I call the city doctor or go right to the dispensary. And it don't cost me a cent," said Mrs. Cassella in 1939. Yet she retained some sense of obligation. She insisted on going home from the hospital after a tonsillectomy in 1938 before the doctor advised her to go because "it didn't seem right to stay there longer than necessary when I wasn't paying for it."

Mr. Cassella had formerly been very successful at dice. He had once won $250 with which they paid for the baby's funeral. With no cash he couldn't gamble in this way. They started a small boy selling papers and with his meager earnings "played the numbers," letting the crippled boy choose the number combination in the hope that his affliction would bring good luck. "Our luck was wretched, but if I had enough to shoot craps, things would be different," was Mr. Cassella's comment.

The principal of the grade school decided to send two of the girls to an "opportunity class" which Mrs. Cassella defined as "the dumb school." This had happened once before in the case of the older daughter. On the former occasion the girl had been taken out of the public school and sent to parochial school. But that step would involve buying books and finding $2 a month for tuition. So the children went to "the dumb school," and Mrs. Cassella had to be content for the time being to speak her mind to the teacher. "I told her," she said, "that I was American-born, not a wop, and she couldn't get away with that stuff on me. But," she added, "she did for the time being. But you wait!"

They heard rumors that a Board of Health inspector was making the rounds and did not approve of children sleeping in the same room as their parents. They lived in fear of his coming for a month. When he did not come, the fear subsided but was not canceled. They vowed to "get out of this cesspool as quick as Joe gets another job."

When the bank took over the mortgage on the house, a representative promised to paint up the kitchen and furnish screens if the Cassellas would pay up the back rent at the rate of $5 a month. "If Joe had a job it would be worth going without something to get that done. As it is, it can't be done, and we'll just have to swat flies," said Mrs. Cassella.

Many problems similar to this would have been met without serious strain if some cash income had been available to the family. Later they were met, as we shall see, when Mr. Cassella obtained work relief and when he realized the value of political influence. As it was, for the time being, they added to the strain on the already disorganized family relations and provided family conversations with new subjects for controversy. The agenda was already well filled. "When we quarrel so much in front of the children they get harder and harder to manage. But it seems as though when everything comes at once this way and everything is too big for us, we don't have any strength left to stop. And we can't keep things to ourselves when we are all crowded in this one room."

Throughout the first six months of unemployment, during the last four and a half of which the family was on relief, such problems were all but overshadowed, however, by a heartbreaking discovery. They learned the truth about the disease, a muscular atrophy, which had afflicted two of the boys. It came about in this way. For years they had spent every cent they could save out of their inadequate means to provide their boys with medical treatment. Four doctors, probably quacks, had promised a cure. The degree of their sacrifice in this matter will be apparent when it is realized that in five years they had spent over $500 on such treatment. No longer able to continue this expenditure, they took John to the dispensary. There they were told that little was known about the disease, save that it was inherited by sons from their mother, and that those afflicted seldom if ever recovered. The case worker who said, "You'd think they'd be glad that they might not as well spend any more money on the boys, but instead they seem to resent it," apparently didn't understand the role of these expenditures in the family life. To be sure, the payments to doctors had helped to keep the family in discouraging poverty. But also they had been the one focus of interest, the one common goal of effort for Mr. and Mrs. Cassella. To restore the boys to their place among their romping former playmates had come to be the persistent purpose of their marital partnership. And now all they had done was proved useless, and the only thing to look forward to was the boys' death and their burial in a pauper's grave since the insurance had had to be dropped.

Mrs. Cassella during the next few months attended the funerals of two boys from John's class in the crippled children's school. Mr. Cassella accompanied her to the second. They lost any ability they had had to manage the household. At a time when all their energies were required for meeting the intensified problems of self-maintenance they were crushed by this blow. "It seemed as though nothing mattered now," was Mr. Cassella's comment.

Added to worry was another factor. This was an hereditary disease. Mrs. Cassella was pregnant. Suppose the new child should be a boy! Filled with anxiety, she induced an abortion which nearly killed her. When she confessed this mortal sin to her priest, he "was furious." The birth of two crippled children, he told her, was probably a visitation from God for former sins. She later went to him for counsel, seeking some assurance that, under the circumstances, birth control would not be sinful. The priest stood firm on the religious principle involved. The Cassellas ceased going to church, their one occasional common association outside the home. In spite of this action, however, sexual intercourse became an unpleasant relationship, beclouded by feelings of dread and guilt. One bright reflection alone remained to them out of this situation, the last three children had been girls.

It is difficult to date the crisis in the Cassellas' family relations, but looking back over the case records, the first changes appear to come at about the time Mr. Cassella was accepted for a C.W.A. job. It is certain that the wages he received supplied the first possibility for adjustment to some of the problems which had been vexing them.

One of the first moves made by the Cassellas was to take out a small loan, pay up their miscellaneous debts to the grocer, and thus reëstablish their credit. Their second move was to call the bank and say they were ready now to pay something on back rent so that the kitchen might be painted and screens furnished. They got the bank to reduce the monthly payment to $3 in exchange for Mr. Cassella's doing the labor on these items. The change in Mrs. Cassella's attitude toward housekeeping was not startling but it was marked. Both of them were very proud of his painting job. Mrs. Cassella went out ironing for several weeks to get enough money for fresh curtains. As soon as the small loan was repaid a new stove and a rocking chair and table were bought on time. (Incidentally we have noticed that shopkeepers in New Haven are perfectly willing to make installment sales to persons on work relief.)

It will be recalled that for many years the Cassellas had lived on a plane very close to bare existence. They had no material symbols of status to lose. These additions to their home were new achievements for them. They were making progress.

As soon as the furniture was paid for in 1937, they moved to a better neighborhood and a four-room flat at an increased rent of $5 a month. The satisfaction of the whole family in this move was obvious. Mrs. Cassella's comment is revealing:

I used to try to keep things up, but I gave up years ago. I was pregnant most of the time, and every new child made things harder. Look at what we had over there on Oak Street. We never could get any better. We had to choose between new curtains and furniture and a decent place to live and a doctor for the boys. But you don't have no fun in keeping up your home with what we could scrape together. But this place now, it's different, don't you think so? And we aren't all on top of each other here. Yes, it looks like we're getting on.

The change in housekeeping noticed in 1937 cannot be ascribed completely to Mrs. Cassella's altered incentives, however. Even more important was the fact that the eldest daughter had reached the age of seventeen, had acquired ideas of orderliness and cleanliness from association with her girl friends, and was running the housekeeping. She was old enough now to enforce her ideas in the matter, also.

Mr. Cassella took $1 a week out of the $15 he received from work relief and began adding an average of about $3 a week to the family exchequer from winnings at dice. When this, together with surplus commodity food and Red Cross clothes, was added to the family income the regular weekly resources were as great as and more regular than the family had had while Mr. Cassella was employed. The large expenditures for the crippled boys were discontinued and free medical service was sought at the dispensary, a sizable saving in this large family.

The steady provision of wages reduced considerably the strain on family harmony. Let Mr. Cassella speak for himself on this matter:

God almighty, it's a terrible thing when the way that you get your grub and things is by going down to the city hall, especially when you need something extra. You come home after asking for it and the wife says, "Well, what luck?" And you say, "Well, they promised to send an investigator." And she says, "Hell! They promised to do that before, and where does it get you? You're a fine provider you are!" And then you sit down and you just rock and rock, and pretty soon she asks you what you're rocking for, and you tell her that it's none of her business. And you keep on rocking and thinking of how queer it is to be getting your living by asking for it at the city hall instead of working for it. And finally when you can't stand it no longer you get up and go over to the Green and sit on a bench that don't rock. That's one reason why you're damned glad when C.W.A. gives you a chance because then it keeps you away from home and your money is your own and you don't have time to think about things like that. And the old woman isn't jumping on your neck all the time.

Almost as important as the income from work relief in the reconstruction of the Cassella family was the discovery that Mr. Cassella's political influence could be used to advantage. His wife had resented the amount of time he spent at the political club and in the service of the party. Until the summer of 1933 this resentment was continued, growing more bitter as she complained that he had better be earning some money instead of "hanging around" the club. Then a succession of events proved to her that political connections could be turned into cash.

In the summer of 1933, the Cassellas were in desperate circumstances, living on a $5-a-week grocery order and had no gas and electricity. Mrs. Cassella was pregnant and no clothing had been accumulated for the baby. John, the older crippled boy, at his father's suggestion, wrote a letter to President Roosevelt describing his own condition, the family's desperate straits, and complaining of the poor way New Haven was providing for the family. "Besides," said the letter, "this is no way to treat honest American people. My father works hard for the Democrats, too." A letter (which they now proudly display) was received from the President's secretary telling them not to worry, that things would be taken care of. Several days later a person whom Mrs. Cassella describes as a "G-man" came to investigate. Their grocery order was increased and that winter Mr. Cassella was accepted for work relief, the results of which change have already been noted.

The frustration to family pride involved in the transfer of two children to "the dumb school" will be recalled. The income was not available for solving the problem by a transfer of the children to a parochial school. Early in the winter of 1934 Mr. Cassella enlisted the services of an influential politician and through him brought pressure on the Board of Education in the matter. The children were given an "achievement test" and promptly restored to their former classes.

An even more obvious demonstration of the value of political connections was made in connection with the death of John. The family had been worried about the possibility of a pauper's burial since they had had to cash in the insurance policy. But a funeral was arranged with an undertaker who was influential in political circles. At the same time Mr. Cassella was raised from a grade of work paying $15 a week to one paying $20.75 per week with the understanding that he was to pay the undertaker $5 a week until the bill was paid. Commented Mrs. Cassella: "I used to raise hell with the old man about his wasting time at the club. But I don't any more. I guess he's got plenty pay for all the time he hung around there. It looks like he has some influence, too, don't you think?"

Both relief work and the use of political connections contributed to the ability of the Cassellas to meet their problems constructively. Two other events made them aware more than ever before of their unity and of their responsibility as a family.

During the time the family was subsisting on direct relief, Mrs. Cassella's sister offered to relieve the family of one of its financial problems by adopting the two-year-old daughter. The material advantage to the girl was obvious. Should they accept the sister's offer? Would that be living up to their responsibilities as parents? Weren't they pretty much failures as parents, anyway? Still didn't they have something to offer which offset the sister's economic contribution? For two months they debated the matter by reference to such questions and finally they decided that the daughter could stay with her aunt for several months, but that they would not give her up. This was the daughter for whom the father had a particular affection. This fact undoubtedly influenced his decision. But the period was one of real exploration of their responsibility as parents. Soon after she had gone, we noticed a picture of the child appeared on the kitchen wall. The conversation was spontaneously directed to cute things Maria had done. They obviously missed her. So did the older children. The minute

Mr. Cassella was taken on C.W.A. they brought Maria home. The celebration at her return was genuine and enthusiastic. Even a bottle of "store wine" was purchased for the occasion.

The second event followed John's death. Since the disease from which he suffered was so rare, the Medical School offered $2,000 for his body. The debate over this matter was short. In their lives $2,000 would make a tremendous difference. But in the words of Mr. Cassella: "No decent family would let one of its children be cut up. We couldn't do much for him while he lived, but we can treat him right, now. We could never hold our heads up if we took that money. He was our boy while he lived and he's still our boy."

The oldest girl declared in 1939 that these debates, carried on in the presence of the children, had had a deep effect on her. For the first time in her life she really felt that her parents had a sincere affection for their children. She believed the other children felt the same way. "We had never realized what a family meant before, but when we saw them fighting the temptation to make things easier by going back on their children, why then we couldn't help knowing that they loved us in spite of everything."

I would not leave the impression that the Cassellas today are a happy and well-integrated family. But they are much closer to that goal than they were in 1932. Their essential regard for each other has been dramatized and tested. They are aware of themselves as a family unit. The children have grown older and have taken responsibilities. One of the boys is selling papers. The eldest girl has practically taken over the management of the housekeeping. The appearance of the house is partly the result of her skill and partly the result of their living in more pleasant and ample quarters which reward her care.

The family is reëstablished in the community economically if not socially. At shops, stores, the movies, and the political club, they are indistinguishable from those whose income is derived from private industry. They are dependent on employment by the federal government. They make use of every free service with which they can make contact. Private industry would have to bid high to attract Mr. Cassella from his present job. In view of the fact that he was always a marginal worker, one doubts that the bid will come soon. No one can deny that this family is dependent on government. Nor can they deny that as a family they are fulfilling their function in the community more successfully than in the days when they were dependent on private industry.

# VII

## *THE CYCLE OF READJUSTMENT*

EVEN a casual reading of these brief case histories would indicate that it is difficult if not impossible to derive a typical pattern of adjustment to unemployment which correctly describes that process in all families. That adjustment must necessarily be made against a background of events and factors which vary from one family to another. What are the clues to each family's stability? What patterns of relationship and authority have been established? How effective are these in meeting the day-by-day needs? By what activities and devices is the family bound together as a functioning unit? How dependent are these on the expenditure of money? What are the family's goals, and what progress and symbols of progress have been achieved in the pursuit of them? How consistent are these goals and evidences of progress with a reduced plane of living? What are the satisfactions members have come to expect from family life and how vulnerable are these to the attack of reduced earnings? Does the family have a conscious conception of its own role in the community? What objective evidences must be presented to others to make this role real? How harmonious are relations within the family, and what are the necessary prerequisites for this harmony? What tactics and customary practices have been devised by the members for carrying on a continuance of the normal division of labor? What resources has the family for the meeting of emergencies? What are the ages of and potential help to be expected from the children? In other words, what equipment do families bring with them to the period of unemployment? What are the weak spots in the pattern of family organization and practice?

Each family is an institution, the nature of which has

been evolved over a period of years from an infinite number of cumulative adjustments. Not only has this evolution produced a wide variety of end products, but the problems of unemployment which the families must face vary. The possibility of another job depends on various factors as we have seen. The steps taken in search of jobs and their success or failure will involve many different sorts of effects on the structure of family life. The adjustments made to unemployment by any particular family are not, therefore, the adjustments of a typical family to a typical unemployment situation.

Nevertheless, all of these families had at least two problems in common. One was the necessity for readjustment of the employment pattern within the family group, and the other was the necessity for making adjustments in expenditure when income was curtailed.

Facing these problems effectively involved adjustments in many of the practices and attitudes upon which family relations are built. It involved adjustments in:

1. Means of support.
2. Employment and job outlook.
3. Expenditures.
4. Community associations and activities.
5. Foresight and planning.
6. Rationalization of position and maintenance of moral standards.

It would not be surprising, therefore, if similarities in the practices and readjustments within families, in response to such problems, were to have certain tendencies in common. These common tendencies did appear, although the length of time which passed before they were distinguishable in any particular case varied from family to family. Several stages are discernible in these adjustments. We have called those stages: (1) Momentum Stability, (2) Unstable Equilibrium, (3) Disorganization, (4) Experimental Readjustment, (5) Permanent Readjustment.

In this chapter we propose to describe briefly the major adjustments which families made in the six areas enumerated above, as they passed through the several stages. In the next chapters we shall trace the effects of these adjustments on the structure and stability of the family institution. Here, then, is our analysis of the processes of readjustment which took place within the twenty-four families whose heads were unemployed upon our first contact and whom we have observed over a period of eight years.[1]

## STAGE I. MOMENTUM STABILITY

### Means of Support and Financial Status.

The final pay envelope, plus an increased proportion of the wages of supplementary earners shared with family, plus small withdrawals from savings (if any) keep resources at approximately the same level as previously.

The terminal point is a reduction of available resources to the point at which abnormal credit must be used, or over half the savings are used, or supplementary earners resist further contributions to the family purse.

### Reëmployment Efforts and Job Outlook.

The unemployed worker expects a recall to his old firm at the same job. He consequently exerts little effort at job hunting other than casual inquiry from friends. His wage and job standards are not affected. Since he has had the same experience before, he is likely to expect the layoff to be merely temporary and to regard it as a chance for a short holiday. The terminus is approached as the possibility of reëmployment by his former employer fades.

1. In fourteen of these families our first contact was immediately after the layoff. We were notified of the discharge by the employment manager of the firm for which the man had worked. In the other ten cases the man had been unemployed from one to two months before our first visit, and the data gathered on the initial stages were therefore memory material.

*Expenditure Choices and Problems.*

Expenditures are on approximately the same level as previously. A few luxuries and minor recreational expenditures are pared, the modification varying with previous luxury patterns; but no basic essentials, such as food, clothing, rent, etc., are curtailed. All "social-front" and family standard expenditures such as clothing, car, furnishings, rent in same location, refreshments for guests, etc., are maintained. "Social-contact" expenditures made for clubs, entertainment of guests, and telephone conversations are also maintained though reduced somewhat in frequency. The parents absorb all readjustment in expenditures.

The terminus is approached with the need for a reduction in basic necessities, failure to make customary replacements, and the need to carry adjustment into the children's expenditures.

*Community Activities and Status.*

The chief change for the head of the family is a lack of working-day association with former workmates; but he still associates with them outside of working hours in the same ways as formerly. If he is a union man, he continues his attendance and activity. Recreational contacts and routine social affairs in the home of the same sort as formerly are continued, though reduced somewhat in frequency. Friendships are maintained on the usual basis, although a new element of the search for a job is introduced. Reading is likely to increase both in the library and at home. Religious associations remain unaltered, if they are customary during employment. Political relations are unchanged, and if the head was active normally, he may even increase these since he has more free time. Neighborhood associations are unchanged.

The terminus is approached when the elimination of contacts rather than a reduction of frequency of contacts seems necessary.

### Foresight and Planning.

No fresh analysis of difficulty is thought necessary, since the same experience has been faced before. Expenditures are slightly curtailed but nothing essential is touched. The chief indications of foresight are a hesitation before spending and an increase in "shopping around." No new employment plans are made. The future of the problem situation is considered short. The imminence of a return of good fortune inhibits any unusual long-range planning. The ordinary values of foresight objectified in savings and lack of large debts are emphasized.

The terminus is approached when customary planning is insufficient and necessity demands a real separation of essential from nonessential expenditures.

### Rationalization and Maintenance of Moral Standards.

Charity is felt to be a disgrace and is not considered on the list of possible adjustments. The family believes that customary adjustments made before in similar circumstances will carry them through, and they retain confidence in these. The head believes he is entitled to a vacation, and makes no attempt to rationalize. Layoffs have been too customary to call for explanation either for the benefit of himself or of others. Since "social-front" and "social-contact" expenditures are maintained, there is little or no need for self-justification in the presence of friends, and the family accepts an explanation blaming loss of work on uncontrollable factors. No moral problems are involved in decisions being made. The customary ethical standards and soundness of social and economic arrangements are unquestioned.

The terminus is approached as the period extends beyond that customary in past experience and as the adjustments necessary involve a violation of former standards.

## STAGE II. UNSTABLE EQUILIBRIUM

### Means of Support and Financial Status.

Skilled craftsmen earn small amounts by "pick-up" jobs. New earners are introduced to gainful employment as an emergency measure only. Usually, however, this employment is a renewal of former earning methods, such as the wife selling cards, baking, or ironing curtains. Children's earnings from paper routes, etc., may be used for family expenditures now, although formerly they were spent by the children. Regular supplementary earners continue to turn over a still larger proportion of their wages, with only minor deductions for personal expenses. Credit, especially from the landlord and grocer, begins to exceed normal amounts. Savings are rapidly diminishing. Small loans from the larger family for particular items are frequent, and outright gifts are made by other members who are "living in."

The terminus of the period is approached as the proportion of assistance from supplementary earners reaches their total earnings; when no rent has been paid for a month; when credit with the grocer becomes twice its normal amount; and when savings are exhausted.

### Reëmployment Efforts and Job Outlook.

Other firms in the same industry are added to the regular firm as sources of job possibilities, and short-time and "pick-up" jobs are sought as "fillers in." The unemployed worker returns to his old place of work with decreasing frequency. Gate-to-gate application for the semi- and unskilled at any plant, and for the skilled at firms in his own industry is the customary technique. Methods known and used formerly are tried out. The worker considers, but does not make extensive use of, other possible avenues, such as friends and political connections. He may register at the

State Employment Office or at the Metal Trades Association (behavior studied prior to introduction of unemployment compensation). The intensity of the search increases, then decreases. Job and wage standards would be *temporarily* foregone, particularly if the job obtained were outside of the normal industry, but the worker is still "choosey" as to jobs. Confidence of work in his own industry nevertheless declines.

The terminus is approached as chances of reëmployment in the same industry or in a similar occupation fade and customary channels of search are unsuccessful.

### Expenditure Choices and Problems.

Expenditures are reduced but not in proportion to available earnings or cash. Credit takes up part of the slack. Luxuries of a nonprestige character are eliminated. Basic necessities, particularly of food, are restudied and considerable substitution is effected providing similar items at a lower cost. The attempt is made to maintain the children's health, but a gradual reduction even in such items as are necessary for this purpose must be made. Other basic expenditures such as rent, medical care, heat, and light are maintained but on an increasingly credit basis. Replacements of clothes, household equipment, etc., are not made. Recreation is drastically cut. "Social-front" expenditures are readjusted to obtain the same effect as previously, if possible. Ways are sought of maintaining these with less cash outlay. "Social-contact" expenditures are considerably reduced, approaching the vanishing point at the end of the period. Those with prestige value are maintained longest. The children's social contacts are reduced but are still effective. Parents still absorb the bulk of the reductions, particularly in clothes and recreation. Earning children are assuming an increasing amount of the burden as their personal allowance is reduced. Expenditures become family controlled and personal choice is discontinued.

The terminus is approached with the necessity for drastic cuts in expenditures for the children, with the disappearance of cherished social contacts, and with the need for foregoing important "social-front" expenditures with no possibility of "covering up."

## Community Activity and Status.

The head of the family makes new contacts with other job seekers among whom exists a common bond of interest at first; but the contacts lose their desirability as the period progresses and these associates have nothing to share but failure. The head of the family reduces his association in clubhouse or poolroom or on the corner with his former workmates. Union meetings are still attended but less frequently. Supplementary earners in new ventures make new contacts with employers and other workers.

Recreational contacts are severely curtailed by supplementary earners, both because of the time and energy spent at work and because of the devotion of a major part of their resources to family maintenance. Social groups and visiting—other than with the family—are reduced to the vanishing point toward the end of the period since most of them involve refreshments and other expenses. Even the children's attendance at parties, etc., is reduced if money or special clothes are involved. "Fair-weather friends" are eliminated from associations. What recreational contacts remain tend to focus on individuals, not on the family. Church associations both for worship and recreation are curtailed if any expenditure is involved. Political associations if normal are increased in the hope of assistance in job getting. Less contact involving visiting is had with neighbors.

The terminus is approached when contacts are actually avoided and when common interests with former friends are no longer sufficient to make association spontaneous.

## Foresight and Planning.

Analysis of the problem is confined largely to reasons for failure to get a job, but the worker and his wife increasingly contemplate past turning points and regret apparent mistakes in choices or mismanagement. The chief attention, however, focuses on impersonal forces over which the worker has little or no control. Regrets are decreasingly modified by the knowledge that resources are available from past foresight.

The methods of foresight tried are customary ones and only infrequently involve new inventions. Considerable planning is evidenced in the distribution of expenditures between essentials and nonessentials, with providing for children's necessities the chief object of the effort. But the tendency is to let the urgency of demand, in terms of its customary orientation, determine the choice. Planning chiefly takes the form of debates over particular items, with long-range factors (save almost unconsciously in the case of the children's requirements) and normal long-range plans temporarily neglected. Any group connections are maintained more from force of habit than from any assessment of their value.

The future still is conceived as containing the possibility of a return to the former standards and practices but confidence is lost in this probability as the period progresses. The uselessness of planning is considered and commented upon.

The terminus is approached as lack of success in the use of customary foresight techniques becomes apparent and long-range plans and temporary readjustments in favor of the children prove inadequate and unsuccessful.

## Rationalization of Position and Maintenance of Moral Standards.

Charity is not yet considered a desirable resource, but a noticeable tendency appears to justify its acceptance by others. Points of justification are developed in the first instance in connection with others.

The need for rationalization is felt in response to attitudes of other family members. Such justifications as the following are developed: It is fate; a certain amount of difficulty is scheduled for one, and it has to be gone through with. One could be worse off; many others are. Those more successful have "pull" or some unusual advantage. Some consideration is given by husband and wife in private to past mistakes and "what would have happened if," but chief attention is paid to the causal impact of forces beyond personal control. "Hard luck" is the catch-all category for most explanations. Few attempts are made by the unemployed to justify themselves to outsiders. No explanation is adequate. Rationalizations, however satisfactory as *self*-justification, do not alter social status. That is not dependent upon explanation but upon fact.

Basic economic beliefs, such as "the value of keeping out of debt," "individual responsibility," "reward proportional to effort," "essential justice of the distribution of income," etc., are increasingly questioned as they run counter to successful rationalization.

The terminus is approached as the decline in resources becomes so obvious and as problems of the future become so desperate that rationalization appears silly in the face of the need for active adjustment.

## STAGE III. DISORGANIZATION

### Means of Support and Financial Status.

Sources of support (with exception of savings which are now exhausted) continue as in period of unstable equilibrium—but are insufficient to maintain a satisfactory standard of living even with the help of readjustments effected in expenditures.

Credit from the landlord, grocer, etc., gets "out of hand."

Creditors become restless. Debts for medical care, light and gas and fuel, mount. Sources of support are sought which undermine anticipated securities, such as loans on, or cashing of, insurance, loans from family beyond amounts for special expenditures, small loans, and sale or pawning or bartering of possessions. Much confused debate about and contemplation of new sources of income, including relief, is carried on without definite decision as to a satisfactory course being reached.

The terminus is approached as a decision is made on new sources of support and on a modification of the plane of living; as settlement with creditors is forced; as opportunities for loans are exhausted; as salable possessions are reduced to the limit permitted by family resistance.

### Reëmployment Efforts and Job Outlook.

The unemployed worker is confused about the source of future work. No source seems likely. He considers a wide variety which are as quickly discarded. Relief work is considered a possibility and is normally accepted if available. He ceases to search, or he merely makes the rounds "from force of habit" and "for something to do." He puts increasing and even desperate pressure on family and friends. He now would take anything; his job standards have completely collapsed. He has completely lost confidence in customary procedures, in former abilities and skills, and in the ability of private industry to supply work opportunities.

The terminus is approached with his decision to try his hand in a new field, including relief work, and with the initial small success of his first efforts.

### Expenditure Choices and Problems.

Greater efforts are made to restrict expenditures to available cash, chiefly from necessity. Since credit is close to the limit, the restriction is forced. The expenditure patterns among the families reveal little uniformity save that purchases are made in small lots as the emergency arises. Customary food choices are no longer made; "cheapness and bulk" are the chief criteria. Health foods, such as milk and eggs, are drastically reduced. House temperature is frequently reduced below the comfort level. Needed medical care is usually foregone. Unmade replacements in furnishings, equipment, and clothes are important enough to disorganize customary domestic and social activities. Readjustments are therefore a definite attack on basic necessities.

Reduction of "social-front" expenditures is so great that appearances can no longer be maintained. Once important symbolic expenditures are foregone. All attempts to "keep a front" rapidly disappear. Mere maintenance is now the goal.

### Community Activities and Status.

Increasingly, contacts of the head of the family are solely with his fellows in misfortune, which contacts produce little social satisfaction and are avoided when unnecessary. The affiliation with the union is broken through failure to pay dues. Supplementary earners continue to make the acquaintance of new workmates, which contacts may offer opportunities for introduction to working associates' social affairs, but on an individual basis.

All recreational contacts involving expenditure are canceled. Even family visiting and inexpensive social contacts are practically stopped because of lack of proper clothes, deterioration of home surroundings, etc. Pressure for assistance on friends who have been retained is increasingly resented by them and hence association is avoided by both parties. The chief attitude of the few remaining friends is sympathy, which only emphasizes the trouble at this stage. Reading is given up as are other forms of self-improvement. Contacts on the Green, in visiting court, at free lectures, etc., do not involve acquaintance with associates. Even in a crowd the unemployed man is alone. Children's friendships continue, although the number of opportunities for association is drastically reduced.

Religious associations may be retained through force of habit if customary, but they give little social satisfaction. If they involve assistance, they tend to destroy the family's former independent status. If the family are church members, probably they have more association with the pastor, chiefly on the latter's initiative.

Normal political activities are given up. Some unemployed attend radical sponsored gatherings. Neighborhood contacts are practically *nil*.

The terminus is approached as the head seeks new contacts or a renewal of old contacts on a less intimate basis, as contacts of supplementary earners grow and open opportunities for drawing in other members of the family, as new forms of family-centered associations are discovered.

### Foresight and Planning.

Attempts at analysis are given up. "Hard luck" is the ultimate explanation. Adjustments heretofore considered inappropriate, such as relief, are now seriously contemplated. The emergency and necessity measures characteristic of this period are forced rather than chosen foresight. Attempts to maintain basic necessities are engulfed in emergency decisions as to immediately necessary expenditures. All attempts to reach goals other than mere maintenance are temporarily given up. Seeking for advice from remaining friends is more frequent, and, if the family are church members, from the pastor or priest. Interest in "direct action" is increased.

The future is limited to "the rest of this day" except where a definite threat of the curtailment of an essential service contains a time-limit ultimatum. Each problem is faced as it arises. Giving up of the results of former foresight, such as insurance, a home in a good neighborhood, and the exhaustion of savings, decreases confidence in the usefulness of planning until little remains.

The terminus is approached as a decision on necessary readjustments is reached and as resentment at the loss of former standards is exhausted.

### Rationalization of Position and Maintenance of Moral Standards.

Relief is considered as a probable necessity. Little attention is paid to a justification of the step. Emphasis is placed on chances of getting it, the problems and relative security of people who are receiving it, and the degree to which it would assist the family in its difficulty. Identification of relief with special funds for the unemployed and the preference for work relief indicates a survival of the feeling that a stigma is attached to ordinary direct relief. The impact of failure and the increasing confusion about possible economic adjustments tends, however, to submerge any attempt to make relief consistent with the maintenance of social status or standards and to encourage its evaluation solely in terms of the support it would provide.

Practical problems of "getting by" absorb most of the family's energy and, together with confusion and dismay, inhibit attention to rationalization. "The less you think about things the better." The failure is so obvious and unprecedented that the reaction is, "What the hell?" rather than further attempts at analysis. Explanations in terms of "general misfortune" and "injustice of the system" are listened to and sometimes repeated, but without conviction; they have not become integrated into a way of thinking. If any consideration at all is given to economic mores and other ethical standards, the attitude is one of cynicism. The abdication of job standards emphasizes the cynicism.

The terminus is approached as a decision on the line of attack on problems breaks through the daze, and as the need for making the facts of the present consistent with a renewed interest in self-respect becomes more prominent.

## STAGE IV. EXPERIMENTAL READJUSTMENT

### Means of Support and Financial Status.

From this point families adopt a variety of courses depending on the cultural standards they share, their degree of inventiveness, the degree of their resistance to loss of social status, the availability of capital resources, and the possession of individual abilities. Some of them are listed: tentative ventures of supplementary earners may be accepted as a continuing necessity; the sale of home products may be undertaken as a regular business; hobbies may be turned to business uses; new methods of selling skills and services of the chief breadwinner may be devised; credit is held to the present level or reduced; if the foregoing expedients are insufficient, relief may be applied for.

The terminus is approached with any reasonable success of the maintenance activities, and with the increasing period of practice during which no opportunity to resume former earning activities appears on the horizon.

### Reëmployment Efforts and Job Outlook.

The sources of job opportunity considered vary from independent work and turning of hobbies to account, through coöperative work-seeking ventures, to work in entirely new occupations or industries, including government work relief. The routine search for jobs may be resumed and even made more systematic during free time. The search is less hectic and the intensity varies with the probable chance of success and with the degree of reinforcement of that hope. Increased use is made of any political connections. The unemployed worker may undertake retraining if such a course offers a reasonable chance of future employment. The inventive experiment with new methods. Former job and wage standards reassert themselves, and the security of any new job offers is measured in comparison with that of the present stop-gap work. Satisfaction is felt in work because it is work. Pride in former work status and skills becomes either a pleasant memory or a source of resentment against forces that have destroyed them.

The terminus is approached with success in stop-gap work and with the disappearance of a hope for more promising employment comparable to one's old job and skills.

### Expenditure Choices and Problems.

Expenditures now fluctuate more directly with available cash resources. Basic needs are progressively redefined. Health foods occupy a larger place in choices. New economies in food and clothing are developed. Medical care expenditures and replacements are made with, and only in case of, "windfalls." The latter are also used occasionally for inexpensive "extras." The use of unexpected funds for "extras" is a certain sign the family is getting out of the disorganization stage. Little attention is paid to "social-front" expenditures even to impress present associates. "Social-contact" expenditures are still meager, but more attention is paid to children's opportunities for such contacts, and free gatherings are occasionally frequented. Parents cut their own expenditures still further, if possible, in the interest of renewed emphasis on provision for their children.

The terminus is approached as future possibilities seem to threaten a necessity for continuing on this level.

### Community Activities and Status.

New self-maintenance activities (coöperative work seeking, relief work, hobby exploitation, independent self-employment, etc.) involve new associations and arouse the interest of all in contacts with new acquaintances. The head of the family, if a former union man, may even return to union gatherings occasionally if he has not too far declassed himself by open violation of union standards. Supplementary earners have made new friends on the job.

Free recreation opportunities are accepted increasingly on a family attendance basis. Individual recreation has developed contact with a few who, although not friends, get used to seeing each other. Much association tends to be with equally unfortunate people, but the stage of dwelling on "hard luck" has passed and makes these contacts more welcome and appreciated. Self-improvement activities may be resumed and result in new acquaintances. The home is still not a center for social events as it was prior to unemployment. Some former friendships are reëstablished, particularly among those sharing a common lot.

Religious associations recover slowly and tend to remain on the same level as in the former stage, with some increase in recreational opportunities made through church organizations.

Political associations may be resumed or undertaken for the first time. If the unemployed worker joins a radical group, he does so now. Political tactics furnish a fresh subject for conversation and debate. Neighborhood associations are still meager, particularly if the family has settled in a new neighborhood, but they are beginning to be reestablished. Shame no longer retards their cultivation.

The terminus is approached as temporary expedients are accepted as probably permanent and as new associates assume approximately the same place in giving social satisfactions as that occupied by former associates.

### Foresight and Planning.

Analysis now focuses on individual responsibility for decision and for "making the best of a bad situation." New interest is displayed in experimental forms of foresight, improving one's ability in new self-maintenance occupations, and in analyzing requirements for success in them, in the development of new job standards, in getting the most out of any new form of support (including relief), in redetermining and devising ways of getting basic necessities, in the distribution of "windfalls," in renewed emphasis on the children's welfare. Older earning children participate more frequently in decisions. New suggestions come from new acquaintances. More attention is paid to building useful contacts, including a restoration of former union associations if possible. Increased interest is displayed in suggested radical alternatives. Foresight takes into account more long-range effects and is less dominated by the expediency of the moment. Fresh thought is given to maintaining family solidarity, to reducing friction in the division of domestic labor and to establishing a comfortable routine.

The future is extended somewhat but is still foreshortened by the possibility that adjustments are merely temporary. Confidence in planning returns to the degree that plans and decisions are successful, but is easily destroyed by failure. The setback is less reinforced, however, by the memory of the collapse of past methods.

The terminus is approached as the conviction is reinforced by the passage of time that temporary experiments are to become permanent adjustments.

### Rationalization of Position and Maintenance of Moral Standards.

Not all have accepted relief as an alternative source of support. For those who have, actual contact has dissipated some of the rumors upon which was based a feeling that a stigma was attached to it. Hence rationalization is less necessary. Families have also given up many associates before whom justification would be necessary and have made increased contacts with those whose similar status provides no necessity for defense. The chief concern is with exploring the possibilities of the new resource and with the practical business of making relief an adequate source of maintenance. Few positive efforts are made to support self-respect with evidence, but the observation of large numbers "in the same boat," of large funds for services to the unemployed, of the fact that relief expenditures form an increasingly normal part of the public outlay, tend to dull any felt need for self-justification. Any justification tends to take the form of an expressed faith that the relief status is only temporary.

Self-maintenance efforts of all sorts are absorbing attention and bringing all family members into contact with individuals unacquainted with the unemployed family's past. The need to defend a changed status is not therefore so vivid. Satisfaction in small successes and in the way the family is meeting the problem is the center of attention, and is made stronger in the light of reaction from previous confusion and dismay. Self-respect is being built out of energy expended on practical adjustments to *present* need with *present* abilities and resources and in connection with the establishment of security at a new level, rather than out of attempts to reëstablish the status and security attained prior to unemployment. Self-congratulation based on a positive advance from a low level is substituted for self-condemnation based on the negative decline from former levels of achievement. Reduction in family tension further reduces the reminders of former status which have to be met by self-justification.

Ethical standards consciously considered are accepted primarily as necessary rules for conduct in meeting successfully new circumstances. These are frequently in conflict with former standards.

The terminus is approached as the probable permanence of the new adjustments becomes apparent and as the need to make the present status consistent with the past and future possibilities becomes more pressing.

*STAGE V. PERMANENT READJUSTMENT*

Experimental adjustments in the means of self-support are accepted as relatively permanent and are exploited with all possible energy and skill.

The temporary job or jobs are accepted as permanent or as one's regular employment.

Expenditures are held to fluctuating cash resources with minor use being made of credit. Any margin in normal resources over the amount necessary for minimum requirements is used to reduce debts. Extras and luxuries are still purchased chiefly with "windfalls." Increasing attention is given to "social-status" expenditures among new associates. Increasing use is made of free social-contact opportunities and of those possible with practically no expenditure. The distribution of expenditure among family members is stabilized on a new pattern.

Community relations are increased. New employment contacts yield increasing satisfaction and opportunities for relationship and become stabilized as a part of regular life. Recreational contacts continue much as in the previous stage with larger emphasis being given to entertainment of new friends in the home. Free entertainment is a definite part of the expected routine. Religious contacts show no dominant trend, save that there is less call on the minister or priest. Many who have moved to new neighborhoods break their contacts completely. Political activities, including radical affiliations, are continued or discarded according to the value they have yielded. Neighborhood contacts are increased.

The scope of foresight and planning is broadened to include consideration of the recurring factors met in new situations. Renewed interest is displayed in the operation of impersonal factors beyond the control of the individual. Those who have stayed with radical groups make use of the slogans and phrases of those groups. Others tend to re-

vert to tools and premises of analysis customary among all
workers with increased emphasis (for them) on impersonal
social and economic factors. Newly acquired methods of
foresight continue and are amplified. Gradually they are
taken for granted, and older methods are revived if possible. Emphasis is definitely increased in long-range planning where some chance of success seems possible. The
children's welfare is still in the center, but consideration of
the parents' future is revived and attention to home surroundings and family solidarity is increased. Increasing
emphasis is put upon building useful contacts. Plans are
still not made for a future as distant as in the period previous to unemployment, but the family contemplates no im-
pending changes. The conviction as to the usefulness of
planning is reinforced according to the degree of success of
any new plans which are made.

If the family has continued on relief, more systematic
attention is paid to making this fact consistent with citizenship through further rationalizations. Such justifications
as: "Relief is after all only another form of community
service available to all citizens," "We have paid taxes (or
made contributions to the Community Chest) for a number of years," etc., are frequently heard. Work-relief clients increasingly look on their work as a regular job and
emphasize, with the help of government publicity, its values
to the community. Efforts to make relief resources more
secure and adequate are looked upon as sensible and normal foresight and initiative. Success in these efforts, particularly if they are undertaken in connection with organizations, bolsters self-respect. Guilt feelings do increase
with the realization that the adjustment is more than temporary, but in most cases they are soon submerged in the
practical business of getting a living.

The awareness that temporary adjustments are becoming permanent stimulates occasional comparison with the
family's former "normal" status, but since the process of

adjustment has involved "accepting the inevitable," comparisons do not arouse sufficient frustration to encourage attempts at impossible rationalization. Increasing concern with the problems of the moment and the contemplation of any success no matter how meager form a basis for renewed confidence that the family has the ability to maintain itself at the new level of living. Increasing stability in family relations and coöperative attention to mutual problems develops a hospitable atmosphere for mutual satisfaction.

New standards of conduct are reinforced by habit; and older standards, particularly among those who have maintained their religious affiliations, reassert themselves. Cynicism continues during the period of any conflict between the new and the old, but gradually decreases with the resolution of the conflict or the definite abandonment of standards proved impracticable by experience.

### *Summary.*

All of the twenty-four families we observed went through these five stages in their attempts to solve the problem of self-maintenance. They varied in the length of time they spent in each period and in the amount of community assistance they received in the process. None of the families, however, applied for such help until they had reached the third stage, that of disorganization. Half never applied at all, and for all but one the receipt of relief was only temporary. This one family appears to have accepted the inevitability of maintenance from the public treasury in the face of a disabling illness in the case of the head and the lack of any family sources of support.

The significant fact is that loss of income through unemployment is followed by the exploration and use of numerous available devices to restore that income by individual and collective effort and to revise the pattern of economic and social life in accordance with the degree of success or failure in this attempt. The early stages of this readjustment are attended by real frustration as present possibilities are compared with the former pattern of life, as the customary techniques of getting a livelihood are proved ineffective, and the pattern of family and community relationships is altered by the removal of the normal amount of cash necessary for its maintenance. The frustration involved in readjustment becomes less acute as the passage of time dulls the sharpness of the comparison of former and present possibilities, and as the need for an active attack on present problems centers the interest and attention on today's opportunities rather than on yesterday's achievements.

The readjustment takes place, however. None of the families stayed for long in the disorganization stage. The end of that period was marked in the economic sphere by the striking of a balance between available income and the accepted standard of living. Adjustment from both angles was important. New earning opportunities or relief allowances on the one hand and revised expenditure wants on the other approached more closely to each other. The amount of relief available set a minimum below which adjustment in expenditure wants need not fall. The adjustment was difficult, but less difficult as time passed and the memory of former standards lost some of its vividness. It is difficult to escape the conclusion that the primary factors involved in the striking of the new balance are the willingness and ability of the workers and their families to readapt their standards, devise new practices, and adjust their relationships and activities to the necessities imposed upon them. The energy and thought of the family itself are the chief resources upon which the community must count for the maintenance of the family as an independent economic unit.

In a monetary economy in an urban industrial setting, however, this process must be undergirded with financial resources sufficient to maintain life. The best efforts some of these families could make did not result in that much financial reward. They turned to the public treasury for help. But it is worth noting that such a move was merely one among the many moves the families were making in their attempts to meet the obligations our culture places upon the family, and that it followed a vigorous attempt to escape recourse to charity.

It is relevant to recall also that the move was taken only after a considerable period of failure to secure sufficient financial resources through individual and collective efforts. Only one fourth of those found unemployed in 1933[2] had applied for relief two years later. Forty per cent of those who finally applied for the first time waited over two years after the layoff before taking that step. Only 30 per cent had applied within twelve months of the beginning of their unemployment. The efforts to find ways of keeping the family a self-supporting unit did not cease; but support itself is a more imperative need than that the form of support should involve no community help.

Another observation concerning the journey of the families through these several stages is relevant. The economic changes are accompanied by social changes in family and community relationships. The two are closely related and react upon each other. Economic resources provide not only food and shelter but also the means of establishing and maintaining the satisfying relationships and status of a social nature within the family and in the community. These in turn support the incentives and standards which stimulate men in their economic practices. A reduction in economic resources undoubtedly tends to undermine somewhat the power of family and community relationships to support economic ambition. At the same time, however, satisfactory "living" is largely defined in terms of these rela-

2. In the sample of 2,007 New Haven families selected for investigation by the Institute of Human Relations in that year.

tionships. The desire to retain or restore them can be counted on to stimulate economic effort directed toward maintaining as nearly as possible the pattern of "living" termed proper and desirable by our culture.

# VIII

## *THE CYCLE OF FAMILY READJUSTMENT*

THE pattern of relations and practices within the family itself must undergo change in order to be consistent with
and to deal with the readjustments recorded in the foregoing chapter. Indeed that pattern tends to evolve through
the same five stages of adjustment we have just described.
The important features of that pattern, the effects of unemployment upon which we shall wish to chart through the
stages from momentum stability to permanent adjustment,
are these:

Relative status and roles of members.

Coöperative practices for meeting problems.

Routine.

Mutual activities within and outside the home.

Discipline and training of children.

Movement of older children into homes of their own.

Foundations for and symbols of family solidarity.

Mutual respect, regard, and affection of members for
each other.

*A priori* it would seem that the adjustments recorded in
the last chapter would exert heavy pressure for change upon
these features and hence have a potentially disruptive effect
upon family solidarity and stability. Unemployment may
promote a shift in status and roles of members inconsistent
with cultural expectancies and hence make of the cultural
pattern a disturbing rather than a stabilizing factor. Unemployment may present problems which are inadequately
solved by customary coöperative practices between husband and wife, parents and children, family and clan. Unemployment may interrupt routine and hence expand the
area of activity in which fresh decisions must be made, and
interfere with the normal comfort of expected action ac-

cording to schedule. This result is likely to surround the whole process of adjustment with an emergency atmosphere and present more numerous opportunities for friction. Unemployment may curtail mutual activities within and outside the home and thus destroy a body of functional interaction supporting the integration of members of the family and of the family with the community. Unemployment may disturb the discipline of and the training of children by parents, and hence modify the ability of the family to organize a common campaign to overcome difficulties and to control members in line with community standards. Unemployment may make necessary new economic arrangements which involve canceling the normal expectancies for children and hence postpone or make impossible for them the establishment of families of their own. Unemployment may curtail or destroy the following foundations for and symbols of family solidarity and hence weaken these as a support for established functions and relationships: common goals of effort; subordination of personal desires to common effort; family pride in social status and adherence to the obligations and privileges accompanying this; well-defined and consistently practiced code of behavior and ideals; regularly practiced ritual; house and home furnishings; devices for relieving tensions. Unemployment may damage the satisfaction involved in mutual association, may decrease the mutual respect, regard, and affection of members and substitute negative attitudes and reactions, thus removing incentives to and lubricants for adjustment. Such effects may also decrease the propensity to marriage and increase the propensity to separation. Unemployment may result in adjustments detrimental to health and hence reduce the physical well-being helpful to harmonious relations.

What evidence do our records bring to bear upon the actual realization of these potential disruptions of family solidarity and upon the adjustments which families make in the relations of members to each other in the face of such danger? The rich variety in the specific practices, relationships, and integrating factors presented by even the small group of twenty-four families whom we studied over a period of years, and by our larger group of two hundred families with whom we did not maintain continuous contact, warns us that any attempt to portray a "typical family" is hazardous. Yet sufficient uniformities in problems and adjustments did appear to verify the following description of the several stages of unemployment and to make it seem a probable indication of trends to be expected in any family. Against this background of general developments each specific family worked out its problem in terms of its own particular history, goals, customs, and characteristics.

### STAGE I. MOMENTUM STABILITY

The description given to this period suggests that the pattern of family relationships remains relatively undisturbed and on very much the same basis as before unemployment. The family proceeds under the momentum of the customary ways evolved when the head of the family was regularly employed. The division of labor within the home is scarcely altered. If the chances of reëmployment at his regular firm are slight, the head may be out looking for a job; nevertheless, this activity is a substitution for the time he formerly spent at work. Since the mornings are the best time to look for work, he is likely to have a considerable amount of time to spend around the home in the afternoon, and in some cases this results in his availability for odd jobs around the place; but he does about the same amount of domestic work as he would ordinarily do on Sundays or holidays. Occasionally he gives more assistance in the matter of shopping. Otherwise, however, the tasks of the several members of the family remain very much the same as before.

There has been no serious challenge to the previously established status of the several members of the family. The new problems and the practices adapted to their solution have not yet gone far enough to raise any serious questions.

Whatever methods have been previously evolved to make a small income stretch over a large potential demand are continued. Any reduction in expenditures involves a change in amount rather than in the type of expenditure, and few if any basic essentials such as food, clothing, rent, or even "social-front" or "social-contact" expenditures are seriously curtailed. Nonfinancial problems of family management are solved in the familiar way.

Some change occurs in the type of relationships and activities in which the family shares. The husband's daily experiences and interest in job possibilities provide the whole family with fresh subjects for conversation. The husband remains at home a greater proportion of the time, and, since his presence there is normally purposeless, it is not particularly satisfactory to anybody concerned except to the younger children. Families are likely to think twice before spending money on recreation, and consequently there is a minor curtailment here of activities normally carried on outside the home.

At this point, new discipline problems or training problems with respect to the children seldom arise. The children and the father see more of each other, and frequently share in more home recreational relationships than before. We find that in almost every case in this initial period the bonds between the father and children were somewhat strengthened.

In general, it is probably true that during this period the necessity of considering the children first and of facing new problems increases the stability of the relationships between the husband and wife. All integrating factors and symbols of family solidarity, such as ritual and established relationships, common goals of effort, family pride, ideals and codes of behavior, the furnishings of the house and the home, remain very much the same. Frequently a common resentment shared by both the husband and the wife, sometimes by the children, that the husband has been discriminated against in the layoff adds to the factors drawing the members closer to each other.

The wife censures or blames her husband very little; she tends to accept whatever explanation he gives for the loss of his job—favoritism, slack work, discrimination, or whatnot—and supports her husband loyally both in his presence and to her friends. We feel certain that, unless this loss of a job is the last of a series of events which has tended to disturb the equilibrium of family life, during this period the integration of family life is actually strengthened.

Eventually, however, worry resulting from lack of success in finding a job and from the increasingly severe adjustments which have to be made to a reduced income increases, and tends to destroy the customary degree of consideration and regard for each other which characterized normal relationships. With such a development this period draws to a close. The most important factor in determining its length is the amount of resources which the family has to call upon. As resources diminish, the severity of the adjustment increases.

## STAGE II. UNSTABLE EQUILIBRIUM

The chief change in the division of labor during this period is likely to result from the fact that the wife tries her hand at gainful work. Usually she is doing something in the home, such as ironing curtains or taking in washings. Less frequently she may be seeking gainful employment outside the home. In any case, her activities take her time away from the domestic duties and make it necessary for her to place those duties upon other members of the family. Usually this means upon the children, because during this

period the husband is engaged in a more intensive search
for work, and hasn't the time to spend around the home even
if he had the inclination or the enthusiasm for such work.
There is some difference of opinion as to whether or not unemployment resulted in a greater amount of domestic work
on the part of the husband. One wife put the impression of
several in these words: "You know, there is something in
the fact that a busy man can always find time to do more.
But a man who isn't doing anything doesn't find time even
to do that." Probably just as important, however, is the
fact that in many cases the hold of custom is strong. Both
husband and wife feel that any thoroughgoing redistribu-
tion of domestic duties somehow is not a proper procedure.

When Mr. C lost his job in Winchester's, his wife was successful in getting a job there, and he did the housework. Mrs. C
thinks that this was a very bitter blow to his pride, and says
that he has been a good sport about it and did not mind until
the neighbors made fun of him. They saw him working outside
the house. He and she have never quarreled over the housework, but she felt very badly when she saw how miserable he
was, and when she is home she protects him from the criticisms
of the neighbors by making certain that he engages in no domestic duties at which they will see him.

Mrs. D tries to think of things that her husband can do around
the house. He's very good at this, but he doesn't like it, and she
doesn't like it, either. "A man's job is to work and bring home
the money. He feels better then. He isn't made for housework,"
she says. Moreover, when he's around the house the family
problems and worries seem to loom bigger to him, and his wife
is constantly calling to his attention family problems that she
never mentioned to him before. "She's always been used to set-
tling those things. I don't know anything about them. All it
does when she mentions them to me now is simply to make me
confused. If I were working I'd not be around so much and
wouldn't have so many family cares to think about, and besides
I'd be earning money so that she'd be able to settle them better

herself. You can't teach an old dog new tricks, even if it would help if he knew them."

The customary division of labor is well rooted. Unemployed men assumed very few tasks commonly accepted by them as "women's work" beyond those with which they normally helped. Household repairs, gardening, and the like received somewhat more attention. But these involved no change in the cultural pattern.

Whatever earnings are coming into the family purse now are channeled through the wife's hands even if before that time she had not managed the purse completely. The wife assumes a greater degree of responsibility for management and for distributing the available income. The husband, considerably discouraged and tired out by his search for work, usually takes this excuse to withdraw from his parental responsibilities in other respects, so that decisions as to the activities of the several members of the family customarily descend upon the mother also.

These changes in the division of labor involve a challenge to the status and the roles of the several members, and these are progressively altered. The husband's status in the eyes of both wife and children tends to decline. Earning children, and in particular the older children who may have been supplementary earners prior to unemployment but who are now contributing a larger share of their earnings to the family purse, find that their function in the family is more important. This increased importance is very frequently out of harmony with the normal submission of their own desires to decisions of the parents. The mother is usually more willing to admit the need for giving them greater prestige and recognition than is the father, who resents this change in status. This is particularly true of Italian fathers. Said Mr. R:

You will notice that many times an Italian father is very strict and very stern, and sometimes he is more stern than he really feels in order to emphasize the fact that he is really the head of the house. Now, as long as everybody recognizes that and as long as it is possible for him to do what a man really is supposed to do, why nothing goes wrong. But as soon as he can't bring in any cash each week, well then you see the thing is different, and he just has to get still more strict and stern in order to show that he is really boss.

It is difficult to predict the effect on the status of members of gifts from the larger family. In some cases the process appeared to bind the clan closer together. In other cases the gift was resented both by the giver and the recipient. In some cases the necessity for the donation confirmed in-laws in their low opinion of their daughter's mate and increased the latter's sense of his own failure and loss of status. In general it can be said that such a result was likely to occur where other events and judgments had paved the way prior to this last evidence of the inability of the man to be "a good provider."

During this period, however, the status of the mother increases in the eyes of her children, and to a somewhat smaller extent in the eyes of her husband. She is not, of course, definitely established as the "head of the house." But her decisions become more important, and her enlarged functions give a basis in reality for her heightened prestige.

No new tactics for the solution of family affairs are highly developed during this period, but there are increasing opportunities for the wife to come into conflict with her husband and for children to come into conflict with their parents over such new tactics as must be used. The wife's methods of earning, whether or not the husband is diligent and active and wise in work-seeking activities, how the available cash shall be distributed, and in particular whether "social-front" and "social-contact" expenditures shall be kept up in preference to expenditures not involving the prestige of the family before the outside world are all troublesome matters. What shall be done about the increasing load of debt and credit? What shall be done about the outside activities of the family, particularly recreational affairs? Decisions on such questions which might have been more or less automatic when regular income was provided by the head of the family now become matters for continued debate. As long as there are still some resources in savings or in credit available to the family these decisions do not become pressing, but the opportunities they offer for conflict are obvious.

We live in a monetary economy, and a great host of our solutions for problems of living involves the decision to make an expenditure and have the matter settled. With the onset of unemployment and the reduction in or elimination of income, old and new problems of livelihood present themselves which cannot be brought to an end by the expenditure of cash. Unsolved or unsatisfactorily solved, they continue to plague the family facing a daily increment of new tasks.

Mr. R earned $4 shoveling snow. They needed coal and could save considerably by buying in bulk rather than in small paper bags. But they also owed an electric bill, and the company threatened to turn off the lights unless it was paid. They must therefore forego the economy on coal.

The gas company threatened to put in a quarter meter unless a payment was made on the L's gas bill. They were afraid they would not have the 25 c. when it was needed. One of their friends had spoiled a whole baking because the gas ran out in the midst of it, and she hadn't the 25 c. to turn on the gas again. But there was nothing they could do about it.

Could the W's conserve on coal by living in one room? They did, and all was well until the family in the apartment below moved out and the heat from their apartment was lost. Then the plumbing froze. They had no money for plumber's bills, so they had to carry water for all purposes.

Mr. T felt that membership in a political club would be helpful, but he could not pay the small dues involved.

The R's had made holidays their primary time of mutual recreation. But how could they make holidays seem like holidays without money for carfare?

Since the G's could not have the customary variety in food on their available resources, they debated whether they could get a bit more variety by eliminating the noon meal.

The burden which lack of money places on customary domestic management is indicated by the statement of the wife of a former rubber worker:

When you have some regular money coming in, you can avoid very many worries. For instance, now you take last week when Dorothy was sick. Ordinarily, I have a doctor in. The doctor says that something is wrong, and then I know that we have done all we could. But now I cannot afford to have the doctor in, so I give her aspirin and then I worry a week until she gets well whether she will get well or not. The doctor relieves your mind very much, but when you do not have the money to spend, you just have to let your mind run.

Every expenditure is likely to involve a campaign for funds:

Every decision now seems to be an emergency decision for us. When it comes to a question of paying the electric-light bill, some unusual source of cash must be found. When the children need new clothes, it's the same thing. When the coal is all used up, again some money must be found somewhere to buy another bag. When I was earning a regular income it was possible to take these expenditures in our stride. We had so much to spend and knew ahead of time how much we could spend on each of these items, but once having decided that, the money was usually ready when the bill came in or when we needed the stuff. Now we have to run a special campaign whenever we need something.

A toolmaker stresses the changed character of the domestic economy:

We used to at the end of the week sit down together and figure up what our expenses had been and how we would pay for them.

We had a regular amount coming in. It varied a little bit this
week and a little bit that, but we always had a minimum amount
we could count on; and what we had left over, well, we'd save
that. We soon got so we knew just what decisions to make and
it wasn't hard. Now when we don't have any money coming in
and we sit down at the end of the week to decide how we are
going to get by, well, we just can't think of anything. We can't
think of what to do. We can't decide to spend money for this
and for that because we haven't got any money. That's all we
used to have to do, you see. There was the money. There was
the bill, and we paid the bill with the money. But now what do
you do?

Another example of the way in which the lack of money
complicates the business of running a home was given by
Mrs. C:

Recently the gas was disconnected so there is no way of heat-
ing the hot-water tank. Today when Mrs. C wanted to wash, she
put on a tub of water at 6 o'clock when they first started the
fire. She hoped that by the afternoon it would be heated sufficiently to do her washing. There was no cover for the tub, and
it takes much longer to heat than a boiler, but she has no boiler.
The whole family routine has been disorganized this day because she could not carry out the process in the normal way.

All of the wives of the unemployed men were worried
about the diets which they were able to furnish their families.

One day when we arrived to visit the T's we found that they
were having for lunch a loaf of bread broken into pieces, mois-
tened with water. Mrs. T then poured a bit of oil over this and
flavored it with garlic. She does not tell anyone about this, not
even her mother. She is very much concerned over her children's diet. She knows that they are not getting enough to eat,
but is helpless to do anything about this. She has trained them
never to say what they have to eat at home. The young son occasionally goes over to his grandmother's and she asks him if
he has eaten. He always says, "Yes." The grandmother asks

what he had to eat. He will answer, "I don't know." Mrs. T is very proud of him for doing this.

The P's have always had a great deal of satisfaction out of the activity and effort involved in raising their children, but, says Mrs. P:

You'd be surprised how little things can take the joy out of it, now. For instance, here's one thing that happens. I bake bread once a week, but since my husband has been unemployed we have had to go practically without butter. I buy a quarter of a pound a week, never more than that. The little girl is especially resentful over this. Some days when the children are home for lunch they yell out that I'm starving them. If anybody would come to the door at that time and hear them, they would feel that I'm mistreating my children. I know I'm not doing this, but it makes me furious to have Angelina make any trouble about it. I hit her when she does it. They are lucky to have bread, and they must learn this, but it is hard to make them learn it when you know they're right, that you're not really providing properly for them.

Another comment from the wife of a rubber worker will illustrate the same challenge to customary ways of carrying on the domestic economy:

It takes all the fun out of raising a family when every little thing has to be so hard to do. For instance, when the two older children were young the school nurse sent home a card saying that they needed glasses. Well, that wasn't much of a problem because we had the money to get the glasses, and we got them immediately and that was the end of it, and we were satisfied, and the children were satisfied, and the school was satisfied. The same thing happened last week with the two younger children. The school nurse said they needed glasses. But what could I do? We've been arguing and working on that problem ever since, and there just isn't any possibility. Finally, I asked the Department of Charities if they couldn't get the glasses, and then I've had to go down there and sign all kinds of forms and they've had to come out and visit, and they've had to consult with the school nurse. I tell you, that's all we've been working on the last week. I've hardly had time enough for anything else.

A large proportion of our problems is solved customarily by the expenditure of money. When the money is available for this, it makes it possible to settle the matter quickly and get on to something else. When no money is available, the whole problem has to be worked out in some other way, and it is of necessity time consuming. Individuals who might have enough energy and enough intelligence to solve problems as long as an expenditure of money is the answer to most of them find themselves overburdened with the tremendous amount of time and attention and thought necessary for getting along without money.

The necessity for undertaking a special campaign for funds every time a necessary expenditure must be made places a tremendous strain upon the organizational and planning abilities of the family. It is little wonder that the usefulness of planning appears to be challenged. Said a former steam fitter: "It just isn't safe to plan. You're tempting Providence in making any sort of plans. It seems that once you do, fate only goes against you."

The rearrangement of domestic affairs necessitated by unemployment must be carried on in the midst of such an emergency-dominated, energy-consuming, and failure-charged atmosphere. It is little wonder that satisfaction in home life is damaged when the customary methods of home building are proved so inadequate. Said Mr. R:

The home is the worker's only real satisfaction. All of the hard work he does, as well as his wish to stand on his own feet, is centered in the desire to see his family enjoy a comfortable life. And he has learned how to do that within his means. Our home isn't much, but it's a place to live in and we're mighty proud of it, and that's that. Now, if I stay out of work too long, I can't keep up that home, and believe me it's going to be an awful blow to my ambition. What gave me ambition before is going to discourage me, now. All I get now is worries.

One of the most serious blows to family stability is found in the way in which the routine of family life is disorganized, even at an early stage in the experience with unemployment. The lack of regularity in the family program is resented, even though silently, by all. It tends to destroy the normal comfort and satisfaction of life within the family group. The case of one family will suggest the problem typical of all.

The T's, since they do not have any regular jobs to do, have very irregular schedules. Mr. T stays up all hours of the night trying to get different stations on the radio. Then in the morning they sleep as late as they want to. That's all right during the summertime, but when the boy goes to school in the winter they have to get up. Mr. T usually lies in bed, anyway, and Mrs. T gets up and gets the boy off to school. She complains that her husband is never on time for meals. "I guess he just forgets about when meals should come when he doesn't have any regular work to do. Then the meals get cold and then we get sore at each other."

"How do you think family life can go on under circumstances of this kind?" asked Mrs. S. We had just come in and found the whole family gathered around the stove, seemingly uninterested in anything except keeping warm. Mrs. S had stuffed a cloth around the window sill in a vain attempt to keep the cold out. They had closed off the kitchen and all were grouped around the fire with their coats and sweaters on. Three of the children had their hats on their heads. Mrs. S had a sweater under a heavy topcoat. "This is a fine thing for a family to be doing, isn't it?" said Mrs. S. "We ought to all be doing things around the house and going about our own business, but here we are just sitting still in front of this fire. I tried to work a little while ago, but all of these people got in my way, and so I just stopped working and I sat down here, too."

At the same time that satisfaction in the home is being decreased by the obvious inadequacy of customary home techniques in dealing with recurring and new problems, and the normal routine in home life is being disrupted, mutual activities outside the home and with friends have to be curtailed. The mutual activities offered opportunity for interaction valuable in making the family a unit and for relieving any tensions and difficulties that might arise. These relationships outside the home now tend to become individual rather than mutual. Two statements, one from a railroad man and the other from a foundry worker's wife, will illustrate the point:[1]

Well, we still have our home around us, but the home doesn't mean what it used to. We used to have just an awful lot of fun having folks in for an evening or going over to their place. But do you know what the chief thing about that evening was? Well, it was that we served wine, and now since I've been unemployed, I can't afford to get the grapes to make the wine, so I don't have any wine any more, so I don't have the folks in, and you see what that means is that our home isn't the happy place that it used to be. I used to look forward to those evenings, but now they're all gone, and the old lady and I just sit here by ourselves. And I suppose that's what our friends are doing too.

Well, it's spring and it wor't be long before summer'll be here again. You know, we used .o look forward to summer. It was a happy family time because if summer came we could all go out to Lighthouse once in a while and have a picnic, and there was always the summer evenings that we would spend out on the porch together. And then my mother and father, they have a garden farm out Westville way, and we'd all go out there and work there when we felt like it. I'm not so crazy for summer to come this time. Where're we going to get the money for carfare and bathing beach? I don't like this new neighborhood we've moved into, and I'll be hanged if I'll be sitting out on the front porch here. It's too far to walk now out to mother's farm, and how are we going to get the carfare to go there? Then, too, where are we going to get money to buy ice this summer? I've never had to worry about that before, but I can't for the life of

1. Further evidence on the decline of mutual activity will be found in chap. i.

me see how I'm going to keep my milk sweet and buy more than little dabs of stuff at the grocery store, which is a very uneconomical way, you know, if I don't have ice. And I don't see where we're going to get the money to have ice. As I was saying, summer was always a kind of a happy family time for us, but there's so many problems coming this summer that I don't know whether it will be happy or not.

The roots of training and discipline problems in the family are grounded in factors which it is not our present task to explore. Yet it is worth noting that at this period in unemployment the customary techniques for the solution to those problems operate with increasing difficulty. The new obstacles which those techniques face are clear.

In the first place, parental authority is geared to the status of parents relative to their children. As we have seen, that status undergoes definite change at this period. The father is no longer performing his basic function of "provider" on which his authority is primarily based. At the same time supplementary earners in view of their increased importance as "providers" frequently expect and demand somewhat less control of their affairs. Elder daughters in particular are resentful of the continued authority of the father when they are actually, in many cases, taking his place as breadwinner. The father, in order to meet this challenge to his authority, is likely to become increasingly arbitrary, and, if his authority had been well established prior to his unemployment, he is likely to be successful for a time, the older children yielding rather than making an open revolt.

The respect for parents was frequently increased, however, by the obvious evidence that they were willing to go without in order to save their children from a too violent adjustment in their manner of life. Indeed in a number of cases children indicated that their regard for their parents had been greatly stimulated by this fact.

In the second place, the subjects in connection with

which it is necessary to exercise authority are increased by unemployment. In this matter also the older children of earning age are most implicated. It is they who have to stop school, curtail their normal social activities most of which involve expenditures, go without adequate clothes for their activities, and in addition devote a larger share of any earnings to supplying the family exchequer. In all these matters they must be persuaded to do the thing necessary for the best interests of the whole family. Frequently dissatisfaction arose between the older and the younger children on the question of what was likely to appear to the former as favoritism. Parents tried to protect the younger children "who couldn't be expected to understand," as much as possible, while expecting coöperation to a larger extent from the others.

In the third place the normal function of expenditures as rewards and punishment is severely handicapped. The case of clothing economies is to the point. Obviously the desires of the children must more frequently meet denial than satisfaction. Decisions must often challenge them. The use of the granting or withholding of new clothes as a reward or punishment is curtailed. The visible evidence of appreciation or disapproval of the children's conduct implicit in the parents' response to the sartorial claims of the children is vitiated by the difficulty of making any expenditure at all. Any existing rivalries between children are difficult to reduce by well-timed and justly distributed expenditures on clothes.

Finally, the atmosphere in the home, charged as it is with discouragement and the preoccupation and weariness of the parents in the face of unaccustomed problems, is not conducive to a happy solution of parent-child relationships. For instance, the ordinary relationships of parents and children with respect to coöperation on their schoolwork or parents' attempts to straighten out social or educational problems of the children are made more difficult when the

parents are under the stress of having to make all these
other decisions. What is ordinarily a somewhat pleasant, if
at times an exhausting undertaking, now is done under a
strain which causes the parents to resent it. Several parents
who had what might be called "problem children" in school
commented on the fact that now they didn't have any energy or patience left for trying to solve their difficulties. "It
was all right when your whole day wasn't a problem, but
when that's the case, then you don't have the same patience and interest as you did before. You resent it. That's
what you do."

In spite of her other worries, however, normally the
mother acts as peacemaker between the father and the
children and bolsters by her increased authority his declin-
ing prestige. Whatever she may say to him, and her criticism of him during this period is likely to increase, she de-
fends the father before the children. Conflicts between parents and children are considerably reduced, also, by the
fact that the parents are trying to absorb the stress of readjustment and save the children from unfortunate and de-
pressing facts, which experience might stimulate their restlessness and revolt.

In every family there exist observable symbols of family
unity which play an effective part in stabilizing family relationships. These symbols are not destroyed at this period
of unemployment, but they are under severe attack.

Any common goals of effort which have existed prior to
unemployment still exist, although the possibility of reaching them has somewhat diminished. In addition to these
goals there is an increased importance now of the effort to
save the children from distress. The common concern of all
members of the family with this problem, including the
elder earners after a first reaction to the situation as "favoritism," tends to give the family an intensified focus for
their common endeavor.

Ritual events are still carried out although on a basis of

somewhat reduced expenditure. The holiday seasons, customary times for much of this ritual, brought a particular awareness of changed circumstances. Christmas trees, exchanges of gifts, family feasts cannot be continued on the old scale. Equally important is the effect of the curtailing of expenditures for such items as Easter baskets and presents for different members of the family.

You know you realize that you're on a tough problem more when you can't pay 2 5 c. for an Easter basket than when you miss the rent. Then too, when I used to go to see my parents I always used to take little gifts to them. When I would be away for a day or two I would always bring the children things. But now I can't do that any more.

Household furnishings and the appearance of the house have not yet deteriorated, and the problem of replacement has not yet become severe. Whenever a family is reduced to the necessity of selling or "hocking" possessions, however, the damage to family stability is clearly evident. These possessions are the visible symbols of the family institution. Living in a family means familiarity with and use of these possessions. It means acquaintance with the mutual efforts to obtain them. When they go out the door they carry with them this part of the imponderable accumulation of experience out of which the family is built.

The evidences of family solidarity involved in common family activities are of course reduced as the recreational interests of the family become more individualized.

Family pride is considerably curtailed by the fact that as the period progresses, the "social-front" and "social-contact" expenditures must be reduced and the inconsistency of any make-believe with the facts becomes increasingly apparent. Interesting examples of adjustment to this situation were in evidence. Families tried to postpone as long as possible their removal to a less desirable neighborhood. Family pride suffered severe injury when removal to a cheaper rent was necessary. We have seen that nearly half of the families in the sample group made this adjustment. "Folks can't see what you eat, but they can't help knowing where you live" is a phrase which reveals one of the problems involved in such a move. Destruction of that symbol of family status is real and removes one of the intangible and taken-for-granted bonds of pride which all members share. Particularly was this true of families who were thoroughly concerned with improving their standards, second-generation families who had moved to an area of second settlement, American families who were determined to live in an American neighborhood. Life in a "good" neighborhood was not only a bulwark for family pride, but it provided opportunities in association, particularly for the children, which provided real foundations for maintaining the family's status. For a number of families, the move of course was to a place "just around the corner," and no change in neighborhood was involved.

Several parents indicated that, from the point of view of maintaining family pride, the children's clothes were almost more important than those of the parents. Said one mother: "We can go to early Mass where no one will see us, but the children are out with other children, and they would bring shame on us if they were not properly dressed."

It was frequently remarked that playmates were very ruthless in their teasing and even ridiculing of children whose fathers were unemployed.

It is not possible now to relieve the tensions arising within the family through outside contact, recreation, small surprises, and like tactics. The forces which are destructive of family integration are constantly in operation.

It can hardly be expected that the satisfaction of husband and wife in mutual association would escape unscathed from such circumstances, or that their mutual affection and regard would be undiminished. It seems clear

that the amount of association that husband and wife want
with each other is conditioned by the customary routine of
the husband's work schedule. That means that he is usually at home in the late afternoon and evening only. Even
if he is on a night schedule, he normally sleeps during the
day, so that he is not in constant contact with his wife. If
their association in the home during unemployment were
to be pleasant, a whole new division of labor would have
to be drawn up, accepted, and practiced until it became
customary and satisfactory. Apparently this shift of the
husband to domestic duties is desired neither by the husband nor by the wife. She is conditioned as much as he is to
the fact that the husband's business is to earn money and
not to do the household tasks. Several of the wives expressed the wish that their husbands would help them
more, but very frequently they would add, "but I suppose
I'd lose my respect for him if he did." Even when some
experimentation is carried on in this matter of getting the
husband accustomed to domestic work, his ineptness and
the mistakes he makes as frequently lead to conflict as to
satisfaction. After a while, the wife is glad to have him out
from under foot and do the work herself. The increased opportunity for association in the home, therefore, while the
husband is unemployed, is not accepted and used with any
degree of satisfaction. As one woman put it, "Just being together is not enough. You have to be together with some
purpose, and when that ain't true it ain't any fun."

Other reasons for lack of satisfaction in mutual association will become evident from the following comments:

You don't have to say anything when the mister is around the
house in order for things to be unpleasant. When my old man
is sitting around the house, I think that he should be out looking for work. I don't tell him this. But he sees my worried look
and suspects that I blame him for not having anything to do. I
don't try to manage to have him away, but I know that he often
goes out to hang around street corners rather than sit at home

and face my silence. He knows what I'm thinking in that silence, or at least he thinks he does, and he probably makes it a lot worse than it really is.

You know, the thing I married my man for partly was the fact that I knew he was a good provider. He had a swell education, and he had a swell job in an office. Well, that was all right as long as he had the job. But now that he doesn't have it, the only kind of work that is available is the sort of thing he can't do. Maybe I should have been better off to marry a man who was just a common ditchdigger, because as I look at it now, all that I can ever hope is that he will be able to earn enough money to carry the rent and the other necessary expenses. Those are not the kind of thoughts that make me glad to have him around.

The following comment is obviously rooted in special circumstances, but it is worth recording nevertheless:

There is a difference between flattery and appreciation. Now, when a man really appreciates you and wants to thank you for something that you've done, he very likely will bring you something from downtown. But if he just wants to flatter you, he'll just say something and won't back it up with any gift. Now, of course you know that when he is unemployed he can't bring you gifts. You know that, all right. But just the same the habit you had of thinking that flattery is only words, and real appreciation is words with something else besides—well, you can't help thinking that it is less sincere than it used to be.

The factors that make any abnormal increase in association pleasant are absent when a man is out of work:

How can you be glad to see your wife and children when you come home when you see debts all around you and that's almost all you can talk about? And every time you think of them you know they cry to heaven that you're a failure. The wife may not say so, but she knows it the same as you do.

Since Mr. C has been unemployed, he doesn't know what to do with himself. He goes down the street to the club, stays a little while, then comes home; stays a bit and goes out. In and out, in and out all day. It makes him nervous and me nervous, too. Even when he's here I can't have any fun with him.

Some wives were very frank in saying that they could hardly expect their husbands to think as much of them as before:

My husband still loves me, I think, but you know it isn't just you that men like, but it's the way you look, as well. Now you take me. I've had these two teeth knocked out and I can't have them changed. I can't have them fixed, because we haven't the $40 that the dentist says it would cost to have them fixed. And then my clothes. Now just look at them! Of course, I don't like them. I keep them clean, but I know they don't look very good. I'm ashamed of my looks, but what can I do about it? And besides, I look all dragged out. Now, you tell me how any man that has any red blood in him can think that I'm as attractive as I used to be. The worst of it is that I could be if I could just have that money to get those teeth and buy some new clothes.

How can I keep looking nice so that my husband will like me when all that we have is macaroni and potatoes to eat? These foods don't cost much and they fill you up. We can't afford to buy fruits and vegetables on the money we have. Then, to make matters worse, my husband says he guesses I don't worry much about his being out of work, because if I did I'd be getting thin. How can I get thin on the kind of food that we eat? It makes me furious when he says I don't take our troubles seriously because if I did I'd be getting thin.

All of the women with whom we talked tried for considerable periods to excuse and to rationalize their husbands' inability to get jobs, but most of them were obviously making an effort to do so. Said one woman: "I don't blame him. I know no one else around here is working, but it's awfully hard not to." Whatever might be said in criticism of the husband at home, however, the wife usually defended him before outsiders.

The chronic worries and the small problems which are always present in family life tend to assume larger proportions and are more likely to lead to disagreement during this period. Two factors, however, save these conflicts from becoming too intense. One is that the interests of both parents are focused on saving the children to a maximum degree from the results of the changes in family life and expenditures and from worry over the family difficulties. They have a common interest in the children, and the common interest is freshly emphasized. The other factor is that the customary methods of avoiding too serious disputes which have developed over a period of years are brought into play in this intensified situation and are usually capable of avoiding a serious and open conflict, although the ingenuity of both persons is strained to the utmost. As compared with the increased desirability of association during the first period, however, husband and wife during this period become definitely less attractive to each other.

As the customary habits enforcing a normal status of members, and as the coöperative methods of dealing with the problems are unable to survive in the midst of increasing difficulties, they are abandoned and are not yet supplanted by substitute habits and methods. Probably the best indication of the terminus of this particular period is the evidence that the children are going to have to face the necessity of marked readjustment.

## STAGE III. DISORGANIZATION

This period is merely an exaggerated manifestation of the tendencies noted in the previous period, that of unstable equilibrium. The family usually does not stay long in this period. Very quickly the forces of readjustment are felt, and those forces, present even from the beginning of unemployment, take hold. A period of temporary readjustment rapidly comes out of the period of disorganization. If the period does not end quickly the likelihood is that the family will be destroyed as a unit.

The division of labor of the previous period is maintained. Unless the husband has found a considerable amount of part-time work, the wife definitely takes over the responsibility for managing and planning. All earnings that are coming into the family are now channeled through her, and she has complete charge of them. Since the husband has not yet found a job, he is so involved in his awareness of his own failure and so frustrated by the surrender of his job standards and so depressed by his loss of confidence in his own ability and his own future that he cannot focus his attention on family problems. The result is that most of the decisions fall to the wife.

Within the family the status of the husband and father as the head of the family has suffered tremendously. He may still maintain his nominal position, but in his own mind and in the minds of other members of the family it is realized that he is not, in fact, the head of the family. The mother finds it necessary to establish more firmly her own prestige on a level sufficient to enable her to fulfill the responsibilities which she now has. In her attempts to do this she frequently withholds any large degree of recognition from the earning children. In turn these earning children try to make themselves independent of both parents, and the situation is much confused. No one at this period has a status which is recognized and customary, and the conflict in claims is a serious handicap to any degree of harmony within the family circle.

The sense of frustration is increased by the fact that customary solutions to economic and social problems, already inadequate, just do not work any longer. The family does not know what to do. They are casting about for new ways, but have not yet found them. In view of the nature of those problems, their lack of preparation for a ready solution is understandable.

Now, you take this sort of a case. The other day I had a toothache, and it was driving me crazy. Now, what would I have done ordinarily? Well, I would have gone down and seen the dentist about it and probably have had that tooth pulled. But I didn't have any money, so before I could have that tooth pulled I had to go to Mother and ask to borrow the money, and she didn't have it, so I had to go over to a friend and ask to borrow the money, and she didn't have it. The result was that I spent two days with that toothache which was nearly driving me crazy, and believe me I wasn't very nice to have around the house when that was happening, either. Finally, in desperation I got my grocer to let me have $1 out of my grocery slip instead of groceries, and with that $1 down the dentist was willing to pull my tooth. But what a job it was to find that money, and for two whole days it was hell in our family, just because I couldn't get that ache stopped.

Decisions which are taken for granted and which require very little discussion when the husband is earning normally are raised to huge proportions and take an inordinate amount of time when the husband is out of work. They furnish, often for long periods of time, the subject for dispute and for interrupting the normal satisfactory character of family life. For instance, the C's have had three children, all of them with a private physician attending. This private physician had charged them $25 each for the previous confinements. Now with Mr. C out of work for about nine months, the C's did not feel that they could afford a private doctor, since they were ashamed to ask him to do it for nothing, and they had no money. Someone suggested that there was free service at the dispensary, so Mrs. C, much against her will, went there. She got more and more disgusted with the prenatal service which she received, and was terrified at the idea of a student doctor attending her when the child was born. This matter became increasingly a subject for irritation between her husband and herself, as the day of the birth of the child approached, but there was nothing either of them could do about it. Finally, Mrs. C's sister-in-law went to the doctor that they had had previ-

ously and told him the situation. He agreed to make the
delivery and to let the C's pay him when they could. After
three months, then, this situation was cleared up, but it
was a situation which never would have occurred had Mr.
C been employed. This process occurred during the period
of unstable equilibrium. Before the child was born the C's
affairs had become thoroughly disorganized and they applied for relief. Their visitor from the relief agency told
them that relief would be cut off unless they used the city's
free service, which eventually they did.

But let us continue their story. They had had three
babies before, all of whom had been born tongue-tied, but
the private doctor had clipped the tongue immediately and
no ill effects had resulted. However, the dispensary doctor
had neglected to clip the tongue. Mrs. C's mother called
this to his attention, and he said he would do it the next
time he came. He made three visits after that, each time
promising to do the tongue clipping the next time, but he
never got around to it. When the visiting nurse came after
his third visit, Mrs. C called it to her attention. She said
the doctor probably did not know how to conduct this operation and was stalling. The baby would have no further
medical attention until she was taken to the dispensary six
weeks later. During this whole period the family was constantly worried for fear failure to clip the baby's tongue
would result in a permanent disability. Mrs. C said: "You
know, he wasn't a real doctor; he was just a student. But,
then, we had to have him; I guess I told you why, because
our relief would have been cut off unless we did have him.
What would you do in a case like that?"

All the same difficulties which were present in the last
period are present in this one also, but their intensity is increased. Pressure from creditors, the judgment of public
opinion and of friends emphasize the failure that they have
made of their domestic economic arrangement. The adjustments taken to get new resources, such as the cashing in of

insurance or taking out loans on insurance up to the full
value of the policy, have undermined their customary anticipated security, and the awareness of this fact makes the
conflict over expenditure decisions even more severe. Various new problems have arisen with respect to new earning
possibilities. It is not certain what these possibilities may
be, but it is certain that some of the alternatives suggested
involve a decrease in the status of the family and involve a
different kind of activity and skill on the part of the potential earners involved. Since no clear line of procedure has
been decided upon, the consideration of such policies is
likely to lead to confusion and disagreement.

The routine of family life is now completely disorganized and in confusion. Irregularity is the dominant note.

By the time the family has reached this period, practically all mutual activities outside the home and with nonmembers of the family have ceased. Even satisfying relations within the home have been reduced to a minimum.
For one thing, "No one has any heart for it"; they cannot
keep their minds off their troubles. In several cases the sale
of items used in such family activities naturally canceled
the activity. A particularly tragic case was that of the
Cardways.

For nine months during unemployment before the Cardways
went on relief, they retained one common activity although
many others had to be dispensed with in view of their cost. The
family had always been a musical family. They had a piano, a
saxophone, a banjo, and a xylophone, and the family would play
together in the evening. When they went on relief, the first
thing that the visitor did was to suggest that they sell some of
the musical instruments. This caused a quarrel, and they told
the visitor to go away, that that was their family, and they were
not going to sell those things. But after another two months,
they were in such desperate straits that they were willing to
take relief on the visitor's terms. They sold the banjo first, then
the xylophone, and now [she pointed to the piano], "that's all

we have left, and the only reason we have that left is because we can't sell it. Now that those things are gone, we don't have anything that we can do together, except quarrel over bills."

The children are disciplined chiefly now by power authority. Both the father and mother have become dogmatic in their orders and seek by arbitrary control to obtain obedience which would not ordinarily be given to them on the basis of the natural respect the children have for them. The supplementary earners are definitely resentful of the amount that they are having to contribute to the family, and are in revolt against any restraint as well as against the obligations that are placed upon them. There is practically no common sharing of activity between the children and parents, and indeed among all the children except very young ones any activity is almost completely individualistic. The children feel an increasing amount of shame for their parents, comparing them, chiefly the father, with those of other children. Shame rather than pity seems to characterize their attitude at this point.

The problem of disciplining the children, to say nothing of enjoying them, is increased by the tiredness and the temper which is encouraged by the lack of rest and the constant pressure under which the parents live. Said Mrs. C:

I used to be willing to reason with the children, but now I just yell at them, and in the afternoon when I really need to rest they get on my nerves until they're driving me crazy. Then I open the winder and I holler out to them to stop making their noise, and of course they're playing with some other children, and then these children's mothers come over and they tell me that I'm stuck up and that I think that I'm too good for this neighborhood, and that don't I know that children have to make noise. So what I used to be able to stand I can't stand any more because I'm so tired, and the fact that I can't gets me into trouble with my neighbors as well as with my children. It's awful.

The future at this period looks so black for the family that the children cannot even offset against present discomfort the possibilities of the future. Particularly is this true with respect to the older children, many of whom in our families were formerly contemplating an early marriage which now seemed to be under the necessity of definite and unlimited postponement.

Very few symbols of family unity remain to give even a superficial indication of family integration. Ritual has been given up with the exception of a few deeply ingrained traditional observances on holidays, and the observance of these is so limited by lack of funds as to give little satisfaction. Many intrafamily activities for mutual aid are now burdens instead of privileges giving reality to the unity of the larger family.

We have a kind of an understanding among our family, and I guess it exists in most families, that we all take care of each other in case we're sick. Now we love each other and we want to do it, and every time mother gets sick I go over and help or my sisters go over and help, and they do the same for me. But now of late whenever I have needed to do that the responsibility has got me down, and there's no fun in it any more. It's just because this is just one more added thing, and I'm already so worried about things that I don't know what to do, so when this comes along it's just the straw that breaks the camel's back. Now isn't that funny? The thing that really used to give me a lot of fun, now makes me sore.

The family pride in its social position now becomes silly and is discarded along with the practices and expenditures which were intended to give some validity to the objective evidence of that status.

In every case where the family moved into a neighborhood inhabited by those whom they have previously considered of a lower social status, this move was preceded by a long period of debate as to whether or not they should do it, primarily because of the feeling that the children would not be in as good and as favorable a neighborhood; second, because it would lower their status; and, third, because they would have to make new associations. In practically every case all these fears were realized, and the fact that they had anticipated them and that the anticipation had increased their fears lent irritation to the adjustments when they had to make them, and continued for a considerable period of time to disturb the comfortable and friendly relations within the family. Here were a new source of debate and a new source of difficulty.

The same objective conditions may have quite different effects upon families in different circumstances. For instance, by chance one of our families was forced to move into a tenement in which another one of the families with which we are in contact had been living for a number of years. They lived across the hall from each other. This morning when we came to the tenement the family which had recently moved in pointed to a leaky roof over the stairway which had been leaking very badly because of melting snow. The hallway was so cold that the water froze on the stairs, and the woman had to put ashes there so that the children would not slip. To her this was a discouraging indication of the change in their status, and for over a week she and her husband had personal difficulties because of such a change in status. The other family across the hall, however, made no mention of this fact and seemed to take it as a matter of course.

It is not only the actual plane of living and the type of service and goods which they are able to get and the discomforts entailed in the shift. Many of these are symbolic of their family status and pride. For instance, when the C's had to go to the dispensary for a doctor, it was not only the fact that Mrs. C feared this, and that she thought she wouldn't get as good service that troubled her, but she was ashamed to let her friends know it because she felt it was a distinct challenge to the status that they had always held before when they had had the private doctor.

The condition of the home is rapidly deteriorating, the sale of belongings has increased this process and has detracted from the home as a source of pride. Replacements cannot be made.

One of the sources of family pride for the R's was a diamond ring which had been the gift of Mr. R to his wife at the time of their marriage. This diamond ring had formerly belonged to his mother, and before that had belonged to his grandmother, and it was the custom in the family to pass it on to the eldest son to give to his bride. The R's had been keeping this diamond ring to give to their eldest daughter when she married. On her wedding day her husband would receive it from Mrs. R and put it on her finger. Thus would the family tradition be carried on. The relief visitor one day accidentally found that the R's possessed this ring and forced them to sell it. Mr. R said:

It was either that or get put off relief, but believe me I would almost rather beg on the streets than to have sold that ring. There are some things that mean more to you than money and the diamond ring was one. Really, it seemed to me that our whole family was represented by that diamond ring.

The family, dissociated from many of its former community contacts, is now thrown in upon itself where conflict and confusion dominate and established relationship patterns have disintegrated. There is no comfort in the family circle. The breaking up of the family unit may be considered at this time by one or both of the parents since there is a present failure to receive satisfaction customarily expected of the family and very little prospect that the future will offer anything different.

Relations between husband and wife are under extraordinary strain during this period. Wives are no longer publicly vocal about their loyalty to their husbands. They more frequently criticize him openly to the family or to "girl friends." Husbands in retaliation blame their wives for poor management, both in the past and in the present. Each blames the other for past mistakes. Old conflicts that have long been suppressed are revived, and much attention is paid to the contemplation of what might have happened if husband or wife had been more wise and foresighted in the past. The wife frequently questions the sincerity of her husband's search for work and expresses suspicion that he is loafing. In return the husband challenges her understanding of his real problem and asks her if she thinks she could do any better. Few criticisms are withheld, even in the presence of children and friends. The mother does not defend the father, as she did prior to this period, from criticism by the children. She herself is now the target for their resentment in view of the fact that her decisions with respect to expenditures and distribution of income and with respect to the kind of activities the minor members of the family can engage in must now severely curtail satisfactory life for those involved. All disagreements are colored by the fact that the husband thoroughly realizes his loss of status and resists this loss. The customary restraints which normally tend to keep relations, even though antagonistic, on a somewhat livable basis, go down, and cooperative habits developed in happier times disintegrate. Mutual activity of the pleasanter sort is practically absent, and most relations are now focused on disagreeable aspects of experience. The potential value of mutual activity therefore as a foundation for harmonious living is decreased, and in place of it there is offered a stimulus to disagreement and unpleasantness. Any pleasant social relations which any member of the family may have are usually on an individual basis and apart from the other members of the family, so that there is no common experience of a pleasant sort upon which their interests can merge. One notable feature of this period is that the chronic worries

and small problems which we saw becoming more important in the last period tend to be submerged by the over-
whelming emergencies of the present and are just not attended to.

During this period both husband and wife are definitely
less attractive to each other than before, and there are very
few factors to compensate for the damaging impact of difficulty. Even the protection of the children which heretofore
had been an important source of satisfaction and coöperative effort loses considerable of its harmonizing effect because it is recognized by both parents that they have failed
to protect the children, and there is no use pretending
about it.

It seems to be clear, however, that breaking up the home
is not considered unless there is an alternative way of maintenance which seems to be more attractive. The difficulties
of home life themselves are not sufficient to cause the man
and wife to separate under any ordinary circumstances. It
is only the presence of an alternative possibility of going
home to mother, or being supported by a rich uncle, or
something of the kind, which causes this matter to be even
seriously considered. The usual reaction is to make some
kind of adjustment to the home situation and make the
best of it. Besides divorces cost money. Separations are
discouraged for those on relief in view of the fact that relief is less likely if there are no dependents. During the period of our survey we did not have opportunity to observe
any possible effects of aid to dependent children or of
mother's aid on this situation.

We have no systematic medical evidence on the developing health problems of the family. But it is during this period that signs of such problems became evident, particularly if the family had been long in the stage of unstable
equilibrium and had tried desperately by cutting food costs
to escape recourse to relief. We learned of notes sent by
teachers to the effect that children were not getting enough

to eat to have any energy. Doctors in discussing an illness would say, "What can you expect? Look at their diet!" Parents and children complained of the monotony and inadequacy of their food to satisfy hunger. Men rationalized their lack of zeal in hunting for work on the basis that "the stuff we eat fills up but puts no pep in a man." But was this entirely rationalization? Obviously needed medical and dental attention were foregone. More complaints of physical ailments were made.

One of the most severe drains upon the physical health is the fact that many of the unemployed cannot sleep at night for thinking about their difficulties. They report that they lie awake staring into the dark wondering what they are going to do. They used to be able to arrive at their decisions during the day they said, but now where there are so many of them to make and they are so impossible to make, they just can't get it all done, and they lie awake thinking. Then in the morning they are tired and cranky, and the chances for arguments and disagreements are increased. Lack of rest must in the end make its effect on health evident.

Since this period of disorganization is normally that in which the family makes appeal to relief agencies, it is appropriate to make special mention of the ways in which life on relief may undermine the integrity of the family. The relief experience comes in addition to the other experiences we have just noted.

Consider the fact that relief investigators or case workers are normally women and deal with the housewife. Already suffering a loss in prestige and authority in the family because of his failure to be the chief breadwinner, the male head of the family feels deeply this obvious transfer of planning for the family's well-being to two women, one of them an outsider. His role is reduced to that of errand boy to and from the relief office.

The customary techniques of self-maintenance are inappropriate for survival on relief. Until the family settles down to the business of developing ways to combat the new situation and make the most of it, the new problems present many questions to which their experience gives no answer. How can the visitor best be pleased? Upon what sort of evidence does she give or withhold relief? How much pressure is wise? Will joining in a petition or demonstration for more adequate relief bring success, or will such methods prejudice the family in the eyes of the agency? Will working out one's grocery order spoil one's chances of work at his own trade? It probably will. Then how get out of it? Will a doctor's certificate do? What doctor can be trusted? What should be done about unexpected windfalls? Should they be reported and the chance taken of having relief reduced? Should one run the risk of "being spotted" as a wearer of relief clothes?

Life on relief, and particularly on a grocery order, presents many problems which the ordinary housewife is not accustomed to face. Here is Mrs. R, for instance, who has a $4 grocery order.

She thinks if she had that $4 in cash so that she could go around from store to store like an ordinary person, she would be much happier and much better off. As it is, the groceryman does not carry everything that she needs, and she has to go to his particular store because his name is on the slip. He has very few vegetables. On Mondays, he has none. On Tuesdays, he has greens. She tried to go in on Tuesdays to get the green vegetables. He has no oranges, only bananas. Her children get very tired of eating bananas, and beg her to buy oranges. The other week her young son started working for $1 a day delivering meat. With this $1 she is able to buy vegetables and fruits which the groceryman does not carry now. Her husband does not like canned foods. He is not accustomed to eating canned vegetables, and she wishes that she could go to some store where she might be able to buy fresh vegetables. This week the visitor found out that the young son was earning $1 and reduced their relief allowance accordingly.

Eventually the family finds the answers to these questions, and in the developing of methods to live as satisfactorily as possible on relief finds a common goal of effort in the winning of which functional integration is secured. But at the moment the questions merely furnish new perplexities to already overburdened minds.

The control over their own affairs which is an acceptable sign of family success and a basis for family pride is, of course, seriously modified, and with the modification comes a decrease in the incentives which impelled the family to coöperative effort. The provision of clothes, furnishings, a decent place to live, improvements in the place, which formerly bound family members to the parents by ties of appreciation, now is partially in the hands of an outside agency. The recreational events, the family dinners, the "surprises," the trips in the family car, the ritual surrounding holidays, must be foregone, or accepted as a gift from an outsider. They do not come to members because the family has been able to produce a surplus over bare necessities solely by its own coöperative efforts.

Innumerable decisions formerly the sole business of the family must now be made in conference with an outsider whose advice, incidentally, had better be followed. The normal pattern of contribution to family funds by supplementary earners must be disturbed far beyond the rearrangement undertaken by families on their own initiative when the head is out of work.

Outsiders are questioned in order to check up on the family's resources and habits, and in the questioning become aware of the affairs of the group, affairs which every self-respecting family expects to keep to itself.

In these and many other ways inherent in life on relief, the process by which the family is integrated into a stable unit is disturbed.

Several things must happen before the family gets out of this particular period of disorganization. The father must change his attitude toward his loss of status and accept it as inevitable, and cease his attempts to reëstablish by dogmatic authority what he has lost in fact. The mother must succeed in establishing her own authority sufficiently so that she can carry on her responsibilities effectively. The children must succeed in realizing their own importance and in getting some recognition for the functions which they are performing. Criticisms which are used must begin to wear thin and no longer have their effect either in stimulating the person criticized or in giving satisfaction to the critic. Some regularity must be established in decisions on expenditures and decisions made on major expenditure adjustments such as rent or tuition. A decision must be made as to new forms of earning or sources of support. As soon as some or all of these developments have taken place, the family is in a position to tackle the problems of adjustment with somewhat more harmony.

Moreover, the family cannot continue to be thrown in upon itself forever and not feel the necessity of defending itself against the judgment of outsiders. As long as there is some possibility that the family may break up, no real organization is possible. When the decision has been made, either to break up or to "stick it out," the family can start on its process of reorganization with some hope of success.

## STAGE IV. EXPERIMENTAL READJUSTMENT

The period we have just described cannot continue for long. If the family continues to live together under the same roof, some working relationships have to be established. An important prerequisite to the reëstablishment of some working harmony is the common, but usually unspoken, acceptance of the fact that the achievements of the past can no longer be made the standards for satisfaction of achievements in the present.

It seems quite evident from our cases that the wife most quickly comes to the decision that she might as well stop looking at the past, start accepting the present, and work for the future, on the assumption that they will never again be able to live on the same standard that they had before. The husband holds most tenaciously to the recovery of these standards, probably because his own status is so severely attacked, whereas that of the wife in managing the household requires that she be realistic about the situation.

The wife's part in management and planning is still most important, but the husband begins to share more in these efforts, particularly if he has succeeded in finding some opportunity to earn. Much depends upon the degree to which the work activities in which he is participating relieve him from contemplation of failure. The division of labor made necessary by the readjustment in contributions to the family welfare has now become somewhat more normal and sufficiently recognized so that the mother can see the gaps in the domestic management provisions and make assignments to them.

The problems involved in status readjustments heretofore have been dominated by the fact that the change was colored by the memory of past status. No adjustment in roles and status seemed to be satisfactory when compared to that which formerly existed. As the memory becomes more faint, however, the attention can be more thoroughly riveted upon the present, and the status can be adjusted to present functional importance with considerably less irritating pressure from memory. The mother's status and authority are recognized, so that she can carry on the management responsibilities which now fall upon her. Usually the earning children have solved their problem of status by securing a nominal, if not real, independence from the decisions of the parents, and they are therefore somewhat more satisfied. Taken all in all, this is a period of status building rather than of status destruction and the adjustment of status recognition to functional reality.

The major decisions necessary to make available resources cover needed expenditures have now been made and accepted as necessary. Therefore one source of debate has been removed, although the adjustments are still novel and continually productive of dissatisfaction. The other sources of conflict are considerably reduced. Either work seeking has become more systematic or the husband has found some new source of earning, or the uselessness of further hunting for work has been recognized by everyone. The ventures of other members of the family in earning are accepted, and the novelty has worn off. The problems of initial entrance to an earning career, particularly in the case of the mother, are not so great. Since the decision has been made and accepted not to undertake the keeping up of a social front and the social contacts, this source of frustration is reduced. Since the expenditures and incomes have been brought more closely together, debts are not increasing and do not continually challenge the family with this evidence of inadequacy in economic matters. The pressure from creditors has been reduced. The decisions about family activities have been accepted as necessary. The husband regains some of his self-confidence, particularly if he has found a place in the working world, no matter how humble that place may be.

The precise mutual activities and interests of the several members, which we saw were so nearly destroyed as unemployment progressed, are seldom restored. But one can witness at this period the process by which such materials are woven into the fabric of family life. The process is a very simple one.

The job activities of the several members of the family have turned up subjects of interest to all. Frequently when the earning activities were in the nature of home industry, mutual interest of all members of the family is displayed. New jobs lead to new associates and experiences which must be shared to be most fully enjoyed. Individual members brought home from these contacts and activities subjects for conversation of interest to all. Frequently the new interests involved problems upon which the advice of other members of the family was sought. Plans for the children have been renewed, albeit on a somewhat lessened standard of expectancy. Numerous new avenues of mutual interest have opened up. It may be that the family has found in settlement-house programs, free concerts, or in some other kind of free entertainment an opportunity for mutual association, not only with each other but with new friends. Even experimentation in new forms of stretching the income has provided fields for common activity productive of a more satisfying relationship. In the doing of these new jobs and in the establishing of new relationships, very frequently new virtues are discovered in each other which had not appeared before, and which tend in some degree to restore the attractiveness of the person in whom the virtue has been observed. One of the most significant characteristics of this period is that minor individual troubles are once more kept to one's self and not spread before the whole group. If separation had been contemplated, the very fact that such thought had entered the mind tends to increase the attempts to develop mutual coöperation. This is not to say that family solidarity is completely restored to its former degree and that the damage done by curtailed mutual activities is completely counteracted. But the restoration of a degree of solidarity does become evident and new resources for functional relationships are found in the natural course of adjustment to necessity.

The routine of family life has become somewhat more satisfactory. Once again the family becomes a help to its members in facing their individual problems. Every point at which such help occurs adds a stone to the foundation of family solidarity.

Whatever pattern of discipline and practice has been established tends to become habitual, and therefore there is less need for the assertion of dogmatic authority. More-

over, since the family is making a somewhat better adjustment to its economic problems, some degree of respect of
children for parents is restored. The older earning children,
now becoming accustomed to their large contribution to
the family exchequer, become less resentful and assist in
discipline problems. The older children have usually been
admitted to the family councils on economic matters, and
this activity in itself offers new opportunity for mutual relationship and assists in the establishment of relations of
customary authority and deference. In many cases the
children's participation in the family maintenance activities and councils has furthered their maturity. Their vanity
is pleased by the evidence of their increased importance
and their ability to make sacrifices. Occasional renewal of
family activities outside the home once more makes pleasant associations possible, and relationships within the home
are considerably less confused and disorganized and offer
more opportunity for pleasant contacts. The school children have somewhat recovered from the shock of having
their parents ridiculed and now begin to defend them. If
not before, the children now frequently realize the sacrifices their parents have made, and the realization contributes to healing the wounds produced by the early strains
of other adjustments to unemployment. This activity and
realization tend to add them to those who are defending
the home against outside critics.

Although it is still difficult to restore completely and
adequately the anticipations and expectancies of the older
children with respect to their future careers, evidence was
increasingly observed that this matter was being more
hopefully considered.

Mr. F brought out a picture of his boy. He also showed us a
picture of his girl on the dresser. He looked at the two and then
said, "The hardest thing about this nine months has been that I
know right now that our only chance to keep our heads above
water and not get on relief is to get these children to work. I've

just got my boy a job pressing collars in a shirt factory. The girl cries and doesn't want to leave school, but I don't see anything we can do. We must be independent, you know. Maybe if she can get a good enough job we could get the boy back to school. Girls only get married, anyway. But this boy, he needs an education. He'll get it, too. We are doing better now.

One of the first signs that the family is recovering from the period of disorganization is the reëstablishment of ritual events although on a somewhat less expensive basis. Typical of such adjustment are the efforts of one family.

It almost seemed as if one by one the things which made us realize that we were one big happy family were being taken away from us. For instance, it's been our custom always on Memorial Day to go down and put flowers on the graves. You know those wreaths that you buy, don't you? Well, that's what we always had. Last year we couldn't afford any such wreaths, and since it was the thing that we'd always done, we just didn't put any on, and it was awfully hard, I'll tell you. This year we decided that we would have to do something about it and we made our own wreaths. I guess we're smarter this year than last, because it felt awfully good to do what we'd always done before.

The importance of common goals of effort reasserts itself as a force binding the family together. One of the O's children had a particular talent for painting. When in the efforts to keep themselves independent of relief allowances the O's had stopped his painting lessons, they had also given up what had been a goal for the whole family. The importance of this goal was recognized when, after the family resorted to relief, the married members who had not been able to contribute to help the family keep up its economic standards now started contributing so that this young boy could continue his painting lessons. Indeed he seemed to be the great hope of all the family. The first thing the father did when he went on W.P.A. was to start paying for the boy's painting lessons himself.

In most families the effort to be self-supporting and to renew or restore the evidences of achievement absorbed the attention. In a few, the attempt to get as much as possible from the community became an engrossing common goal of thought and activity. In any case, the unity of the family in the process was increased.

Very frequently the family becomes more conscious of itself as a unit, defending its members against the impacts of the judgment and the criticism of outsiders. A common enemy, as well as a common goal for action, can act as an integrating factor. This was especially noted in cases where the family had removed to a cheaper rent, involving a marked change in associations and a marked tarnishing of this symbol of status. The forces of reconstruction went to work early. Ashamed to invite former friends to the new home, or realizing the latter's hesitancy to visit the new center of family life, the family was thrown more completely in upon itself. Frequently the increased interaction involved in this situation resulted in a closer association and common interest in presenting a solid front to a supposedly critical community, which interaction can be described as real progress toward the reintegration of the family.

The mutual respect for and appreciation of one's mate so thoroughly challenged in preceding periods cannot be immediately and fully restored. But criticisms once so outspoken are withheld, and each begins to make allowances for the points of view and states of mind and comfort of the other. It seems to be almost inevitable that under circumstances of unemployment criticism will increase. Both husband and wife expect something of the other which that person no longer can give. The amount of attention and skill required in their new problems without sufficient money to help them solve these problems are bound to cause disagreement. Harmonious relations are normally characteristic when the large share of practice and decision is taken for granted, when it is customary, and when both have accepted it. When new problems are faced, and when these problems are so great that they cannot possibly be solved satisfactorily by anybody, the tendency to criticism is amplified. All families indicated that the size of this burden of making plans and solving their problems made them irritable.

Nevertheless, by the time families had reached this period of unemployment they had learned some kind of method for getting around these difficulties and for making it possible to live together even under circumstances of criticism. Although criticisms are well aired, one or the other is very likely to let them go so that they do not cause a continued quarrel.

Husbands in particular played an important role in this situation. In not every case were they willing to grant the wife credit for the way in which she handled her increased responsibilities and functions. Frequently they were quite outspoken on this matter, however, and their appreciation added salve to whatever wounds had been made in the relationship.

Disagreements between husband and wife, and even fights between husband and wife, do not necessarily indicate that the family is not a strong institution. I am reminded of Mrs. S who said:

Me and my man we fight, we fight all the time, but I wouldn't leave him. What you think marriage is for—a love match all the time? It's no good for a woman to go alone. How she have her own home if she go alone? How she hold her head up in the neighborhood if she go alone? How she be a normal woman if she alone? Being married and having a family is doing what you're supposed to do by being married and having a family. You may do it without fighting or you may do it with fighting, but you do it just the same.

Of course by this time any censure has begun to appear as practically useless and as making matters worse. Consequently, if any degree of mental control still exists, criticisms may be reduced for this reason. However, there are very real reasons why blame is not so frequently offered. We are inclined to think that the fact that the wife looks for work is a very important factor in decreasing her criticism of her husband. Once she has been out looking for work and finds out how hard it is, she is less inclined to blame him for not finding work. In every case where the wife looked for work, this result was observed. Blame is normally stimulated by comparison of present achievements with past achievements, and as the distance from the past increases there is less reason and less opportunity for blame. It seems less appropriate than the devotion of attention to the present or future adjustment and the assessment of one's success or failure in terms of his present activities.

Moreover, rationalization of the position of the head of the family has proceeded far enough to take the edge off censure. The decisions of the mother as to expenditures, which were so frequently productive of criticism by the children, have become accepted as necessary, and, in any case, as customary, and criticism of her and of the father is reduced.

Work relief in many cases provided the self-maintenance foundation on which this period of experimental readjustment rested. This fact deserves particular comment. Many of the attacks on the stability of the family unit are weakened when the head of the family is certified for a W.P.A. job. Once more his wages are the chief source of support. He is the breadwinner, the provider. Earnings of supplementary earners can once more be allocated to the personal needs of that individual by family decision. The necessary choices in expenditures can be made in family council from which outsiders are excluded. If those expenditures include items considered important to the satisfactory relations between family members—surprises, symbolic family events, common recreation—the only restraint is one which is self-imposed. Less rationalization is needed to explain the fact that "father can't get a job." To those outside the family circle, he goes daily to work. Even within the family circle the restoration of a more normal division of labor and routine is possible. Lacking a private job for the head, work relief furnishes the family with the best possible substitute under the circumstances. Having observed our families under conditions of unemployment with no public help, or with that help coming from direct and from work relief, we are convinced that after the exhaustion of self-produced resources, work relief is the only type of assistance which can restore the strained bonds of family relationship in a way which promises the continued functioning of that family in meeting the responsibilities imposed upon it by our culture. We have observed a few families finding a new level of integration and stability on the assumption of continued expectancy of direct relief. Stability is not restored in such a case, however, unless family objectives have been severely modified, unless the family has established itself among a group of associates similarly situated and has come to think of the relief check as the probably permanent substitute for the pay envelope. Even so, family stability is scarcely furthered unless agreement on such matters is found among all members. Nor is the institution thus recreated the sort which provides the kind of common life conducive to the satisfactory functioning of its members in a democratic community.

## STAGE V. PERMANENT READJUSTMENT

The aspects of this particular period are not essentially different from those of the last. They are simply continued and strengthened. However, the period is characterized by several features which are worth noting. Conflict situations rooted in the transition in the standard of living and activities and relations dependent upon these have practically disappeared. Instead of concentrating upon a comparison of the past with the present, the attention is focused upon the present and future problems. Rationalizations of the changed position of the family have been accepted without serious question and give a satisfactory explanation of the present status of the family. Goals of common effort once more appear and become the source of common interest and the objective to which individuals will subordinate their own personal wishes. Family activities of a recreational sort are renewed, and such recreation becomes less individualized and more frequently a common enterprise of the whole group. The discipline pattern which is consistent with the new authority relationships within the family is accepted by all and, with exception of the ordinary conflicts arising from the exercise of any discipline, little trouble is found in this quarter.

## IX

## CHALLENGE OF UNEMPLOYMENT
## TO FAMILY STABILITY

WITH this background of recorded effects and adjustments in mind, we may now return to the question we raised at the beginning of this section: What is the observed effect of unemployment on the stability of the family? To provide a basis for comparison among the families we drew up a list of characteristics of family relations which would by their presence give evidence of stability and by their absence suggest a lack of stability.

When we speak of a stable family we mean that that family possesses the following characteristics:

1. The relative status, power, and prestige of the several members are consistent both with their qualities and functions and with cultural expectancies as to the roles of each.

2. The customary coöperative practices developed for the meeting of minor and major problems are serving to solve those problems satisfactorily to the members and to the cultural group of which the family is a part.

3. The routine of family life is regular and provides for automatic dealing with the vast majority of family functions.

4. Mutual activities within and outside the home provide a large area of common interest, and of functional interaction between members with each other and with community associates.

5. The training and discipline of children is sufficient to meet the standards expected of the family by the cultural group of which it is a part and to make possible a united attack upon family problems.

6. The children are being provided with the needed

equipment for and hope of the eventual establishment of homes of their own.

7. The family has succeeded in establishing or acquiring symbolic bases or supports for integrated functions and relationships such as:

    *a*. Common goals of effort.

    *b*. Subordination of personal desires to these.

    *c*. Family pride in social status and adherence to the obligations and privileges accompanying this.

    *d*. Well-defined and consistently practiced code of behavior and ideals.

    *e*. Regularly practiced ritual.

    *f*. House and home furnishings which are the focus of interest and pride.

    *g*. Devices for relieving tensions.

    *h*. Common objectives of attack or resentment.

8. Members desire and gain satisfaction from mutual association and are bound together by common bonds of respect, regard, and admiration.

9. The family is providing successfully for the health of its members and progress toward a plane of living customary to their cultural group.

10. The members accept the conditions and circumstances represented by these characteristics as a satisfactory adjustment to and fulfillment of their basic wants.

### *Effect of Unemployment on Family Stability.*

Using the relative presence or absence of these characteristics as a measuring rod, we found that unemployment affected no two families alike but that in general the group of families with whom we were in continual contact over a period of eight years could be classified into four groups:

1. Those whose stability was undermined, leading to separation in the most extreme case.

2. Those whose stability was increased or reoriented

during unemployment in such a way as to make the family a more effective social institution than before.

3. Those in whose case the tendency toward greater stability in some aspects of family life offset the tendency toward the destruction of stability in other aspects.

4. Those whose stability was reëstablished after a time but on a less effective level of social function.

Since the number of cases was small (24), there is little significance in the proportions who fell into these several classifications. Nor can the generalizations concerning the causal factors which led to these results be more than suggestive hypotheses. The significant fact is that all four results were demonstrated as possible instead of the one which is normally assumed probable, namely, the decrease in family stability. Two of the twenty-four exemplified the decrease in stability to a marked degree, and one in exaggerated form. Two families succeeded in reëstablishing a degree of stability, but on a plane of living and with a dependence on relief agencies which decreased to a marked degree their ability to meet the social and economic obligations the community places on the family. The remaining nineteen of the twenty-four came out of the period of unemployment with, or soon progressed to, a degree of stability equal to or greater than that which characterized them prior to the onset of unemployment.

### Unemployment Not the Sole Cause of Effects.

These variations in results are grounded in the variety of factors which characterized the circumstances of the several families. An examination of the operation of these factors leads to several generalizations. The first generalization is that unemployment cannot be segregated as the sole cause of these effects. Unemployment is a complex phenomenon which acts as a disturbing irritant upon the practices and relationships customary to a particular family. The problems raised by unemployment were injected into a situation the major factors of which were already active.

### *Unemployment As an Irritant: The Loss of Income.*

As an irritant, however, it was powerful. Its chief power to destroy family stability appeared to lie in two unavoidable consequences, the loss of income and the loss of status as a worker. The reduction or elimination of income, particularly after the exhaustion of savings and credit, makes impossible the customary conclusion of family business by the making of an expenditure. When every need for a service or goods must remain unsatisfied until a special campaign for funds has been undertaken or a substitute technique of satisfying the need has been developed, the families' management capacities are taxed beyond their strength. The result is an accumulation of unfinished business, discouraging in its volume, and in the evidence of failure it presents. The usefulness of habit in eliminating large areas of behavior from the category of practices which have to be planned anew for each situation is nowhere better demonstrated than here. It is the exceptional family which, finding so important a set of techniques as spending for self-maintenance no longer available, can develop satisfactory substitute techniques without undermining many of the aspects of family stability we have mentioned. Under the stress of the campaign to develop new techniques for old and new problems involving a minimum of expenditure and the frustration attending almost certain failure, the normal affections and restraints tend to break down, and the confusion produces an atmosphere in which all family relations are less effectively maintained, in which discipline is harder to enforce. In the end, since new sources of income and substitute techniques are unlikely to meet the need, adjustments in expenditures must be made which destroy much of the functional relationships of members of the families with each other and with community associates, and which make difficult if not impossible the maintenance of symbols of family unity.

It is not the necessity for developing substitute techniques for spending which is damaging to family stability. Indeed it is occupation with that task which furnishes one of the main opportunities for interaction which assist in reestablishing that stability. The damage arises from the size rather than from the nature of the problem. The clue to the situation is whether financial resources can be provided sufficient to reduce the number of needs for which new techniques must be developed to reasonable and manageable proportions. If so, habitual practice can continue to solve most problems while mind and effort are freed for the rest.

### Loss of Job Status.

The second major and unavoidable consequence of unemployment is a disturbance of the customary pattern of status and authority of members. Both in the family and the community that pattern is closely related to economic activity. The job of the head of the family provides not only an income but a social role for which there is no adequate substitute in a working-class culture. Every aspect of stability in the normal family is based on the successful performance by the head of this role. It is not impossible to reëstablish the family organization around a different division of labor, but it is difficult to do so, and the period of readjustment witnesses a disrupting attack on the relations, activities, routine, authority, and symbols, based on the customary effectiveness of the head of the family in his normal role.

### Precise Effects Not Predictable.

One may expect therefore an attack on family stability from such factors in every case in which the head of the family is unemployed. But the precise effects cannot be predicted by deducing any logical series of results from these characteristic factors. Even with considerable knowledge of the family history and of the equipment with which the family came to the experience of unemployment we should have found it difficult to predict the precise effects of unemployment on the stability of any particular family. In retrospect we can attempt an explanation, as we did in the cases of the five families described in Chapter VI. But this analysis after the fact leads to the conclusion that no summation of family characteristics would point inevitably to success or failure in maintaining or reëstablishing stability. The reason for this is that the particular combination of characteristics, and their strength in relationship to each other, seemed more significant than the unit characteristics themselves. Furthermore, the elements of the unemployment problem varied, and this observation would cause us to hesitate to say with assurance that even a particularly effective combination of characteristics in the midst of one set of circumstances would lead to equal success if those elements were altered. Moreover, the particular way in which the resources for stability in the family were brought to bear upon the problems depended much on accidental circumstances which could in no way be foreseen.

### Factors Contributing to Family Stability.

Nevertheless, differences in certain resources which families had acquired over a period of years and in certain characteristics of family organization did appear to exercise an important influence in determining the degree of stability[1] retained by families after going through the experience of unemployment. Let us consider some of the most important of these.

1. According to the standards listed on pp. 226–227.

### Degree of Occupational Skill.

The degree of skill in the customary occupation was important in several respects. Skilled craftsmen and factory workers remained longest in the period of momentum stability chiefly because of their possession of larger financial resources. If unemployment continued, they were also more likely to go through more critical disorganization than semiskilled and unskilled workers before readjusting their relations and activities on the basis of lowered standards. For a longer period they held to the hope of returning to their normal work and maintaining their normal standards. Skilled craftsmen were more inventive than any group in developing new earning possibilities. Their skills were most useful in devising odd-job employment, barter arrangements for needed services and commodities, and occupation about the home. Skilled factory workers were least inventive. In the latter case the qualities that made the worker a successful employee served him very inadequately in searching for employment and readjusting to the lack of a regular job.

Likewise the standards of independence and self-support were more thoroughly based on and supported by successful experience for all skilled workers. They consequently postponed longest any readjustment involving a modification of those standards. Unless, however, this postponement was ended by a quick return to private employment, the change in the standard of living was apt to be more destructive to family relations geared to these standards and to the material evidences of their achievement.

### Amount of Experience with Unemployment.

The amount of experience the family has previously had with unemployment is another factor of major importance. The reason for this is contained in the simple aphorism,

"Practice makes perfect." Extended periods of unemployment will, of course, have depleted the family's resources with which to face another spell. Nevertheless the tendency of unemployment to disorganize family relations is least among those who know what to expect and have acquired some of the alternative techniques for dealing with the situation. For instance, the worker who has made occasional or even frequent changes of jobs has become better aware of job possibilities and of the techniques of job hunting, and has acquired a greater variety of skills. One of the first assumptions we were forced to correct was that long and steady employment with one firm indicated qualities useful in any and all emergencies. Such workers and their families demonstrated least facility in meeting the problems of unemployment and in maintaining the stability of family life which had been premised on the expectancy of a continuation of this steady job. The techniques for dealing with misfortune are acquired by dealing with misfortune. Having gone through such experiences before, families had learned what would be required of them, what adjustments were likely to prove effective, and what practices held most promise of filling the gaps in income. They were likely to have had previous contacts with free services. They had learned some of the alternatives to regular earning, and what expenditures could most readily be modified without completely destroying the satisfactions of family life. They had acquired a set of rationalizations which could be brought into play to relieve the tensions and disappointments, and to reduce criticisms. The folklore involved in such sayings as "It never rains but it pours," "Troubles never come alone," "It's no use to tempt fate," "Sold a horse and bought a donkey" have been filled with realistic content for them and are acceptable as possible explanations of their difficulties. Most important, they have developed habits of coöperation in the midst of uncomfortable as well as comfortable circumstances. In other words, the continuity of family stability is not premised on the continuity of good fortune.

### Financial Resources and Obligations.

Financial resources and obligations are of equal significance to practical skills in a monetary economy. We need not repeat the evidence we have already cited to indicate that "laying up for a rainy day" is a universal working-class folkway practiced whenever possible even at the expense of current consumption. The value of such savings and insurance was amply demonstrated in prolonging the period of momentum stability. Equally valuable was a good credit standing, particularly with the corner grocer, and a record of previous indebtedness successfully liquidated. The value of home ownership is debatable. If the home is clear or nearly clear of mortgages, such a resource unquestionably reduced the area of financial adjustments and dispute. But if the interest and taxes were equivalent to rent, the families so situated found the problems of shelter far more challenging than those who were renting. The possibility of postponing a payment for which funds were not immediately available and of moving to a rent more consistent with income possibilities were both involved. The possibility also of supplementary sources of income, either in subsidiary employments, hobbies, more fortunate relatives, or children of earning age, cannot be overlooked as a resource for avoiding the worst effects upon family stability.

### Size of Family.

The stability of the family is obviously more secure in those families whose self-maintenance skills and resources are adapted to the kind of problems presented by unemployment. The same thing can be said with respect to the adaptation of the pattern of family life to the hazard of in-

terrupted income and to a disorganization of the division
of labor. It was early noticed that marked changes in the
existing degree of stability over long periods of unemployment were more likely to occur in small than in large families. Likewise the process of reorganization was likely to
begin earlier in the latter case. The reasons back of this
phenomenon are not wholly correlated in a causal way with
the size of the family. The larger families were likely to be
living on a lower standard of living and hence have less readjustment to effect before community resources were
available. The relief allowances when they did arrive were
scheduled according to the size of the family and hence frequently provided resources not far from those previously
available. Large families were likely to have several supplementary earners whose contributions to the family purse
could be increased. The ties which bound the family together were less likely to depend to so large a degree on
expenditures. A number of minds frequently produced more
ideas about alternative earning possibilities.

Although the changes were more marked in the smaller
families over a period of time, they were less immediately
felt. Small families could cut on many semiluxuries before
getting to basic essentials. If therefore the small family
could have its earning power restored quickly, little change
was noted in its stability. If that event was postponed, however, the changes were ultimately more marked and the re-
vival more tardy.

### Extent of Mutual Activities.

Another element in the pattern of family life is the extent
of mutual activities. The more numerous these were and
the more of them which did not depend on expenditures
the less vulnerable the family appeared to be to the changes
which the impact of unemployment enforced. The conclusion of students of family life that the reality of the family
is to be found in the bonds of interrelationships between

members is demonstrated in this fact. The family is a functioning institution. Its members are bound together by their mutual activities. The greater the number of these which are not premised entirely on expenditures, the larger the core of the institution and the more likely it is to retain its form under the necessity of curtailing these relationships from lack of funds.

### Dependence on Expenditures.

The family whose services to members and whose member satisfactions are not primarily dependent on expenditures is likewise in a better position to withstand the onslaughts of unemployment. The reason for this is obvious.

### Rigidity of Family Roles.

Severe problems of adjustment were presented in those families in which the roles of the husband and wife were rigidly defined and the authority pattern was distinctly based on this specialization of function. All our informants had some conception of "men's work" and "women's work," but the boundaries of such functions were less rigidly set in some cases than in others. Particularly in those cases (chiefly foreign-American families) in which the cultural heritage reinforced distinct boundary lines, unemployment with its disturbance to the division of labor and management brought a change the adjustment to which was not easy. The acceptance of a revised status was particularly difficult for the man in the family, and his resistance to that change clouded the family relations for a considerable time. American families of skilled workmen in which there had been a blurring of functions in earning, in domestic tasks, in parental authority, and in responsibility for planning family activities and relationships, had least trouble in maintaining the stability of family organization in this respect.

## Family Standards.

The effect of relative family standards on the retention or renewal of stability is not clear. Again the factor which seems most crucial in preventing any clear-cut conclusion is the length of time out of work. Families whose previous standard of living had been relatively high, who had a conception of themselves as a "high-class family" maintaining standards, codes, and responsibilities appropriate to that status, and who were in possession of many symbols, material and otherwise, testifying to that status fought most energetically to postpone any departure from that status. If unemployment were ended soon, the stability of the family was unimpaired. But such a family went through tortures and frustrations if unemployment were long continued which were unknown to families with lower standards in these respects. This is perhaps merely to say that "the higher the climb, the harder the fall." The very memories of a status formerly achieved and now lost added irritations disruptive of family stability in all its aspects. Another relevant factor was that the "higher" the families' standards the more they were dependent upon expenditures of money, the more the symbols of family status were likely to be of a material nature, hence the more vulnerable to the primary feature of unemployment—the interruption of money income.

## Extra-Family Relations.

In an interdependent urban community extrafamily relations are an important source of intrafamily stability. Close and helpful integration with the clan is equally useful in urban and rural communities. Greatest resources were had in this respect by Jewish and Italian families, least by Irish-American and "old American" families. Such resources go beyond the availability of financial aid. Even more important at times is the assistance in straightening out difficulties of personal relationship and those connected with sub-stitutes for mutual activities curtailed for lack of funds. Contacts with friends and with community institutions were significant not only because of their value in job hunting, but also because of their potentialities for activi-ties which "took the mind off" the problems of unemploy-ment, and because of the pressure exerted by these groups toward the maintenance by the family of its standing in the community. Again, however, if these contacts could be maintained only by the expenditure of money so that they must be curtailed, the resultant amputation of the rela-tionships which formed a part of the complex of family life raised real obstacles to the restoration of family stability. In this connection it is interesting to observe that the fami-lies who had been most mobile in the past, had pulled up their roots frequently and reëstablished themselves among new associates, reorganized themselves most easily among new acquaintances and in contact with new institutions. Like trees occasionally transplanted, their root systems had become better adapted to a renewal of growth in new soil.

### Miscellaneous Factors.

We have finally to mention several miscellaneous charac-teristics of family members which were helpful in recon-structing the stability of the family. The value of good health should be obvious because of the lessened necessity of medical service, because of the vitality provided for meeting new problems, and because of the physical foun-dation required to reduce worry and the tendency to con-flict in the midst of fresh difficulties. The quality of aggres-siveness was useful if successful, troublesome if aggressive efforts ended in failure. Pride was a useful stimulus in the early attempts to escape a decline in family standards, a handicap to any inevitable need for reorganization on the basis of lowered standards, a factor likely to prolong the period of instability and disorganization. Probably most useful in every period of unemployment were the ability to rationalize, a willingness to modify goals in accordance with realistic possibilities, the tendency to accept the present on its own terms, and inventiveness.

*Summary: Factors Contributing to Family Stability.*

These tentative conclusions should not be taken as an indication that I am proposing that workers would be better off to court a frequent change in jobs, periods of unemployment, misfortunes, large families, mobility, low family standards, lack of pride, constant rationalization, and a tendency to accept fate and to rationalize misfortunes, in order to be better prepared for possible unemployment. I am making or implying no proposals at all. I am merely pointing out the conclusions from the observation of the adjustments of twenty-four families over a period of years checked by our questioning of a sample group of two hundred families unemployed for varying lengths of time, and indicating the factors which in these cases contributed to stability or instability of the family unit.

Certain it is that the problems of unemployment are different from those of employment. Successfully to surmount the obstacles to family stability during a period of no work and earnings requires many items of equipment and skills not equally useful during periods of work. The tests of fitness to survive under both circumstances are in some respects the same, but in many respects different. Certainly additional techniques are required when the normal pattern of self-maintenance is destroyed. It is not surprising therefore to find that frequently families whose characteristics are not judged as socially acceptable under the assumptions of full employment demonstrate their ability to survive the challenge which unemployment raises to family stability. Nor is it surprising to learn that some of the tactics they develop, particularly with respect to getting the maximum assistance from relief agencies, are judged by their effectiveness in solving the problems of the present rather than by their consistency with the standards of the family's past. If we expect men to behave and live according to the standards of a working world, they must be a part of a working world.

We have given ample attention to the negative effects of unemployment on the stability of the family. No one can share intimately the affairs of unemployed families and escape the tremendous impact of interrupted earnings and jobs on the structure of family life which is based on these foundations in a monetary, wage-system economy. We would not minimize these negative effects. But that same observation of the way the family meets unemployment produces another conclusion of equal importance. The family has vast resources for meeting the strain. The institution survives, though its structure and practice are altered. Nor is it too much to say that the family's ability to readjust and survive is the dominant impression which we carry with us from this examination of the families in their battle with unemployment.

The family cannot forever remain disorganized. A rearrangement in status, authority, and function among the several members takes place and is accepted. Time dims the memory of the former character of these. The novelty and conflicts inherent in new earning ventures wear off, and new experiences involved in all adjustments present fresh subjects of interest and new personal problems for common consideration. Routine is reëstablished. Discipline finds a new basis in habitual practice and relations. Cheaper ways of reëstablishing ritual and restoring symbols of family unity are found. Criticisms wear out. Decisions which were a constant source of conflict are made, and the family settles down to life on the basis of living arrangements resulting from these decisions. The decisions slowly reduce the area of adjustment to manageable proportions, and energy becomes sufficient to the task.

A most effective factor in the reorganization process is the functional interaction in solving new difficulties or meeting old problems in a new way. This is an attention-absorbing occupation, and in its doing new bonds of relationship are established, new qualities are revealed in the coöperating members which become the foundation stones of the reconstructed institution.

### Unemployment an Occasional Stimulus to Solidarity.

Nor can we escape the fact that unemployment itself frequently acts as a stimulus to a more successful organization of family life than formerly existed. Occasional examples of this development stand out in our records. An authority relationship in which realities were inconsistent with cultural expectancies is clarified. New responsibilities placed upon older children have frequently stirred them to more faithful and energetic action contributing to the family welfare. Families were forced to move to a new neighborhood or community, which move freed them from factors irritating to stable relations. These adjustments certainly could have been made without the stimulus of unemployment. But they had not been made until the necessities of unemployment forced them.

### The Basis of Family Strength.

The family has within itself great sources of strength for survival because it is furnishing human beings with an adjustment to many of their needs which can be satisfied in no other way. It can survive unemployment because it must survive if the individuals are to continue to derive these benefits from it. Individuals cannot join a new family or lead a minority defection for the establishment of a new institution.

These resources for survival are the chief factors upon which the community must depend for the maintenance during unemployment of its basic economic and social institution. We have already demonstrated that the two major problems, lack of income and lack of jobs, are amenable to reduction through the assistance of unemployment insurance benefits geared to the size of the family and sufficient to keep families off direct relief, and through work relief whose standards of production and industrial relations approximate as closely as possible to those of high-standard private employment. As long as private employment continues to be the only or the chief culturally accepted form of self-maintenance opportunity, of course, less than perfect results may be anticipated from the partnership of these stop-gap devices with the forces working for stability within the family itself.

# SECTION III

## ALLEGED DECAY OF SELF-RELIANCE:
## A SUMMARY

## X

## UNEMPLOYMENT: A BARRIER BEFORE
## THE WORKER'S GOALS

DISQUIETING statements are frequently made that the unemployed are losing their self-reliance. Individual initiative and foresight, it is claimed, are being replaced by a
growing dependence for support upon others, and in particular upon government; a permanently dependent class
is developing. Unquestionably, evidence can be found to
indicate that some families have ceased to be self-supporting and show very little promise of regaining that status.
Generalization from such evidence, however, is likely to be
misleading. A more careful analysis of the process by which
families reach this stage and of the factors which retard or
expedite the change is desirable before generalizations are
made. Certainly any remedy for the decay of self-reliance
must depend upon such analysis.

I wish to conclude this study with an attempt to bring
what evidence we have to focus on this important problem.
This evidence should be considered in the light of the conclusions of the preceding section that, under the impact of
unemployment, families go through several stages of adjustment in the attempt to maintain their independence.
These stages may be likened to the stages of the fight the
physical organism makes against disease and toward the renewal of healthy functioning. Almost as soon as the family
is attacked by the disease of unemployment, the restora-
tive process is set in motion aimed at the renewal of
the ability of the family to fulfill its economic and social
functions. Just as in the case of physical disease the body
sometimes cannot throw off completely the malady and
must continue life in a disabled condition, so in the case of

this economic disease the family does not always completely recover. Yet effective remedial action is dependent in both cases upon coöperation with the normal processes of renewal generated within the organism under treatment. The family is like an organism in this respect at least, that under the stress of the attack made upon its institutional health by unemployment it does develop adjustments which attempt to restore that health.

### The Problem of Defining and Measuring Self-Reliance.

To make a judgment as to whether in going through this process of adjustment workers and their families have lost that quality known as self-reliance is difficult. No one has yet been able to devise an objective measurement for this quality. It is not something visible to the eye, the quantity of which can be measured. One may count those who are on relief and even make a subjective estimate as to the strength or weakness of their desire to support themselves once more. But if that desire appears weak, is he justified in assuming that they have *lost* their self-reliance? How many of them had any large amount of it to lose? Even if one had any confidence in such an assumption, how open to error must be a further judgment that some one factor —say relief or work relief—had caused this change in character!

Even if we were to assume that anyone who applied for relief had lost his self-reliance, public policy and the public attitudes which underlie the giving of relief will profit by a consideration of the incentives to self-reliance which workers bring with them to unemployment, the effect of the readjustments they make (including relief and relief work) on those incentives, the tools of self-support they have acquired in training, customary practices, and foresight, and the self-initiated efforts they make to maintain themselves independent of, and even with the assistance of, community support.

### Basis of Variation in Self-Reliance Before Unemployment.[1]

Not all workers enter a period of unemployment with the same amount of incentive to self-reliance. The first three of the goals we have indicated workers strive to reach furnish stimuli toward the achievement of that status, for self-reliance is an essential part of the definition of these goals. The majority of *socially respected* roles assume a job and self-support. *Economic security* does not involve maintenance guaranteed by others, but that won by one's own efforts. A minimum requirement for an *increasing degree of control* over one's own affairs is a job and an income which one may spend as he chooses. The general character of the goals which workers seek to reach is similar. All want to perform in a *socially respected* role: to be a producer, the holder of a "swell" job, a fellow his mates look to, a thrifty man, a good provider, a man who never lets his family down, the good father of successful kids. *Economic security* means to all a successful achievement of the standard of living customary among one's associates, some hope of lifting that standard to the level of those just beyond one in economic fortune, regularity of income, a comfortable margin of resources beyond mere maintenance, evidence of some progress from the point at which one started, and a sufficient "gearing in" to community relations and institutions so that one is assured of the friendly concern of others in meeting his economic problems. Obtaining *an increasing measure of control* over one's own affairs meant to all an enlarging of the area of life in which one's own decisions determined the outcome of one's efforts and a decreasing of the area in which others had a controlling voice.

1. Following is a summary of chap. i of *The Unemployed Worker*, Yale University Press, New Haven, 1940. Supporting evidence for the generalizations in this section will be found in the indicated chapters of this volume.

But the strength of these goals as incentives to self-reliance varied in accordance with the objective content given them by the experience out of which the worker came to the company of the unemployed.[2] The goals were built out of the actual possibilities available to the workers. They represented no utopian hopes. They were visible on the horizon of the workers' world, and the distance to that horizon was closely related to the nature of the terrain over which the worker must travel in pursuit of them. That terrain was not the same for all workers and each was inclined so to define his objectives that they would not be impossible of achievement *for him*.

True, there are similarities in the problems with which all workers must deal and these similar problems have set general limits to what workers as a group can hope to achieve. The roles in which a worker can perform are limited to those available to wage earners, and to those the trappings for which can be purchased with a wage earner's income. A few may qualify for other roles by getting out of the working class, but the great majority must find their satisfaction in the activities, relationships, and institutions customary among workers. Satisfaction is possible. Work itself keeps a man "normal"; many have kept their families fairly comfortable; a few gain distinction as skillful workers among their associates and as leaders in activities of interest to their own group; many are proud of their connection with particular firms; some are aware of the social usefulness of their work; all are producers. But rewards are doled out in small parcels and satisfaction is extensively possible only by modification of goals so that they are consistent with the possible achievements within a working-class world.

Work-for-another-for-wages is the worker's lot, and who can deny that he who sells his labor for a price must ultimately depend upon the decision of a buyer? Almost at the

2. The following is a summary of chaps. ii, iii, iv, and v, *ibid*.

beginning of their working careers a large number of workers learned that their choice was not the primary determi-
nant of the work they were to do. The most interesting fact
revealed by questions about ambitions was that both those
who had and those who had not any real occupational goal
were eventually distributed in about equal proportions
over all the occupations. There was little relation between
wanting a particular job at the beginning of one's working
life and getting that job later on. That the demand for labor, the accident of fathers' or friends' occupations, rather
than personal choice, determines the job channel into which
these workers' energies flowed is clear. Very few actually
chose their jobs with a planned future in mind. Those who
did stood less than an even chance of following where their
plans led. Even in this important matter of the selection of
an occupation, the worker's decision was not the controlling factor, unless the decision to take what was available,
rather than do nothing, may be considered a controlling
one. How is one to believe that his own decisions are important during his working years in the face of examples
of "pull" and "luck," and in the presence of little understood but powerful impersonal economic events that sweep
upon him almost without warning and rob him of his job?

The response to this practical control "from another
world," as one of them put it, has an important bearing on
the sort of attitude with which the worker approaches the
adjustments to unemployment. He has already had some
practice in rationalizing personal failure and frustration
by reference to the causal factors he does not control.
"Good luck" or "bad luck" has long since actively entered
his explanatory vocabulary. The usefulness of personal
planning has already been seriously questioned on many
occasions. He has become accustomed to watching for evidence that he has satisfied or displeased someone whose
decision as to his fate *does* count.

The degree of economic security he can hope to have is

also limited by the problems peculiar to working-class life. Wages earned roughly in proportion to his usefulness to someone else are designated in our culture as the proper and acceptable means for buying as much of a "living" as possible. His usefulness to another bears little necessary relation, however, to his "living" needs. After meeting the basic physical necessities, the margin left for "bettering" himself and his family is small. He has modified that goal to fit the possibilities of reaching it. The "living" he has been able to buy is in many cases uncomfortably close to the minimum of sustenance which the community feels obligated to supply if the worker can find no job. The latter situation is frequent; irregular earnings present him with a constant problem.

Hanging over every day's satisfactions in meeting a hard problem successfully are many other clouds which at any moment may turn into black storm clouds containing the power to destroy what economic security he has been able to gain for himself and his family. The possibilities that machines or women may get his job; that the pace of work may prove him unqualified; that an accident may decrease his earning power; that old age, as industry counts age, may creep on him before his time, are ever present. What workers mean by "getting ahead," is made real by the possibilities remaining after these obstacles are overcome. It is not surprising that something lower than the sky is the limit of their ambitions: enough to keep the family on the standard familiar to workers; enough to keep out of debt; enough to provide for a rainy day and, if possible, to remain semi-independent when working days are over; enough to make contacts with friends and institutions which one can count on in time of difficulty.

The need for constantly revising goals in the presence of such factors is thoroughly damaging to one of the basic assumptions in American culture that a person "gets ahead" in proportion to his skill and effort and foresight.

The struggle with such forces does not develop an enthusiastic desire for work, nor an intense loyalty to the dispensers of work, nor an exceptional concern for the preservation of all the economic and political arrangements in the midst of which work is carried on. But it does produce a dogged determination to hold on to what one has and a persistent desire to make the best of what is, and, if possible, to do a little better than that. Whatever desire to work hard and to be self-reliant may exist, does not for the majority grow out of any stimulating exceptional success in making progress toward these goals. It grows out of the fact that if any progress at all is to be made or even if present gains are to be held, a job and self-support are necessary.

Financial resources are necessary in order to achieve all these goals, however modified. But the fact that one *works* for those resources is equally necessary. It is to be noted that even if cash equivalent to the standard of living customary among one's associates were guaranteed to a man, the achievement of his limited goals is premised on the holding of a job. If the goals men work for could remain unmodified during the entire period of unemployment, the danger that income without work would appear a satisfactory basis for adjustment would be meager indeed even for the lowest paid unskilled workers. For those whose wages and skill had made possible success at a higher level, still further removed from adjustment to life on a minimum of resources, the danger is of course even more remote.

### Attack of Unemployment on the Bases for Self-Reliance.

Unfortunately, the possibilities for reaching these goals is still more limited when a man is unemployed and the tendency to escape frustration by a modification of goals is ever present. Unemployment is merely an intensification of the hurdles which already block the path of the worker. Ir-

regular work, fluctuating wages, are altogether too familiar an experience to the worker to come as a stunning interruption to steady and satisfactory progress toward these
goals. This statement is no attempt to minimize the effects
of unemployment. Rather it is an indication that those effects which the popular mind reserves for periods of so-
called unemployment are familiar experiences for workers
whose margin of economic independence is not great.

The futility of pretending, when the search for a job is
extended, that one continues to play the roles designated
as respected in the world of labor should be obvious.[3] "A
producer," "the holder of a swell job," "a fellow your
mates look to," "a good provider," "a man who never lets
his family down" are clearly not terms which describe the
man who is wandering from gate to gate begging for a
chance to work. He may be a good fellow among work
seekers, but their opinion of him is not the desired basis for
social status. He is only a sojourner in the company of the
work seekers, his real affinity is with workers. Public recognition that the unemployed are without work through no
fault of their own may salve the hurt for a time. But "a
fellow who deserves our sympathy" is not a description of
the sort of person he wants to be. Such public attitude
toward men with no jobs may make rationalization easier,
and if he does not succeed in recapturing his status as a
producer, may help to ease the transition and enable him
to redefine his goals with less mental pain than might otherwise attend the process. But his whole experience in trying
to measure up to the standards of his working-class associates cries out against the acceptance of anything less
than reinstatement to those roles, the desire for which he
shares with them. The necessity of lowering the standards
of working conditions and wages which are acceptable to
him is fatal evidence to himself as well as to his former associates on the job that "he is slipping."

3. Following is a summary of part of chaps. viii and ix, *ibid.*

Every week he fails to supply the china pitcher with a pay envelope increases his awareness that economic security is escaping him more completely. Nor do the earnings of other members of the family restore his confidence, for he, after all, is head of the family and responsible for its continued well-being.

Most seriously attacked is his desire to control his own affairs. If the belief that his own qualities and decisions were an important determiner of his own destiny could scarcely survive while he was working, how much chance does it have to survive when he is "pounding pavements"? The thing which he seeks is another's to give or withhold. Nothing he can do now will overcome the fact that he lacks the training for a specific job, that "depression opportunists" are "picking off" the jobs he might have had, that firms are taking back only their own men, and that thousands of others like himself are after the jobs that only a few can hope to get. If his search continues unsuccessfully for a long enough period, he will realize that he "doesn't have what it takes," knowledge of the techniques of job hunting, knowledge of available openings, friends who have "pull," an appearance of "not being licked" when he applies for a job. Anyone who "doesn't have what it takes" is certainly fooling himself if he retains any faith in his own ability to be master of his own affairs. He can do something about some of these problems. He can learn from his own experience and from his fellow work seekers about the methods of "running down" work. He can cultivate the "grapevine" news service or visit the Employment Service to learn of possible jobs. He can ask his friends to "speak for him." He can put on a bold front when he asks for a job. But when he has done all this and still cannot "land" a job, what must happen to his faith that what he does is important in the determination of his success or failure? The "iron legions" of economic forces beyond his control must have appeared to the unemployed with renewed emphasis as the real determiners of how he and his family should live.

The efforts of the family to stretch what income they can scrape together retard still further the progress toward previously established objectives.[4] The external evidences symbolic of his role as the successful head of a family are diminished. Those families which had achieved the most obvious symbols of material success found readjustment to the reduced expenditures most difficult. These possessions had become an integral component of their conception of their own worth. Their standing in the community was evidenced by such possessions. The memory of their former status survived long to plague them and to discourage them as one by one the symbols were reduced in potency or completely sacrificed. Acceptance of the new situation was held up for such families longer than in the case of families who possessed fewer outward symbols of success. This acceptance of the need for readjustment on a lower plane of living must precede active and wholehearted attempts to develop means and techniques consistent with actual possibilities. The postponement of that decision usually meant that when such a family did finally recognize the necessity for rebuilding at a different level of life, they were loaded with a burden of debt larger than that of the others who adjusted quickly. Credit and loans had been extended beyond the amounts used by the others in the attempt to maintain possession of the symbols of their former success. Although every attempt is made to save the children from the effects of radical expenditure adjustments, the efforts cannot be successful enough, if unemployment continues for long, to undergird the father's status as "a good provider." Eventually the contacts with associates from whom comes the social recognition desired must be broken; and even if they were maintained the evidence in deterioration of home furnishings, in change of neighborhood, in the cur-

4. Following is a summary of part of chap. x, *ibid.*

tailment of social-front expenditures would result in a negative judgment indicating failure.

The evidences of success in winning a margin of economic security, savings, insurance, and home ownership are eventually exchanged for evidence in the form of debts and loans that one is working from behind. The reduction of social contacts reduces this source of economic security. Even before friendly associations have been curtailed, they have been exploited to the limit and without successful results.

The qualification that economic security shall be won by independent efforts has to be modified. When independent resources are inadequate, the worker resorts to a series of sources of support which, although they do not challenge seriously his status as a self-supporting person, still do prepare the way for his acceptance of forms of assistance which do. Loans from friends and family, debts to landlord and grocer, gifts from several sources are in this category. Since he normally makes use of these possibilities before applying for relief, experience has modified somewhat his original conception of independence before he is forced to make the final declaration of his dependency.

Control is certainly not synonymous with the emergency character of the decisions made on expenditure during the first stages of unemployment. When some degree of planning has been reëstablished, the plans control a pattern of expenditure on a much lower plane of living.

### Attack of Relief Experiences on the Worker's Goals.

Every goal he seeks to reach as a normal worker recedes further from realization when he turns to relief.[5] Until that moment he could in a measure realize that even without current earnings the efforts he had made in the past in the role of a "producer," a "good provider," a "good father"

5. Following is a summary of part of chaps. xii and xiii, *ibid.*

were still contributing to the support of his family. But now he has made a public declaration of his failure, and no rationalization can quite cover up the fact that a "reliefer" is not among those roles which his associates respect. We have seen that shifting public attitudes and altered associations may modify the disgrace involved in this conviction. But such modification does not restore him to the social position demanded by cultural standards.

The goal of economic security which as a worker he was striving for included a margin of safety not present in relief maintenance. It included items beyond food, shelter, and heat permitted to him by maximum relief allowances. It included provision for "a rainy day" and for his old age. It included the awareness that all of these were provided by his own effort. That goal has to be modified with a severity proportional to his previous success in climbing above the plane of mere physical existence.

The most serious damage is done, however, to the goal of control over his own affairs. We need not list again the numerous ways in which, when income depends not upon an evaluation of services but on an assessment of need, the last vestige of control slips from his hands. The worker on relief strives to surmount the high barriers and renew progress toward his goals. He rationalizes his status, and if no improvement can be made accepts the inevitable lowering of the objectives he had worked for. He seeks companions whose standards with respect to social roles are consistent with his own possibilities. He develops appropriate practices to deal with the realistic problems he faces in maintenance from relief sources; and through these practices, if successful, he gains some renewal of faith that he still exercises a measure of control.

Unless, however, he can find a job for wages or hit upon a successful independent venture, his goals must be modified drastically. If that event is postponed too long, the attempt to reach those goals formerly considered "proper" may not seem worth the price, and his attention becomes focused on those objectives possible under his present circumstances. This conviction is likely to come most easily to him from whom the symbols of former success, savings account, insurance, home ownership, comfortable furnishing, etc., have been taken, for as long as some of these are still in his possession they are reminders of the possibility that the present experience is merely a most difficult interruption of his progress. The man "who keeps his chin and his eyes up" after "losing everything" makes good copy for storybook writers; but he does not represent the persistent tendency in the behavior of the unemployed people on relief with whom we were in touch. The loss of the symbols of a measure of success was usually the signal for the modification of goals in order that possible effort might not have to fall too far short of them.

### Effect of Work Relief on the Worker's Goals.

Before the unemployed worker can have a W.P.A. job he must be certified as in need by an agency of direct relief.[6] He has already experienced, therefore, all of the factors present in this original investigation which interrupt his progress toward the goals he seeks. Some workers have been on direct relief for a time and all know from the reported experience of others what the experience means. The reaction to work relief and its benefits is colored by the contrast of this form of assistance with direct relief. Comparatively the former has much to offer. A closer approximation to the possibility of occupying a socially respected role is offered. Particularly for the unskilled this basis for a livelihood is not greatly different from that provided in private employment. In so far as being a producer of useful things; being a person who goes to work daily for wages and has an employer; being a person who has money

6. Following is a summary of part of chap. xv, *ibid.*

of his own, the spending of which is his own business; and being the family's breadwinner are the marks of a normal worker, he finds his status considerably improved, for work relief makes the playing of these roles possible.

When compared with private employment, however, many of the factors lending satisfaction to such effort are lacking. How does this job stand in the eyes of the community and, in particular, in the eyes of his associates among the workers in comparison with "regular work"? Certainly relief work is not rated as a "swell job" by anyone. If the project does not produce what is socially useful, if the quality of the work is poor, and the supervision inefficient, the job provides the holder with little prestige among his mates whose judgment is the foundation for his status as a worker. On the other hand, work on projects which turn out products of recognized value and which are well done and efficiently managed increases his prestige standing among his fellows. On the whole it is difficult for relief work in these respects to compete with jobs initiated and managed under private auspices. For the most part the relief-work projects in the New Haven area were recognized as useful to the community. There are, however, limits to the number of such projects which can be undertaken without supplanting normal government work or without competing in the area normally reserved for private enterprise. We need not recapitulate here the problems involved in keeping the quality of work high and providing efficient supervision on relief-work projects. As we have seen, some of those factors making for poor quality of product and inefficiency of operation are all but inherent in work relief. Such factors are the quality of labor available, the continual withdrawal of the most competent workers into private jobs, the difficulty of rewarding good and punishing bad work through promotion on the one hand and discharge on the other, the necessity for timing of projects to meet the gaps in private employment (undertaken under the most favorable circumstances of weather), the arrangement of work schedules and routine for a constantly shifting proportion of skills (particularly if going wage rates are to be maintained by adjustment in hours), the nonavailability of the best supervisory personnel who are retained by private industry. Certain factors, such as political appointments to "gravy jobs" and the quality of supervision, are subject to correction. If a direct relief system were realistically available to support those discharged from relief work, negative incentives might be more thoroughly applied. Larger allotments for the purchase of equipment and materials would remove one of the major difficulties in efficient work scheduling. Yet when all possible improvements have been made, work relief will offer men superior opportunity to appear before their fellows in a role which is respected only by comparison with the marginal jobs offered by private enterprise, and with the definitely inferior status available to one on direct relief.

Possibly the economic security provided by work relief can also be considered superior only by such comparison. Certainly by comparison with resources available from direct relief those from W.P.A. have for all but the largest families been more adequate. Yet in a community in which 42 per cent of the incomes are less than $1,000 a year, relief wages which would amount to between $780 and $1,116 must have supplied many families with an amount of cash closely approximating their usual income.

As important as income in the production of economic security is the development or retention of skills and abilities. Our testimony revealed an appreciation among the unemployed that their general physical fitness but not their specific skills had been maintained. Men with special skills frequently complained that a period on work relief had actually dulled those skills. This criticism did not come from the unskilled. It is to be remembered also that the latter bulked large among those needing relief work, and that at least some of the skilled were for various reasons facing anyway the necessity for making a living at unskilled work.

Work habits are given some support by relief work, more of course than by the condition of idleness attendant upon the receipt of direct relief. Whether or not the soldiering on the job frequently observed on relief-work projects is damaging to the willingness to exert the effort and speed required by private enterprise is a debatable question. No one can deny that soldiering takes place. We have tried to indicate some reasons for that state of affairs. The reasons may help us to understand the phenomenon, but not to escape its consequences. The only evidence of results beyond the "it stands to reason" type that we could bring to bear on this matter was the report of those employers who had hired former W.P.A., and C.C.C. workers, and who had found no particular difficulty in gearing them in to the production requirements of their firms.

In general, then, our conclusion is that of the possible relief measures available after men have exhausted their own resources, relief work does offer a comparatively adequate degree of economic security, so adequate in fact that it compares favorably with that offered by a considerable number of jobs in private industry held by those "fortunate" enough to be employed.

The most clear-cut contrast between direct and work relief is found in the degree of control which the beneficiary has over his own affairs. After the first investigation of his circumstances, his wages are his own. He may spend them as he chooses. No lady case worker shares the responsibility for the family's decisions. He selects his own grocer and landlord. He does not have to adapt his own desires to the opinion of an outsider as to what is "proper" for a public dependent. His control is by no means complete and, in comparison with the tactics assumed to be appropriate for one who has private employment, it is extremely limited.

It is difficult to see how this situation could be altered, short of a thoroughgoing recognition by the public of the government as an employer undertaking productive enterprise fully comparable in importance to that undertaken by private employers, and under essentially the same conditions of selection and rejection of men on the basis of their proved usefulness in carrying on the work.

## XI

## UNEMPLOYMENT MODIFIES THE WORKER'S TECHNIQUES

EVERY worker brings with him to a period of unemployment not only a stock of incentives to self-reliance, but also a deposit of experience in the form of training, customary practices, and foresight which furnish him with equipment for being self-reliant. Again we note considerable variation in this stock of experience, yet that of most workers can be distinguished from that possessed by more favored economic groups.

### The Worker's Resources in Techniques and Foresight.

What techniques they have developed for mastering the problems of self-maintenance through work and management of expenditures were learned chiefly on the job.[1] Four fifths of our informants among the two hundred unemployed in the sample survey of New Haven families had no formal schooling beyond the eighth grade. They had left school not only because their earnings were needed but because that was the accepted practice and the procedure thought to be most practical for those intending to become industrial workers. More schooling was not considered necessary or particularly useful. Over half of them were trained "on the job" with no particular relationship to apprenticeship or special training. A total of 96 per cent of all unemployed in the sample had been trained by connection with industry or business alone. The remainder had had some preliminary training in trade or commercial school. The economics which they learned was in the "school of

1. Following is a summary of chap. vi, *ibid.*

hard knocks" and the result of induction from personal experience. The typical worker had acquired this experience
within the walls of many factory schools. For over one half
the average job lasted for five years or less; for nearly
three fourths, less than eight years.

Whatever foresight they had learned in the expenditure
of their incomes was adapted to the distribution of meager
funds over a multitude of necessities. Only 3 per cent of
our informants had family incomes of $1,500 or over in
their "best" years prior to this period of unemployment.
Certain self-maintenance practices have been developed
among workers which have become so customary that they
are carried over into economic behavior even when the
basic foundation of a job for wages on which they are built
is removed. Long familiarity with these practices has bred
expectancies that they will be exploited to the limit by the
workers before seeking for new avenues of maintaining life.

First among these is the expectancy that a family takes
care of its own. The male head of the family is the chief
breadwinner, and his status in the family and in the community is geared to the fact that all other earners shall be
supplementary. The earning of children is common among
over half of the working-class families but involves an expectancy either that the money will be used for personal
"extras," or that upon marriage their parents will "set
them up." Woman's place is distinctly "in the home," not
in the shop save in cases of emergency. The distribution of
funds for the meeting of family requirements, however, is
the wife's task. The decisions involved in the fulfillment
thereof give her an important economic role which is much
amplified in importance when customary earnings are reduced. When it is recalled that after the absolutely necessary items of rent, heat, light, and transportation are deducted from an income of $1,000 (a maximum for most of
our informants) all that remained would provide only
12½ c. per person per meal for a family of five, the size of

her job will be realized. And that is reckoning without the expenditures necessary for clothes, household equipment, health, education, benevolence, insurance, and other protection against "a rainy day."

Given a job and the distribution of labor in providing and distributing the income therefrom, workers develop realistic forms of foresight adapted to their way of life.[2] Consideration of these forms and the problems faced in developing them must precede any discussion of the effect of unemployment or unemployment benefits or relief on them. It is the workers' own forms of foresight that are affected, not those of another economic class.

When these practices are examined, they are found among workers to have distinctive characteristics. They are adapted of course to a wage-earning economy. They are defensive rather than aggressive in nature. They are forced rather than chosen foresight.

Many problems arise to plague workers in the practice of foresight. Two practices, each of which seems equally wise, are often not only opposed but mutually exclusive. Rewards are not always proportional to effort expended. Virtue must be its own reward. Tangible rewards are not always sufficiently frequent to overcome the effect of plans proved useless. Rewards are not certain and frequently not worth the price. Observation of the successes and failures about one does not add excessive enthusiasm to any unusual practice of foresight.

The bearing of all this upon the effects of unemployment and relief measures upon such qualities of workers is clear. Men cannot lose more than they actually have of foresight. They do practice foresight, but it bears the stamp of its working-class origin and any change in practice must be measured against such a standard of customary behavior for the group in question.

2. Following is a summary of chap. vii, *ibid.*

### The Attempt To Use Customary Techniques.

Faced with a problem more intense and exaggerated than, but in many respects similar to, a familiar problem, the worker turns first to his experience and exploits those methods which have heretofore proved passingly successful. There will be, of course, great variations between individuals both as to the quantity and serviceability of their experience and as to the tenacity with which they hold to the hope that they can master the situation by the use of familiar techniques.

Only after such devices have failed to prevent the sacrifice of standards the worker is loath to relinquish, will he turn to unfamiliar devices ranging from capitulation to complete dependence on relief to intensified aggressiveness in the form of radical activity. Any social action which can prolong this period of attempted use of past experience will postpone both the hauling down of the workers' colors and the substitution therefor of either the white or the red flag. Indeed the dependence on customary techniques is so strong and the period of struggle to survive by their use so prolonged, that the worker is more than likely to be exhausted by the attempt and come to the end of familiar alternatives with no strength or enthusiasm left to follow a new and untried suggested path of action. Yet the process of adapting means to ends must go on and the record of that process will indicate the new meaning with which appropriate activities during unemployment imbue the phrase "self-reliance."

### Development of New Techniques: Job-Hunting and Earning.

Job-hunting is a job in itself.[3] As we have seen, most workers have felt the necessity of learning how to go about it. This was not the first contact with unemployment. They

3. Following is a summary of a part of chaps. viii and ix, *ibid.*

came to this period of no work with some experience. Yet
the methods they had developed showed very little origi-
nality or inventiveness. They had evolved no familiar
manual of tactics which, if followed, would guarantee success. It would be pleasant to report that unemployed workers faced with this "job" developed a set of practices which
might be summarized to form such a manual. But even
those with previous experience could scarcely be called
skilled in the venture, if skill is to be judged by the measure of success. They were conditioned to conceive of jobs
in terms of work offered by an employer. They therefore
sought to find an employer and to impress him through all
available and customary channels with their qualifications.
They learned to overcome somewhat their lack of knowledge of the labor market by conversations with all possible
informants, by following the news, by registering at the
employment service, by gate-to-gate applications. They exploited the good offices of any friends or acquaintances who
might be useful. But if these customary practices did not
succeed, very few invented new ones. We have reported
the inventions of some. But we cannot fairly ascribe such
initiative to the great majority.

The training which makes a man useful on the job is of
little value in furnishing techniques when the "job" is a
search for work. This is especially true of the "one-firm"
men. Naturally the men who had been most mobile, and in
particular the building tradesmen who had been continually
in search of work, had developed the most successful techniques of job-hunting. Moreover, those with a one-firm record extending say more than five years were inclined to
place undue reliance upon being called back to that firm.

Employment for others creates very little imagination as
to what a man may do "on his own" when no one can use
him. The men who displayed most initiative and inventiveness in finding new work were not always the "best" men
from the point of view of steady work. Techniques are

learned from experience. Techniques in job-hunting are learned from hunting jobs.

Certainly it did not enter the heads of any but a limited few that they might create jobs by undertaking an independent venture. The efforts of these few make interesting stories, but they are not the typical response of New Haven workers to the loss of an employer.

Men who failed to find jobs after the most intensive and energetic personal efforts did not have their faith in the usefulness of their own planning and activity increased. More than occasionally when a job finally was obtained the effective agent was some other person or circumstance. Contemplation of cause and effect in such experiences increased the conviction of many that personal initiative had relatively little to do with final success in finding work.

However, enough of them succeeded in their search for work, even though what they found was of the casual or odd-job nature, so that families as a group still found their major source of income to be earnings of the head of the family at other than his regular work. Next in importance came earnings of other members of the family; then followed in order: credit, particularly for rent and food; savings; assistance from social agencies; loans from insurance companies, small loan companies, friends, and family; the selling or pawning of possessions; cashing of insurance. All of these sources of support are of course used by many families even when the head is employed. The effect of unemployment is to shift the relative importance of them in supplying the family exchequer with funds.

The shift involves new experiences and new problems. When new earners enter the market they have registered for a new course in the school of experience. If they are successful in finding a job, the new routine and contacts present them with new opportunities which require some of the attention which might otherwise be devoted to contemplation of their own hard luck in having a husband or a father who couldn't hold his job. In many cases the new responsibilities placed on young shoulders gave definite signs of advancing the maturation of the individual concerned.

Workers accustomed to depend on steady jobs for a living were forced to develop new techniques of self-maintenance. Many were to develop a skill which hitherto they had not possessed: that of salesmanship, either with respect to their own serviceability in doing odd jobs or with respect to commodities they peddled from door to door. Others, transferring their energies to new occupations and industries, "learned the ropes" in new trades and thus added to their stock of employability. Even though success did not reinforce these new practices in most cases, unemployment did result in the exploration of new techniques of self-maintenance, and left in the possession of the explorers an increased deposit of experience. An enormous quantity of effort and initiative was put into such activities. It is regrettable that the conclusion for many must have been summarized in the words of a foundry worker, "The old ways are impossible for the time being, but the new ways aren't so hot either."

### Finding New Ways of Stretching the Income.

Since earnings furnished less than half of the maintenance, however, the obtaining of the remainder required greater attention to and exploitation of other sources than was normally required.[4] The procedure for getting loans from insurance companies or small loan companies, the dangers involved in "getting tied up" with the papers involved, are learned by many. Others find the pawn shops where the most "generous" loans are given, or the second-hand shops that "Jew you down the least." How one approaches a friend for a loan and what one says to make success more

4. Following is a summary of chap. x, *ibid.*

certain is an important lesson which some learn and others do not. The families must learn how to "put off" the landlord for longer periods than those previously necessary. They must be able to convince the grocer that they are still "good for" purchases made when they have no cash. Such abilities are developed against the opposition of the normal desire to stay out of debt and to "pay as you go." But necessity will not give way to such inhibition for long, and in the end, if success attends these efforts (and it usually did), the families' available techniques of self-maintenance have been enlarged.

The value of foresight exemplified in savings and insurance was amply verified by those fortunate enough to possess such a backlog of security. The prolongation of the period of momentum stability made possible through such means enabled some families to carry themselves over the period of interrupted earning power without serious dislocation to their plane of living. Even when amounts available from such sources were small, the conclusion arrived at was "if we had had more laid up, things might have been different." If Federal Deposit Insurance can curtail the number of losses through bank failures, this one blow to the conviction of the value of savings will have been removed and the testimony of experience during unemployment allowed to reinforce this technique of self-maintenance without serious contradiction.

Similarly membership in mutual loan associations proved its value. It is, naturally, impossible to maintain such membership unless regular earnings are restored, but comments we received indicated that the word had been passed around that "it was a good thing" to belong. From the extent of mutual aid reported one would be inclined to observe that the building up of a wide circle of friends had its importance in self-maintenance reinforced. Gifts were small, but they played a real part at strategic points in providing particular items necessary to relieve the distress not only of the body but of the mind. Moreover, a wide circle of friends meant a large number of persons who could "speak for" one in the quest for a job. The importance of such "pull" is attested to both by the unemployed themselves and by the reliance employers indicated they placed on the recommendations of their own workers. A reduction in associations attending unemployment, therefore, had more than a recreational significance. Increasing atomism meant decreasing chances for success in self-maintenance.

### Development of the Domestic Economy.

It might have been expected that unemployment would stimulate home industry in the raising and preserving of foodstuffs. That such examples of foresight and initiative did not appear with any frequency calls for explanation. That explanation is not hard to find. The adjustment takes cash for garden rental (baked-clay backyards are inhospitable to seed), for equipment, for jars, for fuel, for quantity supplies. Such long-range foresight is permitted to those who can spare the money for such expenditures from diminishing resources. Not many could do that. Even those who customarily engaged in canning and preserving were in many cases forced to cancel the enterprise. Moreover, the housewife who would ordinarily do this work was in many cases working for wages and out of the home.

Nevertheless, families learned many new devices for reducing food bills. Substitute foods were discovered which satisfied the stomach, though not always the palate. Canned goods took the place of fresh fruits and vegetables when special sales made these cheaper. Delicacies were eliminated. Eggs replaced meat, and margarine or drippings replaced butter. It is difficult to escape the conclusion, however, after close association with these families over many months, that such substitutions played a minor role in comparison with the actual reduction in the amount of food consumed. No new technique was developed to reduce to any large degree the necessity for making a reduction in income mean a reduction in the amount of food.

Families did learn that life could go on in one or two rooms around one or two stoves. This concentration of activities involved certain difficulties in carrying on the normal domestic chores, but families were willing to put up with that in order to save on fuel. Only a scattering of families found ways of providing fuel without paying for it. Boxes from behind the stores are soon used up, and even if men knew how to chop wood, an ax and a cart to haul the product of the day's labor would require cash. It is difficult to find in an urban community a neighbor from whom one might borrow an ax, and still more difficult to find a Yankee farmer willing to have his timber cut without adequate compensation.

Half of the families we studied intensively were able by such devices to avoid the journey to the relief office. Accumulated resources and successful efforts at renewed earning, particularly when older children could add their earnings, were sufficient to tide these families over the period in which the earnings of the chief breadwinner were interrupted.

### The Techniques of Obtaining Relief.

Those who finally applied for relief became involved in learning new techniques in self-maintenance.[5] Obtaining relief is not a simple matter. The unemployed must "learn the ropes" if they are to receive the maximum possible assistance from this source. They are not passive recipients of public bounty. Accordingly they set themselves about the task of learning the techniques of obtaining public assistance and of "getting by on relief." How to please, impress, or fool the investigator replaces their interest in how to please, impress, or fool the employer. The investigator

5. Following is a summary of chap. xiv, *ibid.*

now controls the source from which livelihood comes. The worker learns from this experience, as he learned from his working career, the tactics a man must pursue in order to exploit his source of support with advantage. He faces two problems in particular: "how to talk poor mouth," that is, convince the investigator of his need, and how to conceal the small additional sums he might get from nonrelief sources. Upon his freedom to get and to spend these latter sums depends his ability to maintain any margin of satisfaction above the bare minimum of subsistence provided from the public treasury. The conflict involved between the rule that one's relief allowance shall be reduced in proportion to other resources and the tendency to use every effort at one's disposal in an active display of individual initiative to increase the family's standard of living is pronounced. A similar conflict is involved in the rule that those on unemployment compensation shall not earn more than their unemployment benefit (about half their normal earnings). There are reasons for this, of course. That does not alter the fact that in both cases the incentive to the maximum use of one's abilities is severely hampered. That incentive cannot be assumed to operate in the same fashion for men in these circumstances as for those who are independent of such restrictions. Considerations of cost, and administration, and justice to all in need of public help make it necessary for public agencies to require a worker to abate his individual efforts or suffer a reduction in his allowance from the public purse. Not that such a dilemma kills initiative; but it causes it to take new forms, and the new forms are not of the idealized variety pictured in the success literature which has entered into society's judgment of men and their efforts.

Much of a relief applicant's effort must be exerted in proving to an investigator that he is *not* self-supporting. If the worker is supported by grocery orders, he learns ways of getting some few items not scheduled on his slip and even methods of deriving cash from an order for commodities. Others learn what the investigator considers evidence of initiative and foresight, and strive to impress her with their possession of those qualities, insurance against the day when she must cut some off her list. They learn to calculate nicely the amount of insistence which improves their status and the amount which labels them as trouble makers.

In all these efforts the unemployed worker is following a major precept of living, that the man with initiative uses every means at his disposal to increase his standard of livelihood. Practice makes perfect; and the longer he must continue to use his initiative in this way, the more agencies he has to deal with, the more ingrained become the behavior patterns appropriate to the obtaining of a degree of economic security under these circumstances. A multitude of possibilities for support, a variety of community agencies supplying relief are among the factors developing a habit of dependency. If several avenues must be explored, the exploring and learning how to manage the relations with each agency become the unemployed worker's habitual task. Much of his time is taken up by such activity. By habit he becomes, necessarily, concerned with developing skill in exploiting community resources for self-support.

### Appraising Job Opportunities.

Moreover, he learns to appraise with a critical eye the relative security offered by a proffered job and his relief allowance and to calculate the chances of future security bound up with his appraisal. Any mistake may be fatal to the continuance of even the minimum of security he now has. It is no necessary indication of the decline of self-reliance if he tries to avoid this mistake. Remember that he comes to the relief office after a thorough exploration of the labor market. He will be inclined to doubt any reports of jobs. He has been through an experience which has contained many disappointments. He will not believe the first tale he hears about the jobs that are begging for men. Nor will he be inclined to accept at face value the claims that they offer him more security or a greater opportunity to take up his interrupted progress toward his goals than does his present resource. Remember also that his application for relief and the learning of the techniques of making the most of it have followed three successive periods of frustration in attempts to make use of the self-maintenance practices successful under normal conditions.[6] Moreover, the rationalization of these frustrations has left him a bit cynical with respect to ethical standards appropriate enough when their observance was accompanied by success in self-support.

If the relief client is working on W.P.A. and is faced with a decision as to whether or not to look for or accept a job in private industry, if he has not lost all power of discrimination he must compare the relative values in the two jobs.[7] Many of these jobs are so low paid and insecure as to make W.P.A. work comparatively attractive on all counts. When there is added to this fact the uncertainty of again qualifying for a W.P.A. job, the possibility of a return to direct relief with all of its disadvantages, the greater demands from creditors which are expected to follow the return to a private job, the decision in favor of relief work is likely to be pretty thoroughly reinforced. It is unlikely, however, that any large number of job refusals could accumulate in view of the interest of the Employment Service in placing men, if the demand for labor is cleared through the Service and is made with respect to jobs offering a reasonable security. Until such time as private industry feels an actual shortage of labor, which shortage could be relieved *by the hiring of workers now on W.P.A.*, the question is rather academic. In the meantime we may observe that the workers who refuse jobs offering less security than that provided by the

6. See chap. vii, above.
7. Following is a summary of a part of chap. xv, *ibid.*

minimum provided on work relief are exemplifying, according to their standards, a degree of intelligent selection. That quality is not undesirable among the nation's workers.

Another fact must be considered in connection with the effect of W.P.A. work on self-reliance. The latter quality is exemplified not only in the search for a job; it is displayed and practiced in every decision that is made in the distribution of the family's income. The freedom to spend his W.P.A. wages according to the plans and judgments which he himself or members of his family make is a situation in which whatever foresight and intelligence he has in such matters can be preserved and developed.

## *Organizing for Protection.*

At least one distinctive new practice might have been developed by the unemployed who had finally come to depend on relief or relief work.[8] They might have participated in the several organizations available for the representation of their interests. An insignificant number among the direct relief clients, and these chiefly single men, responded to that opportunity. Organization among them found so little favor that, in New Haven at least, such effort may be eliminated as one of the typical adjustments.

A larger proportion of the workers on relief-work projects turned to this alternative for "bettering themselves"— at the height of membership, about one third of those working. Aside from a few mass demonstrations, and irregular meetings, and a few "educational" gatherings, however, actual participation in the activity of this organization was small. What was done in the matter of improvement of conditions and in the coping with complaints was left to the leaders. No doubt this small nucleus of leaders learned a number of lessons about the problems of labor organization and found outlets for their energy in useful activity,

8. Following is a summary of chap. iv above.

but the experience of the rank and file scarcely introduced them to and reinforced them in reliance upon a new form of self-maintenance activity in the form of collective bargaining. Since the great mass of unskilled workers engaged on the projects had had no previous experience with collective bargaining measures, their lack of response to this opportunity is one more evidence that workers turn but slowly, if at all, to forms of self-maintenance adjustments which are inconsistent with their previous experience.

### Was Self-Reliance Retained?

Such is the summarized record of the way in which unemployed workers adapted their equipment in training and customary practices to the tasks of self-maintenance when the normal foundation for that activity—the job—was temporarily removed. Certainly the techniques attempted prior to the receipt of public relief give evidence of resourceful effort to be self-reliant, although few new techniques were invented. When those methods described by the term "self-support" had failed and application was made for relief, a considerable amount of energy and initiative was displayed in getting as much as possible from this source. Whether one calls this "self-reliance" or not will depend on how insistent he is that energy and initiative applied to increasing the plane of living furnished by public funds cannot be *self*-reliance.

Our discussion of the effects on self-reliance of unemployment and unemployment relief has emphasized several considerations. The most important single clue to the nature of those considerations is that the goals which stimulate men to self-reliance, and the practices which are the objectification of that quality are modified by the circumstances under which men live. The modification which takes place during unemployment is an intensification of, but not a radically different process from, that which goes on continuously in the worker's experience. The particular income, work, and institutional relationships outline the foundations to which the structure of ambition and practice must conform for any worker.

The unemployed with whom we have associated exemplified a considerable variety of ambition and practice developed during a lifetime of more nearly normal living. Supporting this variety in superstructure was the variety in income, work, and institutional relationships which characterized the workers' backgrounds. As unemployment continued, the differences between individuals in ambition and practice continued to be displayed. Again our suggested explanation is in terms of the variety in the foundation of experience with which they came to unemployment and of the variety of circumstances they faced in their adjustment to unemployment.

Consider first the variation in the stimuli to self-reliance, that is, the variation in the realistic content of the goals toward which workers direct their efforts. In the attempt to strike a balance between objectives and the possible rewards of effort the normal adjustment is to modify the objectives. Since the possible rewards of effort are geared to income, the nature of the work, and the kinds of institutional relationship available, all workers' goals will be considerably more humble than those of management and professional classes. The former will approximate more closely to the objectives which can be realized on the basis of a relief experience than the latter. Among workers as a group, rewards are doled out in small parcels. The incentive to self-reliance is not the product of exceptional possibilities of rewards for effort, but of the fact that any progress at all toward even their limited goals involves working for an employer and *self*-support. Within the working class itself will of course be found large individual differences in the rewards for work, which in turn support large differences in the distance between the objectives normally within reach and those possible if a worker is forced to rely upon community assistance. Before assuming that men have lost their incentive to self-reliance during unemployment it is well to inquire how powerful were the incentives they had before they became unemployed.

The adjustments to reduced income and to the unsuccessful search for a job still further increase the gap between objectives and possibilities. The sort of a social role he is playing without a job makes necessary, and the breaking of contacts with those whose approval of the former possible roles he counted on makes easier, a modification in such objectives. What is meant by *self*-support has been considerably modified even before he applies for relief by recourse to forms of support which are not strictly the result of his own foresight.

Life on relief contains few possibilities of renewing progress toward his goals. This fact can be counted on to stimulate the development of alternative practices which carry greater promise of success. But the fact can also be counted on, if no alternative is available, to cause the worker to lower his objectives to the level of possibility on relief and reorganize his structure of living on this foundation. The retention of material symbols of former success is a necessary condition for postponing this modification. Loss of these is the signal for modification in order that results may not fall too far short of hopes.

Relief work, in comparison with direct relief and the marginal jobs occasionally offered relief clients in private enterprise, does provide a greater possibility of performing in a socially respected role, or winning a satisfactory degree of economic security, and of gaining control over his own affairs. Such a device, therefore, requires less modification of objectives and hence curtails less their effectiveness in stimulating ambition. It offers greater opportunity for allowing the worker to realize that if he is not making much progress, at least he is not losing ground. He is encouraged, therefore, in his continued efforts to develop practices which form the objective and observable content of the vague phrase, self-reliance.

The close relationship between the objectives which supply the incentive for self-reliance and the income-work boundaries within which they are realistically defined and to which they are shaped suggests an hypothesis which needs further exploration. If objectives are lowered to conform more closely to the possibilities of decreased economic resources, may they not also be raised to conform to *increased* economic resources? The observations we made of the families over the period of their recovery from the disorganization stage of unemployment lead us to suggest that the answer to this question is in the affirmative. What is possible is defined for the worker in terms drawn from observing the accomplishment of those with resources slightly greater than the observer possesses. Goals for one are the realized achievements of another. When economic security is increased by earnings either from private employment or from W.P.A., the worker's conception of what roles he can hope to play, the standards of what possessions, what behavior, what degree of control are required for self-respect is raised to a higher level. He is not satisfied with the level of achievement he had been forced to accept. Ambition starts from a new level. Objectives formerly impossible of realization are once more raised and projected into his future. That they are not completely beyond his reach is made likely by the fact that others with only slightly more resources than he has have reached them.

An important implication of this observation is that it runs counter to a frequently expressed fear that an increase in economic security involves a decrease in the incentives which make men ambitious. Quite the opposite conclusion seems justified, that the degree of ambition is likely to be directly proportional to the degree of economic security. The damage to ambition is not from raising the level of resources from which it may operate, but from the reduction of those resources so that the objectives of ambition must be modified until they have little ability to stimulate effort.

A few years ago I heard of a strange dispute which arose in an English village. An unemployed man had undertaken to enter the poultry and egg business. One of his hens destroyed her eggs so frequently that he built a contraption which rolled the egg off as soon as it was laid. Thereupon a great dispute arose among the villagers as to the effects of the device upon the ambition of the hen. One group contended that it discouraged her. After a few such experiences she would be inclined to say, "What's the use? I'm just going through the motions here." Another group was equally strong in its conviction that the hen was stimulated to greater efforts. When she looked about and found the egg gone, she would say, "That's funny, I thought I just laid an egg! But there's none there now. I'll have to get busy and lay another." The dispute had not been settled when I left.

Whatever may be true of hens, our observations of the reactions of human beings to their economic problems suggest that the first group of villagers would be more nearly correct if their comments referred to workers. That men shall have sufficient economic resources so that some unforeseen event doesn't hurl them into an economic abyss is a necessary foundation for ambition. It is sound common sense to provide them with a platform from which they can climb rather than leave them in the grip of economic quicksand.

A further implication is relevant. This platform is poorly constructed if it provides only a minimum income without the customary practice of work from which income is normally derived. Economic security is one of the major goals of workers we have noted; but it is not the only one. Indeed it is desired chiefly as an advantage in the attempt to perform in a socially respected role and to gain control over one's own affairs. Economic resources are necessary if the latter objectives are to be reached. But cash cannot buy a certificate of attainment—certainly, among workers at least, not cash from any source other than a job. For, as we have seen, the doing of work for wages is an essential component of the practices and relationships out of which come social status and any degree of independence and control. A man receiving $20 a week from wages would still have a real advantage, therefore, over a man receiving $20 from direct relief, for a job is valued only in part for the money which it supplies. Both the money *and the working* are the tools with which the structure of satisfactions are built. With the $20 in hand he must still engage in those practices and establish those relationships which make him a man and a citizen whose decisions and judgments give him what little control over his own affairs experience has taught him he can hope for. He must still conduct himself and gear himself into the life of the community in such a way that he is respected by his fellows. As long as those immediately above him on the economic ladder occupy their place through virtue of work for wages, so long must his ambition be fed not only by economic resources but by the work from which these are "properly" derived. Only during the period of momentum stability immediately following the layoff, a period during which former practices and institutional relationships continue to support normal definitions of objectives, can cash alone hold these stimulating incentives intact. When those supporting practices and relationships have disintegrated sufficiently so that former goals have been severely modified, only a restoration of a *working* relationship in the community can furnish the foundation for amplification of goals assuming a higher level of possible achievement.

Consideration of the techniques developed by the unemployed in their search for work, in stretching their diminishing income, and in exploiting the possibilities of relief does not give much grounds for confidence that unemployment stimulates any unusual inventiveness. That is not to be expected in the light of the equipment workers bring with them to the problem of existing without a job.

The record of the efforts of the unemployed, however, does not give certain evidence that they have lost their self-reliance. Rather it indicates that they have exemplified this quality upon the foundation of the possibilities available to unemployed men and their families. Before assuming that some new effort to get economic security—say while on relief—indicates a change in the character of people, it is well to ask whether the new effort is not merely a method more effectively adapted to getting, under contemporary circumstances, the increasing economic security men have always struggled for, or to restoring a measure of security which they had lost in the sweep of economic and social change. The new effort, far from indicating a loss of self-reliance, may be a new example of the same quality expressing itself in new objective forms adapted to the kind of problems with which the unemployed workers are faced.

It is one of the tragic consequences of the lack of jobs in which the worker can prove he is capable of self-support that many must learn ways of proving that they cannot support themselves. When a man's chief problem, which must be solved if he and his family are to survive, is to prove that he has no resources and has been unable to find ways of renewing them, the stimulus to self-reliance is severely curtailed. The basic cause of this curtailment, however, lies in the nature of the task he must perform and the factors that he must manipulate in the performance. Men become what they practice. What they practice must be adapted to the nature of the problems they face.

## XII

### SOCIAL SERVICES AND SELF-RELIANCE

OUR primary concern in this study has not been to evaluate the effectiveness or efficiency of social-service measures. We have been concerned to describe and to analyze the adjustments which unemployed families undertake when their normal sources of support are reduced and the pattern of their life is disturbed by the loss of a job by the head of the family. Any comments we have made regarding social-service devices and agencies have, therefore, been from this point of view. How do they fit into the processes of self-maintenance and social relationships the family is undertaking under such circumstances? To the degree that our observations and analysis are correct, it would appear that the extent to which social services will support or discourage self-reliance might be anticipated by the answers to the following questions:[1]

1. *Do the services preserve or restore the worker's opportunity to function in socially respected roles?*

Among the incentives to self-reliance such opportunity ranks high. Destroy that opportunity and a strong stimulus is removed. Preserve it and that stimulus, at least, remains. Since working is an essential component of or basis for all socially respected roles among workers, the opportunity cannot be completely preserved during unemployment. Yet some forms of assistance are less destructive of the opportunity than others.

During the first few months after the layoff, when the search for work replaces work itself, some semblance of the former status in the eyes of the family and of friends may

1. Detailed discussion of the evidence upon which the generalizations in this chapter are made will be found in the preceding pages of this book and in chapters xi–xv, *The Unemployed Worker,* Yale University Press, 1940.

be retained in the expenditure of funds the right to which
has been earned by virtue of a previous work record and
which are in reality a prolongation of wages. As long as it
is possible to grant unemployment compensation without
proof of need and as long as this resource, supplemented
by other self-provided resources, can prevent any marked
change in the pattern of former "social-front" and "social-
contact" expenditures, the ability to perform in desired social roles is seriously curtailed only by the failure to go to
work daily for wages. The latter factor is admittedly severe in its effects and must ultimately challenge the status
of the worker before his fellows even if expenditures can be
continued on approximately a normal plane.

If the next step is direct relief involving a thoroughgoing
investigation of the family's resources and a declaration of
dependency, no continuation of the former status is possible. The only path open which provides any degree of satisfaction at all is the drastic redefinition of the desirable
roles and the resignation to association only with those
who have surrendered to the inevitableness of a continued
livelihood furnished by the public bounty. Respected roles
among workers cannot be performed while on direct relief.

Work relief does provide opportunity for a social status
among workers superior to that provided by direct relief.
But the status approximates to that possible in the course
of normal employment only if the work is on products of
recognized social usefulness, if it is well done and efficiently
managed by supervisors appointed on the basis of ability
and not of political affiliations. The maximum values of
work relief in this respect could be realized only if the
qualification did not involve relief certification at all, but
were available as work for the government as employer,
devised as a temporary or permanent occupation for those
who were capable of doing, and willing to do, the tasks required but who were not needed by private enterprise. In
other words, the work would have to be at a job the quali-

fications for which, and the requirements for continued employment on which, were the same as similar work undertaken by private enterprise. In such a case the job could more appropriately be described as government employment rather than as relief work.

Even relief work, however, affords the opportunity to go to work daily for wages, be a comparatively good provider, and remain the head of the family. As such, it supports far more than does direct relief the incentive to self-reliance derived from the ability to perform in a socially respected role before one's family and one's fellows.

2. *Do the services provide for the retention of the symbols of past self-reliance?*

Every family has accumulated a number of such symbols, the home and its furnishings, insurance policies, membership in organizations, and the like. How many of these symbols must be sacrificed before one is eligible for assistance? That is an important question, for the giving up of these symbols is a signal to the worker that he must modify his goals, and a reminder to him of the uselessness of planning and foresight. No such surrender is required by the rules of eligibility for unemployment compensation. It is questionable whether public opinion would support complete retention of all symbols, especially those requiring a continued outlay of cash, when the worker applies for public relief or work relief. Nevertheless, the extent to which such rewards of former foresight and effort can be retained is important, for they stimulate in men an ambition for regaining the opportunities for earning which will support the standard of living which these symbols exemplify.

3. *Are the services realistically designed to postpone as long as possible the necessity of recourse to direct relief?*

We need not labor here the point that life on direct relief offers a minimum of support for the incentives to self-reliance. Recognition of this fact was in large part responsible for the development of new devices in the form of unemployment compensation and work relief. Since the former involves a prolongation of actual earnings while employed, and the latter provides many of the circumstances of actual employment, the fact of self-reliance is not as seriously challenged and the supporting aids to self-reliance are not as drastically undermined as in the case of direct relief. If these beneficial features of the substitute measures are to be preserved for as long a period and for as many workers as possible, they must be geared to the actual problem of keeping workers off the direct relief rolls. What are the realities of that problem?

The chances of the need to have recourse to direct relief vary inversely with the regularity and adequacy of previous earnings and directly with the number of dependents. If unemployment compensation is to fulfill its task of keeping workers off direct relief, it must come to grips with those facts. The worker who has had the most adequate and regular earnings has had the best opportunity to provide himself and his family with safeguards against dependency. The worker who has had the least adequate and the most irregular earnings has had the smallest opportunity to provide himself and his family with safeguards against dependency. The worker with the smallest number of dependents is bound to have the least drain on his resources in providing the bare essentials of food, clothing, and shelter, and consequently is in a better position than the worker with a large number of dependents to conserve whatever resources he has laid up "against a rainy day."

The minimum significance of these facts is that unemployment compensation benefits, if they are to accomplish their purpose of keeping families off direct relief, cannot be geared primarily to previous earnings and cannot neglect the number of dependents for which the worker is responsible. Minimum grants at least must be set above the standards permitted by direct relief and be adjusted to the number of dependents in the family. Since the probable ability of the family to postpone its application for relief is inversely proportional to the amount and regularity of previous earnings, the number of weeks' compensation allowed is poorly designed to assist in this postponement, if it is determined in direct relationship to such earnings. A short waiting period and a uniform period of benefit is called for if those most likely to need direct relief are to be kept from that necessity for a period of time approximating the period of those whose previous earnings have been more adequate and regular.

The present system of unemployment compensation must have prolonged for many workers the period of self-support. But the amount of assistance provided has been in inverse proportion to the probability that the prolongation would be difficult. Common sense would suggest that if a government device is designed to keep workers off relief, it should focus maximum attention on those most likely to need relief. Our present unemployment compensation arrangements which gear the amount and duration of benefits to previous earnings reverses this emphasis. We have set up elaborate machinery presumably for the purpose of keeping workers from the experience of direct relief, and then have scaled down the benefits available in proportion to the very irregularities and inadequacies of wages which provide the effective cause for their need to apply for relief.

Many who advocate the continuance of this present arrangement do so on the basis of the same major objective we are discussing—the maintenance of self-reliance. Their contention is as follows. If we provide no differential in benefits related to the differential in previous earnings, the sense of injustice resulting will tend to decrease the incentives to self-reliance. If the amount men get when they are unemployed gives no advantage to the man who has earned more during employment, what is the use of effort required to earn more than the minimum required for qualification?

The answer to that question should be clear. Why do men desire to earn more when they are employed? Is it merely to increase their benefits when unemployed? The incentives to work and earn are many and complex as we have seen. They are based on the desire to achieve goals and satisfactions dependent on the work and the rewards of work. If in their sum these cannot produce the ambition to earn as much as possible, the promise of a higher benefit when unemployed will not accomplish the result.

Another argument of the defenders of the present arrangements is more relevant. During employment workers have succeeded in winning for themselves a standard of living and a structure of satisfactions proportional to their earnings. We have emphasized that the desire for self-reliance is in part dependent on the maintenance of those standards and that structure. Since they have been built on differences in earnings they will have to be maintained by differences in benefits. That is a sound contention. It may point to the desirability of retaining some limited differential in benefits related to previous earnings. But it is no argument for the focusing of the whole system on the one principle of the establishment of differentials, to the neglect of the basic problem, the establishment of a minimum designed to keep the resources of all workers above relief levels for as long as possible. Differentials ought to be built on the latter minimum, and that minimum if it is to accomplish its purpose will have to take into account the amount the community sets as its obligation for all its citizens and the size of the family a man has to support, regardless of his previous earnings. If, in addition to that minimum, limited differentials can be established, so much the better.

The chief danger that self-reliance will decay is to be found among the low-paid and irregularly employed workers. They are the ones who, when laid off, have least (and probably no) self-provided resources for continuing life on even the low standards they have by choice or force of cir-

cumstances accepted. These will come most quickly to relief and to the experiences damaging to self-reliance accompanying that source of maintenance. This group furnishes
the chief problem; and that problem receives inadequate
attention until the fetish of benefit differentials based on
wage differentials is relegated to its proper place of secondary importance.

It is the function of the wages system to maintain differentials for workers in accordance with their ability in and
usefulness to the productive system. The differences in reward to workers on those bases also result in differences in
ability to support themselves, even when the job ends. Relatively less assistance for maintaining standards already
achieved is needed by those whose earnings are sufficient
to provide a backlog of economic security than by those
whose earnings were low and irregular. On the whole, the
former are likely to have the most savings, the best credit,
the greatest chances of reëmployment, and the smallest
families. It is a function of the wages system to provide opportunity for the realization of such achievement.

But when employment for wages is no longer available
and the need for community supplementation becomes imminent, the function of a device to accomplish this supplementation may properly take account of factors which produce the most pressing need: that wages are not sufficiently
adequate and regular to provide complete maintenance for
many workers, and that we live in a culture in which the
family is the basic unit for economic responsibility. The
managers who pay wages in accordance with the usefulness
and ability of workers need be relatively little concerned
with those facts. A government charged with the responsibility for filling the gaps left by such payments cannot
avoid them. Certainly in setting up arrangements to fill the
gaps a government need not perpetuate the same system
and principles of distribution which led to the need for its
intervention.

Work relief wages are normally well above direct relief allowances granted for the average-sized family. Larger families occasionally face the need for supplementation from direct relief. Inasmuch as direct competition with private enterprise is likely to be involved unless the top limits of "security wages" are less than the normal earnings in private employment, it would probably be difficult to distribute such wages in accordance with the number of dependents. Yet in view of the fact that in certain industrial nations a supplementary "family wage" has been paid even in private employment, it may not be beyond the realm of possibility that some such device will prove worthy of further study in connection with work relief. The degree of pressure for some such arrangement will depend on the amount to which the flat level of security wages falls below the direct relief amounts available to larger families.

4. *Do the services provide sufficient resources so that health and strength are preserved?*

The bearing of health and physical vitality upon the preservation of the ability to be self-reliant and upon the provision of encouragement in the efforts to exemplify this quality is too obvious to need further discussion.

5. *Do the services make possible a retention of the worker's equipment for self-reliance, skills, employability, and work habits?*

Self-reliance has little chance to display itself in objective behavior unless it is implemented by the equipment needed for self-support. It is, therefore, important to inquire whether this equipment is effectively preserved or amplified by the relief measures in question. Since unemployment compensation is received immediately after the loss of a job and continues normally for a short time only, the problem is scarcely relevant. It is our observation that compensation for any period up to six months would not seriously impair whatever equipment in skills, employability, and work habits the worker brings with him from his working experience.

We have seen the shortcomings of work relief in this respect for any but unskilled workers. Any correction of the situation involves as close approximation as possible to the type of work, requirements for employment, and work discipline and rewards available in the best sort of employment in private enterprise. Such approximation, however, raises difficult questions of competition with private enterprise and the necessity of modifying the strictly need basis upon which jobs are assigned and retained. It is unlikely, unless work projects were to be transformed into definite continuing government-sponsored enterprise offering jobs on the basis of skill and efficiency requirements, that such alternative work could reach maximum effectiveness in the preservation of the working equipment of the individuals involved.

Even with its shortcomings, however, work relief offers greater possibilities in this respect than direct relief. One of the most fascinating and deeply significant questions which challenges the skill and thought of management lies in this problem. How can the tools of self-reliance be preserved for men to whom the normal opportunities for acquiring those tools have been closed? It is fascinating because it is pioneer work without the trappings which assist managers in private enterprise. It is significant because in no industrial nation has private enterprise succeeded in absorbing the total available labor force in productive effort which is profitable on the basis of traditional conceptions of profitability. The price of continued freedom for private enterprise to use whom it chooses and in the numbers and for the periods most likely to result in profitable production may be the offering of employment by government to those not needed on the basis of such choice. In such a situation the thought and experimentation on the part of the managers of government enterprise in the development of work standards and incentives, in the building of training and retraining programs, and in the solving of the problems of industrial relations peculiar to such enterprise are as essential as such effort on the part of the management of private enterprise.

If self-reliance is conceived in terms of working for a living, it is useless to expect that the tools of self-reliance will be retained if the worker is supported completely on direct relief. If direct relief is used to undergird programs of maintenance production in workshop or on the land, however, and is coupled with retraining and reconditioning programs, especially for the younger members of relief families, it can conceivably contribute to this end.

6. *Do the services prolong the ability of the worker to pursue his customary practices of foresight for as long as possible?*

Self-reliance implies not only the ability to earn, but the ability to distribute earnings through expenditures which support the physical and social needs of the family. We have seen that during his working years the worker has developed a number of foresight practices consistent with the amount and regularity and source of his income. These practices must be modified under the impact of diminishing resources. If nothing stands between the receipt of a pay envelope and the receipt of a relief check or grocery order, the modification will have been severe. The transition to pauperism will have been marked by the discarding of foresight practices once effective but no longer possible. The ability to be self-reliant will have been diminished by the degree to which such habitual behavior has been interrupted.

To the extent that unemployment compensation supplements the accumulated resources of the family, it postpones the point at which these practices need to be discarded because they are ineffective. The more adequate these payments can be and the longer they can continue, the greater is the chance that the worker will go back to work with his and his family's ability to manage the domestic economy unimpaired.

The practices of foresight developed over a lifetime are the essential stuff of self-reliance. It is likely that they can be prolonged more easily than they can be restored. Even unemployment compensation cannot be expected to provide income sufficient to accomplish this prolongation for longer than six months because of the decay of other factors, such as work routine, customary division of labor, institutional and social contacts. But it can extend the period of momentum stability in which normally the habitual practices, aside from working at a job, are not seriously impaired.

7. *Do the services give the worker a maximum chance to develop foresight and self-reliance through expenditures and activity undertaken on his own initiative?*

The importance of this test lies in two considerations. In the first place, since an increasing control over his own affairs is prominent among the goals toward which the worker is striving, the possibility of such initiative reinforces his faith that that goal has not completely receded beyond his horizon. What incentive is resident in progress toward that goal is not, therefore, completely canceled. In the second place, it is futile to expect that *self*-reliance can be preserved by reliance on another's decisions. Practice makes perfect.

While the worker is receiving unemployment compensation alone no question is raised by another as to how he should spend his money. Work-relief wages may be spent also without answering to anyone outside his own family. Since the art of spending money is an essential requirement for self-reliance in a monetary economy, these forms of assistance further rather than retard the acquisition of abilities needed for self-support. Somewhat more interference with self-initiated decisions is evident when the man is on direct relief. Such interference, wisely administered through suggestions on budgeting, resulted in a few of our cases in a net addition to the families' skills. It is difficult within the boundaries set by relief allowances, however, for the visitor and the agency she represents to escape a degree of arbitrary control of the distribution of those allowances over the essential types of expenditures. The control is most severe in the case of a grocery-order system, least in the case of a relief check. Yet even in the latter situation the amount has been pared to a minimum by the process of surveying irreducible needs, and the family is well aware that the funds had better be spent for the designated purposes lest these importunate needs go unsatisfied. This statement implies no criticism of the administration of relief. It is difficult to see how the matter could be handled any differently and still meet the responsibility placed on relief officials for the administration of public funds. But the very necessity of exercising the amount of control appropriate to that responsibility suggests that it is desirable to postpone for as long as possible the maintenance of the unemployed through the device of direct relief. Practice in self-initiated decision in the expenditure of available income is hard to get while on direct relief.

Another possibility for the maintenance of the habit of initiative lies in the chance to supplement assistance from public funds by earnings from odd jobs. It is understandable that such earnings should be counted as available resources and deducted from the direct relief allowances. Somewhat the same result is accomplished under unemployment compensation by the device of substituting partial for full unemployment benefits in case part-time work has been obtained. W.P.A. officials have never really faced the problem of checking up on this practice of supplementary earning.

It is inevitable, since funds for public assistance are limited, and since taxes for relief as well as unemployment compensation are justified in the public mind by the necessity of community action when self-support is impossible, that some limitation be placed on the possibility of increasing the client's plane of living by earnings derived from odd jobs. Moreover, in view of the fact that odd-job employment shades by almost indistinguishable steps into casual and part-time work in private industry, the danger of subsidizing low and irregular wages is ever present. Yet if the habit of self-reliance is to be encouraged, some compromise will have to be struck between such considerations and the desirability of permitting men to hope for some supplementation of the admittedly low standard of living possible from the amounts available from public sources. The setting of a certain sum which could be earned in subsidiary employment without a reduction in amounts granted from the public treasury would be a step in this direction. Certainly liberality is justified in permitting men to supplement their relief allowances through individual or coöperative production for their own use.

8. *Do the services face the worker with the task of proving he is capable rather than incapable of self-support?*

We have noted that the greater the extent to which assistance is given on proof of complete lack of resources from self-support the greater the stimulus to the development of techniques and skill in proving destitution. Our assumption is that preoccupation with such an endeavor cannot encourage self-reliance in the ordinary meaning of that term. Since public relief is justified in the public mind only under circumstances of destitution, it is difficult to see how such a danger can be avoided, save by the avoidance of the appeal to relief itself. A partial solution to this problem lies in the maximum possible extension of the period of assistance through unemployment compensation, eligibility for which depends on actual attachment to the community's labor force for a qualifying period. The longer this form of assistance can be extended, the fewer workers will be compelled to develop the ability to "talk poor mouth."

Any degree to which qualifications for work relief can increase the emphasis on skill and competence to do the job in hand, and continuation on the job made to depend on the same conditions will also promote the incentive to display the qualities usually consistent with self-reliance rather than with dependence.

9. *Are the agencies through which assistance is secured limited to the smallest possible number?*

The value in the reduction of the number of agencies with which the worker comes in contact lies in the reduction of the amount of attention he must pay to proving his inadequacy for self-support. Habits of dependence are probably increased by the amount of time the worker must spend in "learning the ropes" in his application for relief and in increasing the adequacy and certainty of assistance from public sources. If the will to self-reliance is built on the practice of, and success in, self-support, the attitude of dependence can likewise be increased by the practice of, and success in, dependence on public sources. The fewer the necessary agencies with which the worker must deal in the latter connection, the more the necessity of such practice is reduced.

This situation, among other reasons, justifies as commendable the complete responsibility for individual cases by one agency developed in the course of the depression. It also indicates the desirability of placing minimum unemployment compensation amounts at a level above relief allowances in the community and scaling the amount of benefits to the number of dependents so that supplementation from a relief agency will not be necessary.

10. *Are the services effectively timed?*

Since the experienced needs of the unemployed vary during the several stages in their adjustment to unemployment, it is relevant to ask whether the measures of relief are appropriate and effective if applied at a particular time. Which measures are best adapted to the preservation of self-reliance during the successive stages of (1) momentum stability, (2) unstable equilibrium, (3) disorganization, (4) experimental readjustment, (5) permanent readjustment.

The chief need during the first stage and much of the second is for a cash supplement to self-provided resources (or an amount larger than relief allowances if there are no resources) in order to prolong their adequacy, reduce the need for credit and debt, extend the period over which customary foresight habits continue to determine action and over which normal family and community relations are maintained. If the right to this cash supplement is self-earned by previous work it can perform this function with maximum effectiveness. The need at this period suggests unemployment compensation. Work relief is not appropriate; the worker has not yet felt the need for the restoration of his position as a worker by means of any job carrying a partial stigma of relief. Nor is he prepared to seek work opportunities outside of his normal occupation. It is wise to let whatever incentive he has to regain his status in private industry or business push him in his search for work. Direct relief is certainly not appropriate at this period, for even though it might provide the cash supplement needed, the act of turning to the community for such help and of undergoing the examination of resources, of disposing of symbols of former status, and of making a public declaration of one's impoverishment are designed to induce the modification of goals and cancellation of associations and practices which support self-reliance. It is well to postpone these results for as long as possible and until in the normal course of events other factors will have tended to produce such adjustments. For this reason it is desirable that unemployment compensation be sufficient to obviate the necessity for application for additional relief from sources available only to paupers.

Unfortunately our analysis of the length of time during which workers remained in this stage of momentum stability did not show a high degree of similarity for every family. But the primary factor determining the differences was the variation in accumulated resources. It was the necessity of drastic adjustments in expenditures and the turning to increased contributions from supplementary earners which disturbed the normal pattern of relationships and status and pushed the family from the first to the second stage. If workers were subsidized with funds adequate to keep their plane of living fairly approximate to their normal plane, there are few factors which would make unlikely the passage from the stage of momentum stability to the stage of unstable equilibrium in less than six months.

During the following stage of unstable equilibrium, unemployment compensation might continue to decrease the severity of the adjustments required, but its effectiveness would rapidly decrease. As the stage progresses, more than cash is required to avoid the damage to self-reliance inherent in the modification of goals, disturbance of relations and status, and destruction of self-confidence characteristic of the period. This is the period when the offer of jobs (even involving a shift in normal field of work) from the Employment Service will contribute most to the postponement of the decay of self-reliance. Even an offer of work relief gives an opportunity to escape some of the most serious maladjustments of the disorganization stage, and in any case to shorten it, by providing an alternative source of support which reëstablishes to some degree the status of the unemployed as a worker in the eyes of his family and friends. Moreover, it restores the routine of work, whose lack is one of the most damaging of those factors which disorganize his attempts to be self-reliant and discourage his faith in the efficacy of his own plans.

Among our informants the stage of unstable equilibrium lasted from one to two months before the confusion and discouragement of the stage of disorganization set in. Since the observable sign of getting out of the latter stage was customarily the experimentation with new earning ventures and the reorganization of the economic and social pattern of life on the basis of the activity and income provided therefrom, I am inclined to think that the severity of this period could be reduced considerably, if the stage were not completely eliminated, by the continued offering of work relief. Outside of a job in private industry or business, relief work offers the best basis (better than either unemployment compensation or direct relief) upon which the family may renew practices of self-initiated foresight and management and prevent further decline in status, which up to this point has been partially supported by evidence of past achievements. The regular routine involved does much to restore the comfort of an expected schedule for all the family in the atmosphere of which continued planning and self-reliant effort can take place.

Implicit in this discussion is the conviction that unemployed workers will maintain their incentives to and abilities for self-reliance most thoroughly if they never have to experience contact with direct relief. It is possible that intelligent case work at the stage of disorganization can relieve some of the distress and confusion characteristic of this period. The high respect we have come to have for the self-initiated efforts of the families with whom we have come in contact, however, leads us to conclude that, given an income and work, most families will solve their own problems and set their feet once more on the path toward self-support. In the absence of any resources and of work relief, of course, direct relief is absolutely necessary. If its administration is to lead out of the stage of disorganization to that of temporary readjustment in a way involving an increasing measure of self-reliance, it is desirable that it be accompanied by measures which offer opportunities for which the worker at this stage soon begins to search. Retraining and reconditioning programs, encouragement of individual or coöperative production-for-use enterprise, are efforts of this sort. Intelligent case work can also supply assistance by education in, and understanding of, possibilities of income distribution to produce maximum health with the amount available, and by introducing families to new opportunities for recreational and community activities. It is difficult to determine whether advice on the problems of domestic tensions so intensified during the period of disorganization will help or hinder the reëstablishment of healthy relationships. Any guidance in such matters requires extreme caution and a realization of the possibilities of emphasizing the difficulties by the interference of one outside the family.

The variety of paths followed by the several families in their efforts at experimental and permanent readjustment precludes any precise gearing of relief measures to the self-initiated practices. Work relief continues effective, but unless government employment is to be accepted as a permanent job opportunity an increasing need is evident for transfer to other employment, even for short periods. This is not a suggestion that men be cut off W.P.A. periodically regardless of the availability of openings in private employment. Initial values of work relief in applying the brakes to loss of incentives and to the downward modification of goals, and in providing a possible basis for the reconstruction of foresight practices which work and of satisfactory family and community relations, wear thin with the passage of time. For those whose standards are still geared to the opportunities offered by private employment, these diminishing values are particularly apparent. For those

whose standards have been modified to the level of possibilities from work relief, the danger of becoming "career
men" is obvious. But the latter danger can be avoided, in
line with the desirable economic and social objectives that
every worker shall fill a place in the productive processes
of private enterprise, only by the offering of such a place. It
is questionable whether a "career" on direct relief which is
the only other alternative, lacking a private job, is economically or socially preferable to a "career" on work relief.

11. *Do the services keep the worker and the institutions
of the community together and do they maintain the stability of these institutions and the worker's relationships to
them and to his customary associates?*

The scene has been repeated so many times that it need
be given no specific setting. Two men in worker's garb are
talking outside a "flop house." One of them is the author.
The other, whom I shall call Joe Stark, is a single man receiving a small weekly sum in the form of a meal ticket and
a ticket good for shelter in one of the numerous "flop
houses" of the city. The value of this relief is probably
about $3. Joe Stark is a native of New Haven who had
been employed by Winchester's for ten years. A prospect
of a better job opened up in Waterbury three years ago.
He left "to better himself." The job lasted six months. He
returned to New Haven and found Winchester's wrestling
with a reorganization and a depression. His old job had
been abolished. All New Haven factories were cutting pay
rolls. His small savings lasted six months. After these were
gone he gave up looking for a "regular" job and started
taking anything he could get. "Anything" included weed-
ing in a truck garden, mowing a few lawns, substituting for
a friend as a hod carrier, and working for the city as a
street sweeper. Even these work opportunities gradually
disappeared. The truck gardener stopped employing anyone but his own wife and children; his lawn-mowing cus-

tomers started doing their own cutting; the business agent
found out that he didn't belong to the union; and his friend
the alderman was defeated. Two years on the streets and
picking up occasional odd jobs had gradually broken his
self-respect and had isolated him from his former friends.
He was alone. He knew it, and anyone who talked with him
for five minutes knew it.

I left him and walked across the viaduct to Olive Street,
knocked on the door of another Winchester man. His wife
opened the door. I sat down with him in the kitchen while
he poured some powerful alcoholic beverage into a cup of
black coffee made of coffee beans, the roasting of which
gives a characteristic fragrance to this block of tenements.
We talked of many things. His work history was not un-
like that of Joe Stark. He had a large family and although
he had been a bit more fortunate in picking up "anything"
than Joe, he had been forced to supplement his small earnings with a $3 a week subsidy from a local charity organi-
zation. He had kept his home about him, however, although
some of the better pieces of furniture had been sold. He
had dropped his membership in an Italian benefit society
although he occasionally met his former pals on the street
or in a back yard leveled off for a game of bowls. He still
attended church and his wife had many things to report
about the affairs of the community collected at a sewing
club in one of the local settlement houses. His children
were still in school and one of them showed promise of
musical ability. He spoke with considerable satisfaction of
a school affair which he and his wife had attended at which
Flora had performed with distinction. He went occasionally
to a political club which met in a small hall over "Fred's
Pool Room" for a game of cards, and during election week
distributed fliers for the Democrats. His contacts were not
as many, or as satisfying as during the fifteen years he
had worked for Winchester's. He no longer was on friendly
terms with the bank teller to whom he had carried small

and irregular savings. He had moved to his present tenement from a three-family house in a better neighborhood,
and the move resulted in less association with his former
neighbors. The evenings of pinochle had become more and
more infrequent. The clubhouse at the factory was no
longer a natural meeting place. He felt like a "piker" if he
went to any of the community festivals. The former friends
he met on the street didn't seem anxious to stop and talk
as long. Yet compared to Joe Stark he was still geared in in
a number of ways to the institutions of the community in
which he lived and of which he felt himself a citizen. Joe
was isolated, no question about that. Giovanni was still
tied in by several bonds to the life of the people of his
group.

Both were receiving practically the same amount of community assistance. In the case of Giovanni the amount provided a measure of security, in the other it merely saved
Joe from starving. The difference was not in the amount.
Rather it was due to the fact that in the one case it worked
in partnership with a set of forces and relationships which
supported the life of the Sellanos at many points. In the
other case it performed its function of maintenance alone,
in isolation from the relations to men and institutions which
furnished the Sellanos with what degree of social security
they possessed.

During the eight years that we have followed the fortunes of a small group of New Haven families whose head
was unemployed in 1933, during which we have lived as
workers and unemployed men for several periods, participating in their search for jobs, in their club meetings, in
their social affairs, in their park meetings, and during which
we have checked our impressions and findings by extensive
interviews in their homes with representative samples of
the unemployed in New Haven, first in 1933 and again in
1938, this clue to the reactions and adjustments of the unemployed has been so persistently prominent that we can-

not escape recording it as the major explanation for the results which we observed.

The income a family has to spend is important, for in a monetary urban economy most of the support for the satisfactions which life yields and for the maintenance of the symbols of self-reliance must be bought. The job and the activities of working are important, for on this basis is built the worker's claim to normal social status in a culture in which men must work for a living. But income and the job are only the foundations for, not the structure of, security, whether that noun be preceded by the adjective "economic" or "social." The clue to that security lies in the structure of goals and satisfactions which that income supports, in the conditions of a livelihood under which it is obtained, and for the mastering of which it is spent, in the relations it sustains, and in the activities necessary to obtain it and the interests which, in other-than-economic fields, it makes possible. Those men and women and children impressed one as secure and as most thoroughly motivated toward self-reliance who in these ways were geared into the life of their community. The degree of their insecurity and the loss of their desire to be self-reliant appeared to be almost directly proportional to the extent of the breaking of these ties.

The relevance of this observation to the determination of appropriate measures of assistance to the unemployed is this. Unemployment compensation which is available almost immediately upon the cessation of wages from work operates in coöperation with the multitude of practices and relationships supporting social security and self-reliance. Earned by former work, its acceptance involves no real challenge to the continuation of the status and control assigned to workers. As a device for perpetuating the degree of gearing in with the life of the community already attained, it therefore has no peer. If it provides enough to keep the family off direct relief and continues for all initially eligible as long as possible up to six months, it is a sound device. But its benefits in this respect do not continue indefinitely. The problem at the end of six months of unemployment is not only the maintenance of former relationships and status. These have begun to disintegrate in spite of the cash subsidy. Renewed establishment of his position as a worker is necessary if the disintegration is not to proceed rapidly. At this point work relief is the appropriate device. If eventually direct relief is necessary, its administrators, if interested in the retention of incentives to self-reliance, may well pause before insisting on the necessity of complete destitution, which in reality means first, surrender of the evidences of past achievements which remind the worker that effort is not entirely futile, second, withdrawal from those associations where judgments of one exert pressure for the renewal of those achievements via the road of self-support. If these are gone the relief allowance is robbed of valuable partners in the effort to restore self-reliance.

The effects of and adjustments to unemployment among the working class are meaningless unless they are seen as the products of men's attempts to maintain what comfort and assurance can be had from participation in the ways of the folk. The study of unemployment becomes therefore a problem in searching for an accurate description of the normal course of working-class life which the lack of earnings and work interrupts. It becomes a problem in interpreting observed reactions under the stress of misfortune in the light of the customary goals toward which workers are striving, the normal conditions under which that striving is carried on, and the habitual relations and practices which have grown out of the effort to reach them. The arrangements established by the community to deal with the effects of unemployment are bound to be inadequate unless they are shaped with the purpose of restoring as nearly as possible the normal structure of societal living.

No end of misunderstanding and misdirected action has been the product of judgments made about the unemployed by assuming that such facts are universally the same for all groups in the population. It has been assumed that the workers are motivated by essentially the same incentives and trained in the same school of experience, and are subject to the same opportunities and conditions as bankers and professors. Or if common sense makes such an assumption difficult, it is assumed that such matters make no difference. If this book does nothing else I hope it will furnish middle-class Americans with a realistic picture of the circumstances which furnish the actual content of the background from which a worker comes to face any one of the numerous problems which beset his struggle for existence, including the particular problem with which we are concerned, unemployment, and from which he acquires the habits, initiative, and foresight with which he must effect a readjustment once more labeled by public opinion as self-reliance. For the content of that background is essential to an understanding of his reactions and adjustments in any of the areas in which his problems affect the lives of other groups in the community, whether it be industrial relations, unionization, housing, radical political activity, or unemployment.

# INDEX

Associations, institutional, as evidence of working-class status, 94. *See also* Community associations

Benevolence, attitude toward, among unemployed, 30–32
Birth control, 146
Building Laborers' Union, 74, 79–80

Children, ambitions of parents for, 120; discipline of, 114. *See also* Unemployment, effect of, on discipline and training of children
Church, activities of, 36; assistance of, in job seeking, 24, 25; attitude of pastor toward unemployed, 25; class status within, 39–40; effect of unemployment on participation in, 14; financial contributions to, 37–39; as a group-making factor, 35–36; importance of pastor in, 26–27, 42–43; parochial schools, 124, 125, 144; participation in, 44, 124, 132, 135, 160, 165, 169; Protestant, 22–23, 27, 28, 29, 32–33, 37, 40, 41, 42; relief practices of, 26; requirements for participation in life of, 37–42; Roman Catholic, 21–22, 27, 28, 29, 32–33, 37, 40, 41, 42, 63. *See also* Religion; Pastor
Class consciousness, evidence of, 99–102; requirements for, 102–103. *See also* Working class
Cliques, basis for, 9–10
Clubs, effect of unemployment on participation in, 14
Communism, 44, 60–61, 62–63, 65
Communist party, influence in unemployed organizations, 72, 73, 74
Community associations, 3–17, 238; among unemployed, 168; effect of social services on, 301–305; readjustments in, due to unemployment, 156, 160, 164, 172
Community relations, of a religious nature, 35–36

Control, by others, as evidence of working-class status, 90–92
Control of own affairs, effect of relief on, 214; effect of unemployment on, 253
Cultural activities, 14, 16, 17
Cultural conflicts, 124, 129–130, 132
Culture, political aspects of, 46–55; working-class, v, ix–x, 85–86, 102–103, 122, 306. *See also* Working class

Debts, among unemployed, 163
Dependency, need for gearing social services to, 285–290
Disorganization, 299–300; as stage in cycle of readjustment to unemployment, 162–167; as stage in cycle of readjustment within family, 201–215

Economic security, 279; effect of unemployment on, 16, 253, 255
Education, of children, 120, 133, 138, 144, 219–220
Employability. *See* Work habits
Expenditures, adjustments in, due to unemployment, 156, 159, 163–164, 168, 172, 181, 186–190; adjustment in control of, 184; foresight in, 263; handling of, within family, 113, 121, 134; need for personal decisions in, among clients of social agencies, 293–295
Experimental readjustment, 300; as stage in cycle of readjustment to unemployment, 167–171; as stage in cycle of readjustment within family, 215–224

Family, common life of, 112; conflicts within, due to unemployment, 135–136; division of labor within, 113, 121, 122, 123, 130, 134–135, 180, 182–184, 215–216, 263; as an economic and social unit, 109; effect of religion on, 32–34; effect of unemployment on, cases, 110–152; effect